The American Wilderness

The American Wilderness

Essays by JOHN MUIR
Photographs by ANSEL ADAMS

Edited, with an introduction,
by JOHN THAXTON

BARNES
&NOBLE
BOOKS
NEW YORK

Introduction and compilation copyright © 1993 by Barnes & Noble, Inc.
All rights reserved.

This edition published by Barnes & Noble, Inc.

1993 Barnes & Noble Books

Book design by Charles Ziga, Ziga Design

ISBN 1-56619-103-3

Printed and bound in the United States of America

M 9 8 7 6 5 4 3 2 1

CONTENTS

Ansel Adams' photographs follow pages 50 and 178

*N*ow my eye roved over the piny hills and dales as over fields of waving grain, and felt the light running in ripples and broad swelling undulations across the valley from ridge to ridge, as the shining foliage was stirred by corresponding waves of air. Oftentimes, these waves of reflected light would break up suddenly into a kind of beaten foam, and again, after chasing one another in regular order, they would seem to bend forward in concentric curves, and disappear on some hillside, like sea waves on a shelving shore.

—JOHN MUIR

*A*t one place along the Highway One roadside, I photographed from a cliff top, directing my camera almost straight down to the surf patterns washing upon the beach below in a continuing sequence of beautiful images. As I became aware of the relations between the changing light and surf, I began making exposure after exposure.

—ANSEL ADAMS

INTRODUCTION

More than anything, more than even their profound love of nature, John Muir and Ansel Adams shared an uncanny, almost intuitive ability simply to watch, to notice, to see. Each of them observed, in his way, the subtlest rhythms and patterns, the faintest nuances, of the wild and threatened wildernesses they haunted like spirits. And they haunt them still, for they recorded what they saw on their watch, Muir in his essays and Adams in his photographs, and to this day their work makes our eyes wide with wonder at the sublime and fragile grandeur of the American wilderness.

The Green Movement currently sweeping the world was in John Muir's day the stuff of crackpots and eccentrics. Who in their right mind would climb to the summit of a hundred-foot Douglas spruce in the middle of an intense High Sierra windstorm, the better to watch a climax forest bending in the gusts like fields of waving grain? The same sort of man, obviously, who would spend the whole morning whistling old Scottish airs to an audience of squirrels, only to disperse "the whole hairy tribe" with a too solemn song: "They at once stopped eating, stood erect, and listened patiently until I came to 'Old Hundredth,' when with ludicrous haste every one of them rushed to their holes and bolted in, their feet twinkling in the air for a moment as they vanished." The same sort of man, indeed, who would run out-of-doors in the midst of a devastating earthquake to revel in the fearful symmetry of its chaos, or charge a grizzly bear foraging contentedly in a field of wildflowers—to see what it would look like when it ran. The same sort of man who would smile when the bear held its ground, and describe the encounter as one of great love rather than dread. The startled bear confronted the startled John Muir for a few minutes, and then retreated slowly, turning back frequently to let the human know his presence was being noted. The sort of man a grizzly wouldn't want to meet in a dark canyon.

In short, a crackpot. But a crackpot with a wicked pen and a stunning repertoire of natural wonders to describe: birds that sing all year, walk under water, build nests of living mosses within the spray of waterfalls and trace in their daily and seasonal wanderings the precise paths of the ancient glaciers; talus slopes of gigantic boulders with two-hundred-year-old trees growing on their tops; other-worldly patterns of shadow and light in a cone of ice five hundred feet tall; rainbows arching out of thunderous falls; an unexpected, exhilarating ride on an avalanche; the fairyland golds of the alpen-glow on snow-capped mountains. Numerous industrialists and de-velopers of his day labeled Muir a crazed crackpot, a wild, bearded mountain man who stood in the way of progress—who opposed the sheep herders and the natural devastations of their "hoofed locusts," the timber companies and their wasteful harvesting of thousand-year-old trees, the city of San Francisco and its damming of a spec-tacular Sierra valley.

A one-man-band of a conservation movement, John Muir fell in love with Yosemite Valley and America fell in love with what he saw and felt there, and with how powerfully he showed it. America fell in love with Muir because here was the real thing: the genuine crackpot holy man living in a prelapsarian wilderness, bonding with water ouzels and Douglas squirrels, remembering the glaciers, probably living on nothing but locusts and wild honey, firing out essays the public eagerly awaited. Sometimes he sounded like Saint Francis communing with the animals, at others like Jeremiah declaiming the nighness of the end. The first essay he ever submitted for publication was accepted immediately, and so was everything else he ever of-fered. The man never wrote a bad sentence, and by all accounts his conversation was even more infectious and mesmerizing than his prose. At age eleven he could recite the New Testament verbatim, and even though he didn't attend any formal school between sixth

Introduction

grade and college, he steeped himself in a few classic authors—
Shakespeare, Milton, Burns, Wordsworth. Weaned on the glorious
poetry of the King James Bible and his handful of English Roman-
tics, John Muir developed a naturally graceful and muscular style,
beautifully cadenced.

Muir's best writing has the immediacy of experience itself, the
supple freshness of impressions graduating into thoughts, the spon-
taneity of recognition, the ah-hah smile in the mind's eye. His most
compelling essays leave everybody slack-jawed with amazement,
smiling at how damned articulate the man could be, how full of love,
how smart. His magical piece on the Water-Ouzel is a tour de force,
a dazzling combination of scientific observation and gorgeous English prose. Moreover, it's full of fun and laughter and a trove of
unforgettable images:

> He seems to be expecially fond of the larvae of mosquitoes, found in abun-
> dance attached to the bottom of smooth rock channels where the current is
> shallow. When feeding in such places he wades upstream, and often while
> his head is under water the swift current is deflected upward along the
> glossy curves of his neck and shoulders, in the form of a clear, crystalline
> shell, which fairly incloses him like a bell-glass, the shell being broken and
> reformed as he lifts and dips his head; while ever and anon he sidles out to
> where the too powerful current carries him off his feet; then he dexterously
> rises on the wing and goes gleaning again in shallower places.

For his admirers, the question begging is whether John Muir was a
greater writer or a greater storyteller, a greater journalist or a greater
outdoorsman, a greater man or a greater spirit?

Published in *The Atlantic Monthly*, Muir's essays created a ground-
swell of environmental concern and made him a legend in his own
time. He described natural things so clearly they seemed in his prose
freshly-minted, sparkling icons of the wild, and the depth of his love
for all of creation burnished everything he wrote with a luminous,
almost spiritual glow. He had the ear of a poet and the eye of a

scientist, and he saw things nobody else did. A botanist with no formal training in geology, and with no other tool than the sheer power of his observations in the wild, Muir concluded that Yosemite Valley was sculpted by a glacier, probably by several of them. This theory flew in the face of the accepted wisdom of the day, with the result that Muir was denounced in a cataract of academic papers and lectures. The academes defended their theory of a giant primordial cataclysm forming the valley, but Muir had studied the shadows there and had evidence to the contrary. On his wanderings, he noticed such details as the way a certain mountain perenially cast a shadow on a sheer rock wall of the valley, and how the section of wall within the shadow displayed the smooth polished surface of glacial action while that above it, rougher and in the sun, did not. He saw the shadow as the glacier's ghost, and he was right.

Ansel Adams was also a keen observer of shadows and light—so keen, arguably, that for two generations of photographers now he seems largely responsible for having invented them. His famous Zone System, which correlates areas of varying luminance in a scene with values of gray as they appear in a finished print, enabled him, as it has many of his students, to visualize in the field the latent image that develops in the darkroom. Totally commited to "seeing" the final image in advance, Adams embodied the spirit of "making" rather than "taking" photographs, and he studied his landscapes with a visionary sensitivity that speaks for itself. The depth and range of tone he achieves in his prints continues to dazzle even the technologically blasé. How on earth did he expose for the highlights in those billowing clouds and capture the details in that mountain's shadow? How come this photograph is so sharp, so perfect?

Adams' wilderness photographs have a quality of always having existed. Ansel Adams didn't really take them, our collective memory took them and Ansel Adams just happened to be there, with an

Introduction

8 × 10 inch view camera and a few sheets of film, a couple of filters maybe, sixty, sixty-five pounds of stuff. And wouldn't you know it, on that perfect evening when the clouds gathered like that behind Grand Teton and that morning when the Grand Canyon looked like that? And that afternoon in Glacier National Park, when of all the mountains only Heaven's Peak caught the light, snowcapped and under a darkening sky layered with luminous horsetail clouds? Yes, Ansel Adams was there, and wouldn't it have been marvelous to have been standing beside him, gazing at the wilderness when it looked precisely like what it was supposed to look like? Or would you have missed it, even as it displayed its glory right before your eyes?

Ansel Adams is a great artist because he had a great eye, a sense of seeing, in the same glance, the boldest and subtlest gradations of reality, the forest and the trees at the same time. Even his most dramatic images—like snow-besplattered Grand Teton, erupting into dramatic layers of clouds and a dark blue sky, above the luminous curve of the Snake River in the foreground—become as you study them incredibly subtle statements, silent fields and bands of slightly differing charcoal grays, bold geometric swaths of almost white. As you observe them, Adams' photographs begin to look more three-dimensional than others, as if their depth and tonal range were a gimmick, a fancy, stereoscopic effect. A trick. But study them longer and they begin to look like exactly the opposite, like some undeniable truth about the world—the fact, not the fiction.

Ansel Adams took pictures at the perfect moment because he understood the perfect moment, because he observed his favorite landscapes with such assiduous care that he knew beneath a certain slant of light the aspens and spruces were ten shades of gray apart, the river a band of dazzling light, the clouds a nacreous glory. He worked for the most part with large format cameras, not firing off hundreds of exposures and editing them later for the perfect shot, but watching and waiting until the perfect shot appeared in the ground glass, until the perfect slant of light illumined his composition. Some of his photographs capture ineffably delicate atmospheric moments, the clarity of air just after a storm, the chiaroscuro of cloud shadows, the stratified clouds of a desert evening. Adams captured such moments because he anticipated them. He loved the wilderness and he watched it like a hawk, scanning again and again from the ideal eyrie, seeing things more clearly than others.

For Adams, the ultimate image, the realization of the photographer's vision, was the print. The purest tonal values, the strongest and subtlest contrasts, the richest textures, were the province of the original print, made by the photographer. Adams' technical virtuosity in the darkroom remains as legendary as his virtuosity in the field. He did it right: He controlled his images from the wilderness to the print washer, capturing, along the way, more nuances than the eye could normally see. When you look at a landscape of bright spots and shadows, the pupils of your eyes dilate and contract as they pass from one to the other, arriving, as you fix your stare for a moment, at a compromise—the brights darken a bit, details emerge in the shadows. A skilled darkroom technician can coax out of a first-rate negative more details than the keenest observer could detect in a single glance. Sure enough, if you disregard the sky and peer into the enshadowed Grand Canyon you can see vast subtleties of shape and color, litmus-like graduations of tone on a gargantuan scale. But if you look up quickly at the luminous sky, you will see only a blinding field of light. Gradually the clouds and the sky and the pale gray snow-capped peaks in the distance come into focus as the eyes adjust, and by then the shadows are lost.

In an Ansel Adams print you can see the darkness and light at the same time, for his mastery of technique compensated for our imperfect vision. He would "burn-in" sections of his prints, exposing them longer than others, to bring out the details usually lost in shadows or bright light, and "dodge out" others, exposing them less,

Introduction

to maintain tonal balance. As a result, his work has a preternatural texture and clarity, a sort of hyper-reality, a classic, timeless dignity.

John Muir and Ansel Adams never met, but they looked at many of the same landscapes, and they loved them.

John Thaxton
1993

The Wild Parks and Forest Reservations of the West

Keep not standing fix'd and rooted,
  Briskly venture, briskly roam;
Head and hand, where'er thou foot it,
  And stout heart are still at home.
In each land the sun does visit
  We are gay, whate'er betide:
To give room for wandering is it
  That the world was made so wide.

The tendency nowadays to wander in wildernesses is delightful to see. Thousands of tired, nerve-shaken, over-civilized people are beginning to find out that going to the mountains is going home; that wildness is a necessity; and that mountain parks and reservations are useful not only as fountains of timber and irrigating rivers, but as fountains of life. Awakening from the stupefying effects of the vice of over-industry and the deadly apathy of luxury, they are trying as best they can to mix and enrich their own little ongoings with those of Nature, and to get rid of rust and disease. Briskly venturing and roaming, some are washing off sins and cobweb cares of the devil's spinning in all-day storms on mountains; sauntering in rosiny pinewoods or in gentian meadows, brushing through chapar-

1

ral, bending down and parting sweet, flowery sprays; tracing rivers to their sources, getting in touch with the nerves of Mother Earth; jumping from rock to rock, feeling the life of them, learning the songs of them, panting in whole-souled exercise, and rejoicing in deep, long-drawn breaths of pure wildness. This is fine and natural and full of promise. So also is the growing interest in the care and preservation of forests and wild places in general, and in the half wild parks and gardens of towns. Even the scenery habit in its most artificial forms, mixed with spectacles, silliness, and kodaks; its devotees arrayed more gorgeously than scarlet tanagers, frightening the wild game with red umbrellas—even this is encouraging, and may well be regarded as a hopeful sign of the times.

All the Western mountains are still rich in wildness, and by means of good roads are being brought nearer civilization every year. To the sane and free it will hardly seem necessary to cross the continent in search of wild beauty, however easy the way, for they find it in abundance wherever they chance to be. Like Thoreau they see forests in orchards and patches of huckleberry brush, and oceans in ponds and drops of dew. Few in these hot, dim, strenuous times are quite sane or free; choked with care like clocks full of dust, laboriously doing so much good and making so much money—or so little— they are no longer good for themselves.

When, like a merchant taking a list of his goods, we take stock of our wildness, we are glad to see how much of even the most destructible kind is still unspoiled. Looking at our continent as scenery when it was all wild, lying between beautiful seas, the starry sky above it, the starry rocks beneath it, to compare its sides, the East and the West, would be like comparing the sides of a rainbow. But it is no longer equally beautiful. The rainbows of today are, I suppose, as bright as those that first spanned the sky; and some of our landscapes are growing more beautiful from year to year, notwithstanding the clearing, trampling work of civilization. New plants and animals are enriching woods and gardens, and many landscapes wholly new, with divine sculpture and architecture, are just now coming to the light of day as the mantling folds of creative glaciers are being withdrawn, and life in a thousand cheerful, beautiful forms is pushing into them, and new-born rivers are beginning to sing and shine in them. The old rivers, too, are growing longer, like healthy trees, gaining new branches and lakes as the residual glaciers at their highest sources on the mountains recede, while the rootlike branches in their flat deltas are at the same time spreading farther and wider into the seas and making new lands.

Under the control of the vast mysterious forces of the interior of the earth all the continents and islands are slowly rising or sinking. Most of the mountains are diminishing in size under the wearing action of the weather, though a few are increasing in height and girth, especially the volcanic ones, as fresh floods of molten rocks are piled on their summits and spread in successive layers, like the wood-rings of trees, on their sides. New mountains, also, are being created from time to time as islands in lakes and seas, or as subordinate cones on the slopes of old ones, thus in some measure balancing the waste of old beauty with new. Man, too, is making many far-reaching changes. This most influential half animal, half angel is rapidly multiplying and spreading, covering the seas and lakes with ships, the land with huts, hotels, cathedrals, and clustered city shops and homes, so that soon, it would seem, we may have to go farther than Nansen to find a good sound solitude. None of Nature's landscapes are ugly so long as they are wild; and much, we can say comfortingly, must always be in great part wild, particularly the sea and the sky, the floods of light from the stars, and the warm, unspoilable heart of the earth, infinitely beautiful, though only dimly visible to the eye of imagination. The geysers, too, spouting from the hot underworld; the steady, long-lasting glaciers on the mountains, obedient only to the sun; Yosemite domes and the tremendous grandeur of rocky cañons and mountains in general—these must always be wild, for man can change them and mar them hardly more than can the butterflies that hover above them. But the continent's outer beauty is fast passing away, especially the plant part of it, the most destructible and most universally charming of all.

Only thirty years ago, the great Central Valley of California, five hundred miles long and fifty miles wide, was one bed of golden and purple flowers. Now it is ploughed and pastured out of existence, gone forever—scarce a memory of it left in fence corners and along the bluffs of the streams. The gardens of the Sierra, also, and the noble forests in both the reserved and unreserved portions are sadly hacked and trampled, notwithstanding the ruggedness of the topography—all excepting those of the parks guarded by a few soldiers. In the noblest forests of the world, the ground, once divinely beautiful, is desolate and repulsive, like a face ravaged by disease. This is true also of many other Pacific Coast and Rocky Mountain valleys and forests. The same fate, sooner or later, is awaiting them all, unless awakening public opinion comes forward to stop it. Even the great deserts in Arizona, Nevada, Utah, and New Mexico, which offer so little to attract settlers, and which a few years ago pioneers were afraid of, as places of desolation and death, are now taken as pastures at the rate of one or two square miles per cow, and of course their plant treasures are passing away—the delicate abronias, phloxes, gilias, etc. Only a few of the bitter, thorny, unbitable shrubs are left, and the sturdy cactuses that defend themselves with bayonets and spears.

Most of the wild plant wealth of the East also has vanished—gone into dusty history. Only vestiges of its glorious prairie and woodland wealth remain to bless humanity in boggy, rocky, unploughable places. Fortunately, some of these are purely wild, and go far to keep Nature's love visible. White water-lilies, with root-stocks deep and safe in mud, still send up every summer a Milky Way of starry, fragrant flowers around a thousand lakes, and many a tuft of wild grass waves its panicles on mossy rocks, beyond reach of trampling feet, in company with saxifrages, bluebells, and ferns. Even in the midst of farmers' fields, precious sphagnum bogs, too soft for the feet of cattle, are preserved with their charming plants unchanged—chiogenes, Andromeda, Kalmia, Linnaea, Arethusa, etc. Calypso borealis still hides in the arbor vitae swamps of Canada, and away to the southward there are a few unspoiled swamps, big ones, where miasma, snakes, and alligators, like guardian angels, defend their treasures and keep them as pure as paradise. And beside a' that and a' that, the East is blessed with good winters and blossoming clouds that shed white flowers over all the land, covering every scar and making the saddest landscape divine at least once a year.

The most extensive, least spoiled, and most unspoilable of the gardens of the continent are the vast tundras of Alaska. In summer they extend smooth, even, undulating, continuous beds of flowers and leaves from about lat. 62° to the shores of the Arctic Ocean; and in winter sheets of snowflowers make all the country shine, one mass of white radiance like a star. Nor are these Arctic plant people the pitiful frost-pinched unfortunates they are guessed to be by those who have never seen them. Though lowly in stature, keeping near the frozen ground as if loving it, they are bright and cheery, and speak Nature's love as plainly as their big relatives of the South. Tenderly happed and tucked in beneath downy snow to sleep through the long, white winter, they make haste to bloom in the spring without trying to grow tall, though some rise high enough to ripple and wave in the wind, and display masses of color—yellow, purple, and blue—so rich that they look like beds of rainbows, and are visible miles and miles away.

As early as June one may find the showy Geum glaciale in flower, and the dwarf willows putting forth myriads of fuzzy catkins, to be followed quickly, especially on the dryer ground, by mertensia, eritrichium, polemonium, oxytropis, astragalus, lathyrus, lupinus, myosotis, dodecatheon, arnica, chrysanthemum, nardosmia, saussurea, senecio, erigeron, matrecaria, caltha, valeriana, stellaria, Tofieldia, polygonum, papaver, phlox, lychnis, cheiranthus, Linnaea, and a

5

host of drabas, saxifrages, and heathworts, with bright stars and bells in glorious profusion, particularly Cassiope, Andromeda, ledum, pyrola, and vaccinium—Cassiope the most abundant and beautiful of them all. Many grasses also grow here, and wave fine purple spikes and panicles over the other flowers—poa, aira, calamagrostis, alopecurus, trisetum, elymus, festuca, glyceria, etc. Even ferns are found thus far north, carefully and comfortably unrolling their precious fronds—aspidium, cystopteris, and woodsia, all growing on a sumptuous bed of mosses and lichens; not the scaly lichens seen on rails and trees and fallen logs to the southward, but massive, round-headed, finely colored plants like corals, wonderfully beautiful, worth going round the world to see. I should like to mention all the plant friends I found in a summer's wanderings in this cool reserve, but I fear few would care to read their names, although everybody, I am sure, would love them could they see them blooming and rejoicing at home.

On my last visit to the region about Kotzebue Sound, near the middle of September, 1881, the weather was so fine and mellow that it suggested the Indian summer of the Eastern States. The winds were hushed, the tundra glowed in creamy golden sunshine, and the colors of the ripe foliage of the heathworts, willows, and birch—red, purple, and yellow, in pure bright tones—were enriched with those of berries which were scattered everywhere, as if they had been showered from the clouds like hail. When I was back a mile or two from the shore, reveling in this color-glory, and thinking how fine it would be could I cut a square of the tundra sod of conventional picture size, frame it, and hang it among the paintings on my study walls at home, saying to myself, "Such a Nature painting taken at random from any part of the thousand-mile bog would make the other pictures look dim and coarse," I heard merry shouting, and, looking round, saw a band of Eskimos—men, women, and children, loose and hairy like wild animals—running towards me. I could not guess at first what they were seeking, for they seldom leave the shore;

6

but soon they told me, as they threw themselves down, sprawling and laughing, on the mellow bog, and began to feast on the berries. A lively picture they made, and a pleasant one, as they frightened the whirring ptarmigans, and surprised their oily stomachs with the beautiful acid berries of many kinds, and filled sealskin bags with them to carry away for festive days in winter.

Nowhere else on my travels have I seen so much warm-blooded, rejoicing life as in this grand Arctic reservation, by so many regarded as desolate. Not only are there whales in abundance along the shores, and innumerable seals, walruses, and white bears, but on the tundras great herds of fat reindeer and wild sheep, foxes, hares, mice, piping marmots, and birds. Perhaps more birds are born here than in any other region of equal extent on the continent. Not only do strong-winged hawks, eagles, and water-fowl, to whom the length of the continent is merely a pleasant excursion, come up here every summer in great numbers, but also many short-winged warblers, thrushes, and finches, repairing hither to rear their young in safety, reinforce the plant bloom with their plumage, and sweeten the wilderness with song; flying all the way, some of them, from Florida, Mexico, and Central America. In coming north they are coming home, for they were born here, and they go south only to spend the winter months, as New Englanders go to Florida. Sweet-voiced troubadours, they sing in orange groves and vine-clad magnolia woods in winter, in thickets of dwarf, birch and alder in summer, and sing and chatter more or less all the way back and forth, keeping the whole country glad. Oftentimes, in New England, just as the last snow-patches are melting and the sap in the maples begins to flow, the blessed wanderers may be heard about orchards and the edges of fields where they have stopped to glean a scanty meal, not tarrying long, knowing they have far to go. Tracing the footsteps of spring, they arrive in their tundra homes in June or July, and set out on their return journey in September, or as soon as their families are able to fly well.

THE AMERICAN WILDERNESS

This is Nature's own reservation, and every lover of wildness will rejoice with me that by kindly frost it is so well defended. The discovery lately made that it is sprinkled with gold may cause some alarm; for the strangely exciting stuff makes the timid bold enough for anything, and the lazy destructively industrious. Thousands at least half insane are now pushing their way into it, some by the southern passes over the mountains, perchance the first mountains they have ever seen—sprawling, struggling, gasping for breath, as, laden with awkward, merciless burdens of provisions and tools, they climb over rough-angled boulders and cross thin miry bogs. Some are going by the mountains and rivers to the eastward through Canada, tracing the old romantic ways of the Hudson Bay traders; others by Bering Sea and the Yukon, sailing all the way, getting glimpses perhaps of the famous fur-seals, the ice-floes, and the innumerable islands and bars of the great Alaska river. In spite of frowning hardships and the frozen ground, the Klondike gold will increase the crusading crowds for years to come, but comparatively little harm will be done. Holes will be burned and dug into the hard ground here and there, and into the quartz-ribbed mountains and hills; ragged towns like beaver and muskrat villages will be built, and mills and locomotives will make rumbling, screeching, disenchanting noises; but the miner's pick will not be followed far by the plough, at least not until Nature is ready to unlock the frozen soil-beds with her slow-turning climate key. On the other hand, the roads of the pioneer miners will lead many a lover of wildness into the heart of the reserve, who without them would never see it.

In the meantime, the wildest health and pleasure grounds accessible and available to tourists seeking escape from care and dust and early death are the parks and reservations of the West. There are four national parks—the Yellowstone, Yosemite, General Grant, and Sequoia—all within easy reach, and thirty forest reservations, a magnificent realm of woods, most of which, by railroads and trails and open ridges, is also fairly accessible, not only to the determined traveler rejoicing in difficulties, but to those, (may their tribe increase) who, not tired, not sick, just naturally, take wing every summer in search of wildness. The forty million acres of these reserves are in the main unspoiled as yet, though sadly wasted and threatened on their more open margins by the axe and fire of the lumberman and prospector, and by hoofed locusts, which, like the winged ones, devour every leaf within reach, while the shepherds and owners set fires with the intention of making a blade of grass grow in the place of every tree, but with the result of killing both the grass and the trees.

In the million acre Black Hills Reserve of South Dakota, the easternmost of the great forest reserves, made for the sake of the farmers and miners, there are delightful, reviving sauntering-grounds in open parks of yellow pine, planted well apart, allowing plenty of sunshine to warm the ground. This tree is one of the most variable and most widely distributed of American pines. It grows sturdily on all kinds of soil and rocks, and, protected by a mail of thick bark, defies frost and fire and disease alike, daring every danger in firm, calm beauty and strength. It occurs here mostly on the outer hills and slopes where no other tree can grow. The ground beneath it is yellow most of the summer with showy Wythia, arnica, applopappus, solidago, and other sun-loving plants, which, though they form no heavy entangling growth, yet give abundance of color and make all the woods a garden. Beyond the yellow pine woods there lies a world of rocks of wildest architecture, broken, splintery, and spiky, not very high, but the strangest in form and style of grouping imaginable. Countless towers and spires, pinnacles and slender domed columns, are crowded together, and feathered with sharp-pointed Engelmann spruces, making curiously mixed forests—half trees, half rocks. Level gardens here and there in the midst of them offer charming surprises, and so do the many small lakes with lilies on their meadowy borders, and bluebells, anemones, daisies, castilleias, comandras, etc., together forming landscapes delightfully novel, and

9

made still wilder by many interesting animals—elk, deer, beavers, wolves, squirrels, and birds. Not very long ago this was the richest of all the red man's hunting-grounds hereabout. After the season's buffalo hunts were over—as described by Parkman, who, with a picturesque cavalcade of Sioux savages, passed through these famous hills in 1846—every winter deficiency was here made good, and hunger was unknown until, in spite of most determined, fighting, killing opposition, the white gold-hunters entered the fat game reserve and spoiled it. The Indians are dead now, and so are most of the hardly less striking free trappers of the early romantic Rocky Mountain times. Arrows, bullets, scalping-knives, need no longer be feared; and all the wilderness is peacefully open.

The Rocky Mountain reserves are the Teton, Yellowstone, Lewis and Clark, Bitter Root, Priest River and Flathead, comprehending more than twelve million acres of mostly unclaimed, rough, forest-covered mountains in which the great rivers of the country take their rise. The commonest tree in most of them is the brave, indomitable, and altogether admirable Pinus contorta, widely distributed in all kinds of climate and soil, growing cheerily in frosty Alaska, breathing the damp salt air of the sea as well as the dry biting blasts of the Arctic interior, and making itself at home on the most dangerous flame-swept slopes and ridges of the Rocky Mountains in immeasurable abundance and variety of forms. Thousands of acres of this species are destroyed by running fires nearly every summer, but a new growth springs quickly from the ashes. It is generally small, and yields few sawlogs of commercial value, but is of incalculable importance to the farmer and miner; supplying fencing, mine timbers, and firewood, holding the porous soil on steep slopes, preventing land-slips and avalanches, and giving kindly, nourishing shelter to animals and the widely outspread sources of the life-giving rivers. The other trees are mostly spruce, mountain pine, cedar, juniper, larch, and balsam fir; some of them, especially on the western slopes of the

The Wild Parks and Forest Reservations

mountains, attaining grand size and furnishing abundance of fine timber.

Perhaps the least known of all this grand group of reserves is the Bitter Root, of more than four million acres. It is the wildest, shaggiest block of forest wildness in the Rocky Mountains, full of happy, healthy, storm-loving trees, full of streams that dance and sing in glorious array, and full of Nature's animals—elk, deer, wild sheep, bears, cats, and innumerable smaller people.

In calm Indian summer, when the heavy winds are hushed, the vast forests covering hill and dale, rising and falling over the rough topography and vanishing in the distance, seem lifeless. No moving thing is seen as we climb the peaks, and only the low, mellow murmur of falling water is heard, which seems to thicken the silence. Nevertheless, how many hearts with warm red blood in them are beating under cover of the woods, and how many teeth and eyes are shining! A multitude of animal people, intimately related to us, but of whose lives we know almost nothing are as busy about their own affairs as we are about ours: beavers are building and mending dams and huts for winter, and storing them with food; bears are studying winter quarters as they stand thoughtful in open spaces, while the gentle breeze ruffles the long hair on their backs; elk and deer, assembling on the heights, are considering cold pastures where they will be farthest away from the wolves; squirrels and marmots are busily laying up provisions and lining their nests against coming frost and snow foreseen; and countless thousands of birds are forming parties and gathering their young about them for flight to the southlands; while butterflies and bees, apparently with no thought of hard times to come, are hovering above the late-blooming goldenrods, and, with countless other insect folk, are dancing and humming right merrily in the sunbeams and shaking all the air into music.

Wander here a whole summer, if you can. Thousands of God's wild blessings will search you and soak you as if you were a sponge, and the big days will go by uncounted. If you are business-tangled, and so burdened with duty that only weeks can be got out of the heavy-laden year, then go to the Flathead Reserve; for it is easily and quickly reached by the Great Northern Railroad. Get off the track at Belton Station, and in a few minutes you will find yourself in the midst of what you are sure to say is the best care-killing scenery on the continent—beautiful lakes derived straight from glaciers, lofty mountains steeped in lovely nemophila-blue skies and clad with forests and glaciers, mossy, ferny waterfalls in their hollows, nameless and numberless, and meadowy gardens abounding in the best of everything. When you are calm enough for discriminating observation, you will find the king of the larches, one of the best of the Western giants, beautiful, picturesque, and regal in port, easily the grandest of all the larches in the world. It grows to a height of one hundred and fifty to two hundred feet, with a diameter at the ground of five to eight feet, throwing out its branches into the light as no other tree does. To those who before have seen only the European larch or the Lyall species of the eastern Rocky Mountains, or the little tamarack or hackmatack of the Eastern States and Canada, this Western king must be a revelation.

Associated with this grand tree in the making of the Flathead forests is the large and beautiful mountain pine, or Western white pine (*Pinus monticola*), the invincible contorta or lodge-pole pine, and spruce and cedar. The forest floor is covered with the richest beds of Linnaea borealis I ever saw, thick fragrant carpets, enriched with shining mosses here and there, and with Clintonia, pyrola, moneses, and vaccinium, weaving hundred-mile beds of bloom that would have made blessed old Linnaeus weep for joy.

Lake McDonald, full of brisk trout, is in the heart of this forest, and Avalanche Lake is ten miles above McDonald, at the feet of a group of glacier-laden mountains. Give a month at least to this precious reserve. The time will not be taken from the sum of your life. Instead of shortening, it will indefinitely lengthen it and make you truly immortal. Nevermore will time seem short or long, and cares will never again fall heavily on you, but gently and kindly as gifts from heaven.

The vast Pacific Coast reserves in Washington and Oregon—the Cascade, Washington, Mount Rainier, Olympic, Bull Run, and Ashland, named in order of size—include more than 12,500,000 acres of magnificent forests of beautiful and gigantic trees. They extend over the wild, unexplored Olympic Mountains and both flanks of the Cascade Range, the wet and the dry. On the east side of the Cascades the woods are sunny and open, and contain principally yellow pine, of moderate size, but of great value as a cover for the irrigating streams that flow into the dry interior, where agriculture on a grand scale is being carried on. Along the moist, balmy, foggy, west flank of the mountains, facing the sea, the woods reach their highest development, and, excepting the California redwoods, are the heaviest on the continent. They are made up mostly of the Douglas spruce (*Pseudotsuga taxifolia*), with the giant arbor vitae, or cedar, and several species of fir and hemlock in varying abundance, forming a forest kingdom unlike any other, in which limb meets limb, touching and overlapping in bright, lively, triumphant exuberance, two hundred and fifty, three hundred, and even four hundred feet above the shady, mossy ground. Over all the other species the Douglas spruce reigns supreme. It is not only a large tree, the tallest in America next to the redwood, but a very beautiful one, with bright green drooping foliage, handsome pendent cones, and a shaft exquisitely straight and round and regular. Forming extensive forests by itself in many places, it lifts its spiry tops into the sky close together with as even a growth as a well-tilled field of grain. No ground has been better tilled for wheat than these Cascade Mountains for trees: they were ploughed by mighty glaciers, and harrowed and mellowed and outspread by the broad streams that flowed from the ice-ploughs as they were withdrawn at the close of the glacial period.

In proportion to its weight when dry, Douglas spruce timber is

13

perhaps stronger than that of any other large conifer in the country, and being tough, durable, and elastic, it is admirably suited for shipbuilding, piles, and heavy timbers in general; but its hardness and liability to warp when it is cut into boards render it unfit for fine work. In the lumber markets of California it is called "Oregon pine." When lumbering is going on in the best Douglas woods, especially about Puget Sound, many of the long, slender boles are saved for spars; and so superior is their quality that they are called for in almost every shipyard in the world, and it is interesting to follow their fortunes. Felled and peeled and dragged to tide-water, they are raised again as yards and masts for ships, given iron roots and canvas foliage, decorated with flags, and sent to sea, where in glad motion they go cheerily over the ocean prairie in every latitude and longitude, singing and bowing responsive to the same winds that waved them when they were in the woods. After standing in one place for centuries they thus go round the world like tourists, meeting many a friend from the old home forest; some traveling like themselves, some standing head downward in muddy harbors, holding up the platforms of wharves, and others doing all kinds of hard timber work, showy or hidden.

This wonderful tree also grows far northward in British Columbia, and southward along the coast and middle regions of Oregon and California; flourishing with the redwood wherever it can find an opening, and with the sugar pine, yellow pine, and libocedrus in the Sierra. It extends into the San Gabriel, San Bernardino, and San Jacinto Mountains of southern California. It also grows well on the Wasatch Mountains, where it is called "red pine," and on many parts of the Rocky Mountains and short interior ranges of the Great Basin. But though thus widely distributed, only in Oregon, Washington, and some parts of British Columbia does it reach perfect development.

To one who looks from some high standpoint over its vast breadth, the forest on the west side of the Cascades seems all one dim, dark, monotonous field, broken only by the white volcanic cones along the summit of the range. Back in the untrodden wilderness a deep furred carpet of brown and yellow mosses covers the ground like a garment, pressing about the feet of the trees, and rising in rich bosses softly and kindly over every rock and mouldering trunk, leaving no spot uncared for; and dotting small prairies, and fringing the meadows and the banks of streams not seen in general views, we find, besides the great conifers, a considerable number of hardwood trees—oak, ash, maple, alder, wild apple, cherry, arbutus, Nuttall's flowering dogwood, and in some places chestnut. In a few favored spots the broad-leaved maple grows to a height of a hundred feet in forests by itself, sending out large limbs in magnificent interlacing arches covered with mosses and ferns, thus forming lofty sky-gardens, and rendering the underwoods delightfully cool. No finer forest ceiling is to be found than these maple arches, while the floor, ornamented with tall ferns and rubus vines, and cast into hillocks by the bulging, moss-covered roots of the trees, matches it well.

Passing from beneath the heavy shadows of the woods, almost anywhere one steps into lovely gardens of lilies, orchids, heathworts, and wild roses. Along the lower slopes, especially in Oregon, where the woods are less dense, there are miles of rhododendron, making glorious masses of purple in the spring, while all about the streams and the lakes and the beaver meadows there is a rich tangle of hazel, plum, cherry, crab-apple, cornel, gaultheria, and rubus, with myriads of flowers and abundance of other more delicate bloomers, such as erythronium, brodiaea, fritillaria, calochortus, Clintonia, and the lovely hider of the north, Calypso. Beside all these bloomers there are wonderful ferneries about the many misty waterfalls, some of the fronds ten feet high, others the most delicate of their tribe, the maidenhair fringing the rocks within reach of the lightest dust of the spray, while the shading trees on the cliffs above them, leaning over, look like eager listeners anxious to catch every tone of the restless waters. In the autumn berries of every color and flavor abound, enough for birds, bears, and everybody, particularly about the stream-sides and meadows where sunshine reaches the ground: huckleberries, red, blue, and black, some growing close to the ground, others on bushes ten feet high; gaultheria berries, called "sal-al" by the Indians; salmon berries, an inch in diameter, growing in dense prickly tangles, the flowers, like wild roses, still more beautiful than the fruit; raspberries, gooseberries, currants, blackberries, and strawberries. The underbrush and meadow fringes are in great part made up of these berry bushes and vines; but in the depths of the woods there is not much underbrush of any kind—only a thin growth of rubus, huckleberry, and vine-maple.

Notwithstanding the outcry against the reservations last winter in Washington, that uncounted farms, towns, and villages were included in them, and that all business was threatened or blocked, nearly all the mountains in which the reserves lie are still covered with virgin forests. Though lumbering has long been carried on with tremendous energy along their boundaries, and home-seekers have explored the woods for openings available for farms, however small, one may wander in the heart of the reserves for weeks without meeting a human being, Indian or white man, or any conspicuous trace of one. Indians used to ascend the main streams on their way to the mountains for wild goats, whose wool furnished them clothing. But with food in abundance on the coast there was little to draw them into the woods, and the monuments they have left there are scarcely more conspicuous than those of birds and squirrels; far less so than those of the beavers, which have dammed streams and made clearings that will endure for centuries. Nor is there much in these woods to attract cattle-keepers. Some of the first settlers made farms on the small bits of prairie and in the comparatively open Cowlitz and Chehalis valleys of Washington; but before the gold period most of the immigrants from the Eastern States settled in the fertile and open Willamette Valley of Oregon. Even now, when the search for tillable land is so keen, excepting the bottomlands of the rivers

The Wild Parks and Forest Reservations

around Puget Sound, there are few cleared spots in all western Washington. On every meadow or opening of any sort some one will be found keeping cattle, raising hops, or cultivating patches of grain, but these spots are few and far between. All the larger spaces were taken long ago; therefore most of the newcomers build their cabins where the beavers built theirs. They keep a few cows, laboriously widen their little meadow openings by hacking, girdling, and burning the rim of the close-pressing forest, and scratch and plant among the huge blackened logs and stumps, girdling and killing themselves in killing the trees.

Most of the farm lands of Washington and Oregon, excepting the valleys of the Willamette and Rogue rivers, lie on the east side of the mountains. The forests on the eastern slopes of the Cascades fail altogether ere the foot of the range is reached, stayed by drought as suddenly as on the west side they are stopped by the sea; showing strikingly how dependent are these forest giants on the generous rains and fogs so often complained of in the coast climate. The lower portions of the reserves are solemnly soaked and poulticed in rain and fog during the winter months, and there is a sad dearth of sunshine, but with a little knowledge of woodcraft any one may enjoy an excursion into these woods even in the rainy season. The big, gray days are exhilarating, and the colors of leaf and branch and mossy bole are then at their best. The mighty trees getting their food are seen to be wide-awake, every needle thrilling in the welcome nourishing storms, chanting and bowing low in glorious harmony, while every raindrop and snowflake is seen as a beneficent messenger from the sky. The snow that falls on the lower woods is mostly soft, coming through the trees in downy tufts, loading their branches, and bending them down against the trunks until they look like arrows, while a strange muffled silence prevails, making everything impressively solemn. But these lowland snowstorms and their effects quickly vanish. The snow melts in a day or two, sometimes in a few hours, the bent branches spring up again, and all the forest work is left to the fog and the rain. At the same time, dry snow is falling on the upper forests and mountain tops. Day after day, often for weeks, the big clouds give their flowers without ceasing, as if knowing how important is the work they have to do. The glinting, swirling swarms thicken the blast, and the trees and rocks are covered to a depth of ten to twenty feet. Then the mountaineer, snug in a grove with bread and fire, has nothing to do but gaze and listen and enjoy. Ever and anon the deep, low roar of the storm is broken by the booming of avalanches, as the snow slips from the overladen heights and rushes down the long white slopes to fill the fountain hollows. All the smaller streams are hushed and buried, and the young groves of spruce and fir near the edge of the timber-line are gently bowed to the ground and put to sleep, not again to see the light of day or stir branch or leaf until the spring.

These grand reservations should draw thousands of admiring visitors at least in summer, yet they are neglected as if of no account, and spoilers are allowed to ruin them as fast as they like. A few peeled spars cut here were set up in London, Philadelphia, and Chicago, where they excited wondering attention; but the countless hosts of living trees rejoicing at home on the mountains are scarce considered at all. Most travelers here are content with what they can see from car windows or the verandas of hotels, and in going from place to place cling to their precious trains and stages like wrecked sailors to rafts. When an excursion into the woods is proposed, all sorts of dangers are imagined—snakes, bears, Indians. Yet it is far safer to wander in God's woods than to travel on black highways or to stay at home. The snake danger is so slight it is hardly worth mentioning. Bears are a peaceable people, and mind their own business, instead of going about like the devil seeking whom they may devour. Poor fellows, they have been poisoned, trapped, and shot at until they have lost confidence in brother man, and it is not now easy to make their acquaintance. As to Indians, most of them are dead or civilized into useless innocence. No American wilderness that I know of is so dangerous as a city home "with all the modern improvements." One should go to the woods for safety, if for nothing else. Lewis and Clark, in their famous trip across the continent in 1804–1805, did not lose a single man by Indians or animals, though all the West was then wild. Captain Clark was bitten on the hand as he lay asleep. That was one bite among more than a hundred men while traveling nine thousand miles. Loggers are far more likely to be met than Indians or bears in the reserves or about their boundaries, brown weather-tanned men with faces furrowed like bark, tired-looking, moving slowly, swaying like the trees they chop. A little of everything in the woods is fastened to their clothing, rosiny and smeared with balsam, and rubbed into it, so that their scanty outer garments grow thicker with use and never wear out. Many a forest giant have these old woodmen felled, but, round-shouldered and stooping, they too are leaning over and tottering to their fall. Others, however, stand ready to take their places, stout young fellows, erect as saplings; and always the foes of trees outnumber their friends. Far up the white peaks one can hardly fail to meet the wild goat, or American chamois—an admirable mountaineer, familiar with woods and glaciers as well as rocks—and in leafy thickets deer will be found; while gliding about unseen there are many sleek furred animals enjoying their beautiful lives, and birds also, notwithstanding few are noticed in hasty walks. The ousel sweetens the glens and gorges where the streams flow fastest, and every grove has its singers, however silent it seems—thrushes, linnets, warblers; humming-birds glint about the fringing bloom of the meadows and peaks, and the lakes are stirred into lively pictures by water-fowl.

The Mount Rainier Forest Reserve should be made a national park and guarded while yet its bloom is on; for if in the making of the West Nature had what we call parks in mind—places for rest, inspiration, and prayers—this Rainier region must surely be one of them.

In the centre of it there is a lonely mountain capped with ice; from the ice-cap glaciers radiate in every direction, and young rivers from the glaciers; while its flanks, sweeping down in beautiful curves, are clad with forests and gardens, and filled with birds and animals. Specimens of the best of Nature's treasures have been lovingly gathered here and arranged in simple symmetrical beauty within regular bounds.

Of all the fire-mountains which, like beacons, once blazed along the Pacific Coast, Mount Rainier is the noblest in form, has the most interesting forest cover, and, with perhaps the exception of Shasta, is the highest and most flowery. Its massive white dome rises out of its forests, like a world by itself, to a height of fourteen thousand to fifteen thousand feet. The forests reach to a height of a little over six thousand feet, and above the forests there is a zone of the loveliest flowers, fifty miles in circuit and nearly two miles wide, so closely planted and luxuriant that it seems as if Nature, glad to make an open space between woods so dense and ice so deep, were economizing the precious ground, and trying to see how many of her darlings she can get together in one mountain wreath—daisies, anemones, geraniums, columbines, erythroniums, larkspurs, etc., among which we wade knee-deep and waist-deep, the bright corollas in myriads touching petal to petal. Picturesque detached groups of the spiry Abies lasiocarpa stand like islands along the lower margin of the garden zone, while on the upper margin there are extensive beds of bryanthus, cassiope, kalmia, and other heathworts, and higher still saxifrages and drabas, more and more lowly, reach up to the edge of the ice. Altogether this is the richest subalpine garden I ever found, a perfect floral elysium. The icy dome needs none of man's care, but unless the reserve is guarded the flower bloom will soon be killed, and nothing of the forests will be left but black stump monuments.

The Sierra of California is the most openly beautiful and useful of all the forest reserves, and the largest excepting the Cascade Reserve

The Wild Parks and Forest Reservations

of Oregon and the Bitter Root of Montana and Idaho. It embraces over four million acres of the grandest scenery and grandest trees on the continent, and its forests are planted just where they do the most good, not only for beauty, but for farming in the great San Joaquin Valley beneath them. It extends southward from the Yosemite National Park to the end of the range, a distance of nearly two hundred miles. No other coniferous forest in the world contains so many species or so many large and beautiful trees—Sequoia gigantea, king of conifers, "the noblest of a noble race," as Sir Joseph Hooker well says; the sugar pine, king of all the world's pines, living or extinct; the yellow pine, next in rank, which here reaches most perfect development, forming noble towers of verdure two hundred feet high; the mountain pine, which braves the coldest blasts far up the mountains on grim, rocky slopes and five others, flourishing each in its place, making eight species of pine in one forest, which is still further enriched by the great Douglas spruce, libocedrus, two species of silver fir, large trees and exquisitely beautiful, the Paton hemlock, the most graceful of evergreens, the curious tumion, oaks of many species, maples, alders, poplars, and flowering dogwood, all fringed with flowery underbrush, manzanita, ceanothus, wild rose, cherry, chestnut, and rhododendron. Wandering at random through these friendly approachable woods, one comes here and there to the loveliest lily gardens, some of the lilies ten feet high, and the smoothest gentian meadows, and Yosemite valleys known only to mountaineers. Once I spent a night by a camp-fire on Mount Shasta with Asa Gray and Sir Joseph Hooker, and, knowing that they were acquainted with all the great forests of the world, I asked whether they knew any coniferous forest that rivaled that of the Sierra. They unhesitatingly said: "No. In the beauty and grandeur of individual trees, and in number and variety of species, the Sierra forests surpass all others."

This Sierra Reserve, proclaimed by the President of the United

States in September, 1893, is worth the most thoughtful care of the government for its own sake, without considering its value as the fountain of the rivers on which the fertility of the great San Joaquin Valley depends. Yet it gets no care at all. In the fog of tariff, silver, and annexation politics it is left wholly unguarded, though the management of the adjacent national parks by a few soldiers shows how well and how easily it can be preserved. In the meantime, lumbermen are allowed to spoil it at their will, and sheep in uncountable ravenous hordes to trample it and devour every green leaf within reach; while the shepherds, like destroying angels, set innumerable fires, which burn not only the undergrowth of seedlings on which the permanence of the forest depends, but countless thousands of the venerable giants. If every citizen could take one walk through this reserve, there would be no more trouble about its care; for only in darkness does vandalism flourish.

The reserves of southern California—the San Gabriel, San Bernardino, San Jacinto, and Trabuco—though not large, only about two million acres together, are perhaps the best appreciated. Their slopes are covered with a close, almost impenetrable growth of flowery bushes, beginning on the sides of the fertile coast valleys and the dry interior plains. Their higher ridges, however, and mountains are open, and fairly well forested with sugar pine, yellow pine, Douglas spruce, libocedrus, and white fir. As timber fountains they amount to little, but as bird and bee pastures, cover for the precious streams that irrigate the lowlands, and quickly available retreats from dust and heat and care, their value is incalculable. Good roads have been graded into them, by which in a few hours lowlanders can get well up into the sky and find refuge in hospitable camps and club-houses, where, while breathing reviving ozone, they may absorb the beauty about them, and look comfortably down on the busy towns and the most beautiful orange groves ever planted since gardening began.

The Grand Cañon Reserve of Arizona, of nearly two million acres,

The Wild Parks and Forest Reservations

or the most interesting part of it, as well as the Rainier region, should be made into a national park, on account of their supreme grandeur and beauty. Setting out from Flagstaff, a station on the Atchison, Topeka, and Santa Fé Railroad, on the way to the cañon you pass through beautiful forests of yellow pine—like those of the Black Hills, but more extensive—and curious dwarf forests of nut pine and juniper, the spaces between the miniature trees planted with many interesting species of eriogonum, yucca, and cactus. After riding or walking seventy-five miles through these pleasure-grounds, the San Francisco and other mountains, abounding in flowery park-like openings and smooth shallow valleys with long vistas which in fineness of finish and arrangement suggest the work of a consummate landscape artist, watching you all the way, you come to the most tremendous cañon in the world. It is abruptly countersunk in the forest plateau, so that you see nothing of it until you are suddenly stopped on its brink, with its immeasurable wealth of divinely colored and sculptured buildings before you and beneath you. No matter how far you have wandered hitherto, or how many famous gorges and valleys you have seen, this one, the Grand Cañon of the Colorado, will seem as novel to you, as unearthly in the color and grandeur and quantity of its architecture, as if you had found it after death, on some other star; so incomparably lovely and grand and supreme is it above all the other cañons in our fire-moulded, earth-quake-shaken, rain-washed, wave-washed, river and glacier sculptured world. It is about six thousand feet deep where you first see it, and from rim to rim ten to fifteen miles wide. Instead of being dependent for interest upon waterfalls, depth, wall sculpture, and beauty of parklike floor, like most other great cañons, it has no waterfalls in sight, and no appreciable floor spaces. The big river has just room enough to flow and roar obscurely, here and there groping its way as best it can, like a weary, murmuring, overladen traveler trying to escape from the tremendous, bewildering labyrinthic abyss, while its roar serves only to deepen the silence. Instead of being filled with air, the vast space between the walls is crowded with Nature's grandest buildings—a sublime city of them, painted in every color, and adorned with richly fretted cornice and battlement spire and tower in endless variety of style and architecture. Every architectural invention of man has been anticipated, and far more, in this grandest of God's terrestrial cities.

The Yellowstone National Park

Of the four national parks of the West, the Yellowstone is far the largest. It is a big, wholesome wilderness on the broad summit of the Rocky Mountains, favored with abundance of rain and snow—a place of fountains where the greatest of the American rivers take their rise. The central portion is a densely forested and comparatively level volcanic plateau with an average elevation of about eight thousand feet above the sea, surrounded by an imposing host of mountains belonging to the subordinate Gallatin, Wind River, Teton, Absaroka, and Snowy ranges. Unnumbered lakes shine in it, united by a famous band of streams that rush up out of hot lava beds, or fall from the frosty peaks in channels rocky and bare, mossy and bosky, to the main rivers, singing cheerily on through every difficulty, cunningly dividing and finding their way east and west to the two far-off seas.

Glacier meadows and beaver meadows are out-spread with charming effect along the banks of the streams, parklike expanses in the woods, and innumerable small gardens in rocky recesses of the mountains, some of them containing more petals than leaves, while the whole wilderness is enlivened with happy animals.

Beside the treasures common to most mountain regions that are wild and blessed with a kind climate, the park is full of exciting wonders. The wildest geysers in the world, in bright, triumphant bands, are dancing and singing in it amid thousands of boiling springs, beautiful and awful, their basins arrayed in gorgeous colors like gigantic flowers; and hot paint-pots, mud springs, mud volcanoes, mush and broth caldrons whose contents are of every color and consistency, plash and heave and roar in bewildering abundance. In the adjacent mountains, beneath the living trees the edges of petrified forests are exposed to view, like specimens on the shelves of a museum, standing on ledges tier above tier where they grew, solemnly silent in rigid crystalline beauty after swaying in the winds thousands of centuries ago, opening marvelous views back into the years and climates and life of the past. Here, too, are hills of sparkling crystals, hills of sulphur, hills of glass, hills of cinders and ashes, mountains of every style of architecture, icy or forested, mountains covered with honey-bloom sweet as Hymettus, mountains boiled soft like potatoes and colored like a sunset sky. A' that and a' that, and twice as muckle's a' that, Nature has on show in the Yellowstone Park. Therefore it is called Wonderland, and thousands of tourists and travelers stream into it every summer, and wander about in it enchanted.

Fortunately, almost as soon as it was discovered it was dedicated and set apart for the benefit of the people, a piece of legislation that shines benignly amid the common dust-and-ashes history of the public domain, for which the world must thank Professor Hayden above all others; for he led the first scientific exploring party into it, described it, and with admirable enthusiasm urged Congress to preserve it. As delineated in the year 1872, the park contained about 3344 square miles. On March 30, 1891, it was to all intents and purposes enlarged by the Yellowstone National Park Timber Reserve, and in December, 1897, by the Teton Forest Reserve; thus nearly doubling its original area, and extending the southern boundary far enough to take in the sublime Teton range and the famous pasture-lands of the big Rocky Mountain game animals. The withdrawal of this large tract from the public domain did no harm to any one; for its height,

The Yellowstone National Park

6000 to over 13,000 feet above the sea, and its thick mantle of volcanic rocks, prevent its ever being available for agriculture or mining, while on the other hand its geographical position, reviving climate, and wonderful scenery combine to make it a grand health, pleasure, and study resort—a gathering-place for travelers from all the world.

The national parks are not only withdrawn from sale and entry like the forest reservations, but are efficiently managed and guarded by small troops of United States cavalry, directed by the Secretary of the Interior. Under this care the forests are flourishing, protected from both axe and fire; and so, of course, are the shaggy beds of underbrush and the herbaceous vegetation. The so-called curiosities, also, are preserved, and the furred and feathered tribes, many of which, in danger of extinction a short time ago, are now increasing in numbers—a refreshing thing to see amid the blind, ruthless destruction that is going on in the adjacent regions. In pleasing contrast to the noisy, ever changing management, or mismanagement, of blundering, plundering, money-making vote-sellers who receive their places from boss politicians as purchased goods, the soldiers do their duty so quietly that the traveler is scarce aware of their presence.

This is the coolest and highest of the parks. Frosts occur every month of the year. Nevertheless, the tenderest tourist finds it warm enough in summer. The air is electric and full of ozone, healing, reviving, exhilarating, kept pure by frost and fire, while the scenery is wild enough to awaken the dead. It is a glorious place to grow in and rest in; camping on the shores of the lakes, in the warm openings of the woods golden with sunflowers, on the banks of the streams, by the snowy waterfalls, beside the exciting wonders or away from them in the scallops of the mountain walls sheltered from every wind, on smooth silky lawns enameled with gentians, up in the fountain hollows of the ancient glaciers between the peaks, where cool pools and brooks and gardens of precious plants charmingly embowered are never wanting, and good rough rocks with every variety of cliff and scaur are invitingly near for outlooks and exercise.

From these lovely dens you make make excursions whenever you like into the middle of the park, where the geysers and hot springs are reeking and spouting in their beautiful basins, displaying an exuberance of color and strange motion and energy admirably calculated to surprise and frighten, charm and shake up the least sensitive out of apathy into newness of life.

However orderly your excursions or aimless, again and again amid the calmest, stillest scenery you will be brought to a standstill hushed and awe-stricken before phenomena wholly new to you. Boiling springs and huge deep pools of purest green and azure water, thousands of them, are plashing and heaving in these high, cool mountains as if a fierce furnace fire were burning beneath each one of them; and a hundred geysers, white torrents of boiling water and steam, like inverted waterfalls, are ever and anon rushing up out of the hot, black underworld. Some of these ponderous geyser columns are as large as sequoias—five to sixty feet in diameter, one hundred and fifty to three hundred feet high—and are sustained at this great height with tremendous energy for a few minutes, or perhaps nearly an hour, standing rigid and erect, hissing, throbbing, booming, as if thunderstorms were raging beneath their roots, their sides roughened or fluted like the furrowed boles of trees, their tops dissolving in feathery branches, while the irised spray, like misty bloom is at times blown aside, revealing the massive shafts shining against a background of pine-covered hills. Some of them lean more or less, as if storm-bent, and instead of being round are flat or fan-shaped, issuing from irregular slits in silex pavements with radiate structure, the sunbeams sifting through them in ravishing splendor. Some are broad and round-headed like oaks; others are low and bunchy, branching near the ground like bushes; and a few are hollow in the centre like big daisies or water-lilies. No frost cools them, snow never covers them nor lodges in their branches; winter and summer they welcome alike; all of them, of whatever form or size, faithfully rising and sinking in fairy rhythmic dance night and day, in all sorts of weather, at varying periods of minutes, hours, or weeks, growing up rapidly, uncontrollable as fate, tossing their pearly branches in the wind, bursting into bloom and vanishing like the frailest flowers —plants of which Nature raises hundreds or thousands of crops a year with no apparent exhaustion of the fiery soil.

The so-called geyser basins, in which this rare sort of vegetation is growing, are mostly open valleys on the central plateau that were eroded by glaciers after the greater volcanic fires had ceased to burn. Looking down over the forests as you approach them from the surrounding heights, you see a multitude of white columns, broad, reeking masses, and irregular jets and puffs of misty vapor ascending from the bottom of the valley, or entangled like smoke among the neighboring trees, suggesting the factories of some busy town or the camp-fires of an army. These mark the position of each mush-pot, paint-pot, hot spring, and geyser, or gusher, as the Icelandic words mean. And when you saunter into the midst of them over the bright sinter pavements, and see how pure and white and pearly gray they are in the shade of the mountains, and how radiant in the sunshine, you are fairly enchanted. So numerous they are and varied, Nature seems to have gathered them from all the world as specimens of her rarest fountains, to show in one place what she can do. Over four thousand hot springs have been counted in the park, and a hundred geysers; how many more there are nobody knows.

These valleys at the heads of the great rivers may be regarded as laboratories and kitchens, in which, amid a thousand retorts and pots, we may see Nature at work as chemist or cook, cunningly compounding an infinite variety of mineral messes; cooking whole mountains; boiling and steaming flinty rocks to smooth paste and mush—yellow, brown, red, pink, lavender, gray, and creamy white— making the most beautiful mud in the world; and distilling the most ethereal essences. Many of these pots and caldrons have been boiling thousands of years. Pots of sulphurous mush, stringy and lumpy, and pots of broth as black as ink, are tossed and stirred with constant care, and thin transparent essences, too pure and fine to be called water, are kept simmering gently in beautiful sinter cups and bowls that grow ever more beautiful the longer they are used. In some of the spring basins, the waters, though still warm, are perfectly calm, and shine blandly in a sod of overleaning grass and flowers, as if they were thoroughly cooked at last, and set aside to settle and cool. Others are wildly boiling over as if running to waste, thousands of tons of the precious liquids being thrown into the air to fall in scalding floods on the clean coral floor of the establishment, keeping onlookers at a distance. Instead of holding limpid pale green or azure water, other pots and craters are filled with scalding mud, which is tossed up from three or four feet to thirty feet, in sticky, rank-smelling masses, with gasping, belching, thudding sounds, plastering the branches of neighboring trees; every flask, retort, hot spring, and geyser has something special in it, no two being the same in temperature, color, or composition.

In these natural laboratories one needs stout faith to feel at ease. The ground sounds hollow underfoot, and the awful subterranean thunder shakes one's mind as the ground is shaken, especially at night in the pale moonlight, or when the sky is overcast with storm-clouds. In the solemn gloom, the geysers, dimly visible, look like monstrous dancing ghosts, and their wild songs and the earthquake thunder replying to the storms overhead seem doubly terrible, as if divine government were at an end. But the trembling hills keep their places. The sky clears, the rosy dawn is reassuring, and up comes the sun like a god, pouring his faithful beams across the mountains and forest, lighting each peak and tree and ghastly geyser alike, and shining into the eyes of the reeking springs, clothing them with rainbow light, and dissolving the seeming chaos of darkness into varied forms of harmony. The ordinary work of the world goes on. Gladly we see the flies dancing in the sunbeams, birds feeding their young, squirrels gathering nuts, and hear the blessed ouzel singing confidingly in the shallows of the river—most faithful evangel, calming every fear, reducing everything to love.

The variously tinted sinter and travertine formations, outspread like pavements over large areas of the geyser valleys, lining the spring basins and throats of the craters, and forming beautiful coral-like rims and curbs about them, always excite admiring attention; so also does the play of the waters from which they are deposited. The various minerals in them are rich in colors, and these are greatly heightened by a smooth, silky growth of brilliantly colored confervae which lines many of the pools and channels and terraces. No bed of flower-bloom is more exquisite than these myriads of minute plants, visible only in mass, growing in the hot waters. Most of the spring borders are low and daintily scalloped, crenelated, and beaded with sinter pearls. Some of the geyser craters are massive and picturesque, like ruined castles or old burned-out sequoia stumps, and are adorned on a grand scale with outbulging, cauliflowerlike formations. From these as centres the silex pavements slope gently away in thin, crusty, overlapping layers, slightly interrupted in some places by low terraces. Or, as in the case of the Mammoth Hot Springs, at the north end of the park, where the building waters issue from the side of a steep hill, the deposits form a succession of higher and broader terraces of white travertine tinged with purple, like the famous Pink Terrace at Rotomahana, New Zealand, draped in front with clustering stalactites, each terrace having a pool of indescribably beautiful water upon it in a basin with a raised rim that glistens with confervae—the whole, when viewed at a distance of a mile or two, looking like a broad, massive cascade pouring over shelving rocks in snowy purpled foam.

The stones of this divine masonry, invisible particles of lime or silex, mined in quarries no eye has seen, go to their appointed places in gentle, tinkling, transparent currents or through the dashing tur-

31

moil of floods, as surely guided as the sap of plants streaming into bole and branch, leaf and flower. And thus from century to century this beauty-work has gone on and is going on.

Passing through many a mile of pine and spruce woods, toward the centre of the park you come to the famous Yellowstone Lake. It is about twenty miles long and fifteen wide, and lies at a height of nearly 8000 feet above the level of the sea, amid dense black forests and snowy mountains. Around its winding, wavering shores, closely forested and picturesquely varied with promontories and bays, the distance is more than 100 miles. It is not very deep, only from 200 to 300 feet, and contains less water than the celebrated Lake Tahoe of the California Sierra, which is nearly the same size, lies at a height of 6400 feet, and is over 1600 feet deep. But no other lake in North America of equal area lies so high as the Yellowstone, or gives birth to so noble a river. The terraces around its shores show that at the close of the glacial period its surface was about 160 feet higher than it is now, and its area nearly twice as great.

It is full of trout, and a vast multitude of birds—swans, pelicans, geese, ducks, cranes, herons, curlews, plovers, snipe—feed in it and upon its shores; and many forest animals come out of the woods, and wade a little way in shallow, sandy places to drink and look about them, and cool themselves in the free flowing breezes.

In calm weather it is a magnificent mirror for the woods and mountains and sky, now pattered with hail and rain, now roughened with sudden storms that send waves to fringe the shores and wash its border of gravel and sand. The Absaroka Mountains and the Wind River Plateau on the east and south pour their gathered waters into it, and the river issues from the north side in a broad, smooth, stately current, silently gliding with such serene majesty that one fancies it knows the vast journey of four thousand miles that lies before it; and the work it has to do. For the first twenty miles its course is in a level, sunny valley lightly fringed with trees, through which it flows in silvery reaches stirred into spangles here and there by ducks and leaping trout, making no sound save a low whispering among the pebbles and the dipping willows and sedges of its banks. Then suddenly, as if preparing for hard work, it rushes eagerly, impetuously forward rejoicing in its strength, breaks into foam-bloom, and goes thundering down into the Grand Cañon in two magnificent falls, one hundred and three hundred feet high.

The cañon is so tremendously wild and impressive that even these great falls cannot hold your attention. It is about twenty miles long and a thousand feet deep—a weird, unearthly-looking gorge of jagged, fantastic architecture, and most brilliantly colored. Here the Washburn range, forming the northern rim of the Yellowstone basin, made up mostly of beds of rhyolite decomposed by the action of thermal waters, has been cut through and laid open to view by the river; and a famous section it has made. It is not the depth or the shape of the cañon, nor the waterfall, nor the green and gray river chanting its brave song as it goes foaming on its way, that most impresses the observer, but the colors of the decomposed volcanic rocks. With few exceptions, the traveler in strange lands finds that, however much the scenery and vegetation in different countries may change, Mother Earth is ever familiar and the same. But here the very ground is changed, as if belonging to some other world. The walls of the cañon from top to bottom burn in a perfect glory of color, confounding and dazzling when the sun is shining—white, yellow, green, blue, vermilion, and various other shades of red indefinitely blending. All the earth hereabouts seems to be paint. Millions of tons of it lie in sight, exposed to wind and weather as if of no account, yet marvelously fresh and bright, fast colors not to be washed out or bleached out by either sunshine or storms. The effect is so novel and awful, we imagine that even a river might be afraid to enter such a place. But the rich and gentle beauty of the vegetation is reassuring. The lovely Linnaea borealis hangs her twin bells over the brink of the cliffs, forests and gardens extend their treasures in smiling confidence on either side, nuts and berries ripen well whatever

33

may be going on below; blind fears vanish, and the grand gorge seems a kindly, beautiful part of the general harmony, full of peace and joy and good will.

The park is easy of access. Locomotives drag you to its northern boundary at Cinnabar, and horses and guides do the rest. From Cinnabar you will be whirled in coaches along the foaming Gardiner River to Mammoth Hot Springs; thence through woods and meadows, gulches and ravines along branches of the Upper Gallatin, Madison, and Firehole rivers to the main geyser basins; thence over the Continental Divide and back again, up and down through dense pine, spruce, and fir woods to the magnificent Yellowstone Lake, along its northern shore to the outlet, down the river to the falls and Grand Cañon, and thence back through the woods to Mammoth Hot Springs and Cinnabar; stopping here and there at the so-called points of interest among the geysers, springs, paint-pots, mud volcanoes, etc., where you will be allowed a few minutes or hours to saunter over the sinter pavements, watch the play of a few of the geysers, and peer into some of the most beautiful and terrible of the craters and pools. These wonders you will enjoy, and also the views of the mountains, especially the Gallatin and Absaroka ranges, the long, willowy glacier and beaver meadows, the beds of violets, gentians, phloxes, asters, phacelias, goldenrods, eriogonums, and many other flowers, some species giving color to whole meadows and hillsides. And you will enjoy your short views of the great lake and river and cañon. No scalping Indians will you see. The Blackfeet and Bannocks that once roamed here are gone; so are the old beaver-catchers, the Coulters and Bridgers, with all their attractive buckskin and romance. There are several bands of buffaloes in the park, but you will not thus cheaply in tourist fashion see them nor many of the other large animals hidden in the wilderness. The song-birds, too, keep mostly out of sight of the rushing tourist, though off the roads thrushes, warblers, orioles, grosbeaks, etc., keep the air sweet and merry. Perhaps in passing rapids and falls you may catch

The Yellowstone National Park

glimpses of the water-ouzel, but in the whirling noise you will not hear his song. Fortunately, no road noise frightens the Douglas squirrel, and his merry play and gossip will amuse you all through the woods. Here and there a deer may be seen crossing the road, or a bear. Most likely, however, the only bears you will see are the half tame ones that go to the hotels every night for dinner-table scraps— yeast-powder biscuit, Chicago canned stuff, mixed pickles, and beefsteaks that have proved too tough for the tourists.

Among the gains of a coach trip are the acquaintances made and the fresh views into human nature; for the wilderness is a shrewd touchstone, even thus lightly approached, and brings many a curious trait to view. Setting out, the driver cracks his whip, and the four horses go off at half gallop, half trot, in trained, showy style, until out of sight of the hotel. The coach is crowded, old and young side by side, blooming and fading, full of hope and fun and care. Some look at the scenery or the horses, and all ask questions, an odd mixed lot of them: "Where is the umbrella? What is the name of that blue flower over there? Are you sure the little bag is aboard? Is that hollow yonder a crater? How is your throat this morning? How high did you say the geysers spout? How does the elevation affect your head? Is that a geyser reeking over there in the rocks, or only a hot spring?" A long ascent is made, the solemn mountains come to view, small cares are quenched, and all become natural and silent, save perhaps some unfortunate expounder who has been reading guide-book geology, and rumbles forth foggy subsidences and upheavals until he is in danger of being heaved overboard. The driver will give you the names of the peaks and meadows and streams as you come to them, call attention to the glass road, tell how hard it was to build —how the obsidian cliffs naturally pushed the surveyor's lines to the right, and the industrious beavers, by flooding the valley in front of the cliff, pushed them to the left.

Geysers, however, are the main objects, and as soon as they come in sight other wonders are forgotten. All gather around the crater of

35

the one that is expected to play first. During the eruptions of the smaller geysers, such as the Beehive and Old Faithful, though a little frightened at first, all welcome the glorious show with enthusiasm, and shout, "Oh, how wonderful, beautiful, splendid, majestic!" Some venture near enough to stroke the column with a stick, as if it were a stone pillar or a tree, so firm and substantial and permanent it seems. While tourists wait around a large geyser, such as the Castle or the Giant, there is a chatter of small talk in anything but solemn mood; and during the intervals between the preliminary splashes and upheavals some adventurer occasionally looks down the throat of the crater, admiring the silex formations and wondering whether Hades is as beautiful. But when, with awful uproar as if avalanches were falling and storms thundering in the depths, the tremendous outburst begins, all run away to a safe distance, and look on, awe-stricken and silent, in devout, worshiping wonder.

The largest and one of the most wonderfully beautiful of the springs is the Prismatic, which the guide will be sure to show you. With a circumference of 300 yards, it is more like a lake than a spring. The water is pure deep blue in the centre, fading to green on the edges, and its basin and the slightly terraced pavement about it are astonishingly bright and varied in color. This one of the multitude of Yellowstone fountains is of itself object enough for a trip across the continent. No wonder that so many fine myths have originated in springs; that so many fountains were held sacred in the youth of the world, and had miraculous virtues ascribed to them. Even in these cold, doubting, questioning, scientific times many of the Yellowstone fountains seem able to work miracles. Near the Prismatic Spring is the great Excelsior Geyser, which is said to throw a column of boiling water 60 to 70 feet in diameter to a height of from 50 to 300 feet, at irregular periods. This is the greatest of all the geysers yet discovered anywhere. The Firehole River, which sweeps past it, is, at ordinary stages, a stream about 100 yards wide and 3 feet deep; but when the geyser is in eruption, so great is the quantity of water discharged that the volume of the river is doubled, and it is rendered too hot and rapid to be forded.

Geysers are found in many other volcanic regions—in Iceland, New Zealand, Japan, the Himalayas, the Eastern Archipelago, South America, the Azores, and elsewhere; but only in Iceland, New Zealand, and this Rocky Mountain park do they display their grandest forms, and of these three famous regions the Yellowstone is easily first, both in the number and in the size of its geysers. The greatest height of the column of the Great Geyser of Iceland actually measured was 212 feet, and of the Strokhr 162 feet.

In New Zealand, the Te Pueia at Lake Taupo, the Waikite at Rotorna, and two others are said to lift their waters occasionally to a height of 100 feet, while the celebrated Te Tarata at Rotomahana sometimes lifts a boiling column 20 feet in diameter to a height of 60 feet. But all these are far surpassed by the Excelsior. Few tourists, however, will see the Excelsior in action, or a thousand other interesting features of the park that lie beyond the wagon-roads and the hotels. The regular trips—from three to five days—are too short. Nothing can be done well at a speed of forty miles a day. The multitude of mixed, novel impressions rapidly piled on one another make only a dreamy, bewildering, swirling blur, most of which is unrememberable. Far more time should be taken. Walk away quietly in any direction and taste the freedom of the mountaineer. Camp out among the grass and gentians of glacier meadows, in craggy garden nooks full of Nature's darlings. Climb the mountains and get their good tidings. Nature's peace will flow into you as sunshine flows into trees. The winds will blow their own freshness into you, and the storms their energy, while cares will drop off like autumn leaves. As age comes on, one source of enjoyment after another is closed, but Nature's sources never fail. Like a generous host, she offers here brimming cups in endless variety, served in a grand hall, the sky its ceiling, the mountains its walls, decorated with glorious paintings and enlivened with bands of music ever playing. The petty discomforts that beset the awkward guest, the unskilled camper, are quickly forgotten, while all that is precious remains. Fears vanish as soon as one is fairly free in the wilderness.

Most of the dangers that haunt the unseasoned citizen are imaginary; the real ones are perhaps too few rather than too many for his good. The bears that always seem to spring up thick as trees, in fighting, devouring attitudes before the frightened tourist whenever a camping trip is proposed, are gentle now, finding they are no longer likely to be shot; and rattlesnakes, the other big irrational dread of over-civilized people, are scarce here, for most of the park lies above the snake-line. Poor creatures, loved only by their Maker, they are timid and bashful, as mountaineers know; and though perhaps not possessed of much of that charity that suffers long and is kind, seldom, either by mistake or by mishap, do harm to any one. Certainly they cause not the hundredth part of the pain and death that follow the footsteps of the admired Rocky Mountain trapper. Nevertheless, again and again, in season and out of season, the question comes up, "What are rattlesnakes good for?" As if nothing that does not obviously make for the benefit of man had any right to exist; as if our ways were God's ways. Long ago, an Indian to whom a French traveler put this old question replied that their tails were good for toothache, and their heads for fever. Anyhow, they are all, head and tail, good for themselves, and we need not begrudge them their share of life.

Fear nothing. No town park you have been accustomed to saunter in is so free from danger as the Yellowstone. It is a hard place to leave. Even its names in your guidebook are attractive, and should draw you far from wagon-roads—all save the early ones, derived from the infernal regions: Hell Roaring River, Hell Broth Springs, The Devil's Caldron, etc. Indeed, the whole region was at first called Coulter's Hell, from the fiery brimstone stories told by trapper Coulter, who left the Lewis and Clark expedition and wandered through the park, in the year 1807, with a band of Bannock Indians.

The Yellowstone National Park

The later names, many of which we owe to Mr. Arnold Hague of the U.S. Geological Survey, are so telling and exhilarating that they set our pulses dancing and make us begin to enjoy the pleasures of excursions ere they are commenced. Three River Peak, Two Ocean Pass, Continental Divide, are capital geographical descriptions, suggesting thousands of miles of rejoicing streams and all that belongs to them. Big Horn Pass, Bison Peak, Big Game Ridge, bring brave mountain animals to mind. Birch Hills, Garnet Hills, Amethyst Mountain, Storm Peak, Electric Peak, Roaring Mountain, are bright, bracing names. Wapiti, Beaver, Tern, and Swan lakes conjure up fine pictures, and so also do Osprey and Ouzel falls. Antelope Creek, Otter, Mink, and Grayling creeks, Geode, Jasper, Opal, Carnelian, and Chalcedony creeks, are lively and sparkling names that help the streams to shine; and Azalea, Stellaria, Arnica, Aster, and Phlox creeks, what pictures these bring up! Violet, Morning Mist, Hygeia, Beryl, Vermilion, and Indigo springs, and many beside, give us visions of fountains more beautifully arrayed than Solomon in all his purple and golden glory. All these and a host of others call you to camp. You may be a little cold some nights, on mountain tops above the timber-line, but you will see the stars, and by and by you can sleep enough in your town bed, or at least in your grave. Keep awake while you may in mountain mansions so rare.

If you are not very strong, try to climb Electric Peak when a big bossy, well-charged thunder-cloud is on it, to breathe the ozone set free, and get yourself kindly shaken and shocked. You are sure to be lost in wonder and praise, and every hair of your head will stand up and hum and sing like an enthusiastic congregation.

After this reviving experience, you should take a look into a few of the tertiary volumes of the grand geological library of the park, and see how God writes history. No technical knowledge is required; only a calm day and a calm mind. Perhaps nowhere else in the Rocky Mountains have the volcanic forces been so busy. More than ten thousand square miles hereabouts have been covered to a depth of at least five thousand feet with material spouted from chasms and craters during the tertiary period, forming broad sheets of basalt, andesite, rhyolite, etc., and marvelous masses of ashes, sand, cinders, and stones now consolidated into conglomerates, charged with the remains of plants and animals that lived in the calm, genial periods that separated the volcanic outbursts.

Perhaps the most interesting and telling of these rocks, to the hasty tourist, are those that make up the mass of Amethyst Mountain. On its north side it presents a section two thousand feet high of roughly stratified beds of sand, ashes, and conglomerates coarse and fine, forming the untrimmed edges of a wonderful set of volumes lying on their sides—books a million years old, well bound, miles in size, with full-page illustrations. On the ledges of this one section we see trunks and stumps of fifteen or twenty ancient forests ranged one above another, standing where they grew, or prostrate and broken like the pillars of ruined temples in desert sands—a forest fifteen or twenty stories high, the roots of each spread above the tops of the next beneath it, telling wonderful tales of the bygone centuries, with their winters and summers, growth and death, fire, ice, and flood.

There were giants in those days. The largest of the standing opal and agate stumps and prostrate sections of the trunks are from two or three to fifty feet in height or length, and from five to ten feet in diameter; and so perfect is the petrifaction that the annual rings and ducts are clearer and more easily counted than those of living trees, centuries of burial having brightened the records instead of blurring them. They show that the winters of the tertiary period gave as decided a check to vegetable growth as do those of the present time. Some trees favorably located grew rapidly, increasing twenty inches in diameter in as many years, while others of the same species, on poorer soil or overshadowed, increased only two or three inches in the same time.

Among the roots and stumps on the old forest floors we find the remains of ferns and bushes, and the seeds and leaves of trees like those now growing on the southern Alleghanies—such as magnolia, sassafras, laurel, linden, persimmon, ash, alder, dogwood. Studying the lowest of these forests, the soil it grew on and the deposits it is buried in, we see that it was rich in species, and flourished in a genial, sunny climate. When its stately trees were in their glory, volcanic fires broke forth from chasms and craters, like larger geysers, spouting ashes, cinders, stones, and mud, which fell on the doomed forest like hail and snow; sifting, hurtling through the leaves and branches, choking the streams, covering the ground, crushing bushes and ferns, rapidly deepening, packing around the trees and breaking them, rising higher until the topmost boughs of the giants were buried, leaving not a leaf or twig in sight, so complete was the desolation. At last the volcanic storm began to abate, the fiery soil settled; mud floods and boulder floods passed over it, enriching it, cooling it; rains fell and mellow sunshine, and it became fertile and ready for another crop. Birds, and the winds, and roaming animals brought seeds from more fortunate woods, and a new forest grew up on the top of the buried one. Centuries of genial growing seasons passed. The seedling trees became giants, and with strong outreaching branches spread a leafy canopy over the gray land.

The sleeping subterranean fires again awake and shake the mountains, and every leaf trembles. The old craters, with perhaps new ones, are opened, and immense quantities of ashes, pumice, and cinders are again thrown into the sky. The sun, shorn of his beams, glows like a dull red ball, until hidden in sulphurous clouds. Volcanic snow, hail, and floods fall on the new forest, burying it alive, like the one beneath its roots. Then come another noisy band of mud floods and boulder floods, mixing, settling, enriching the new ground, more seeds, quickening sunshine and showers; and a third noble magnolia forest is carefully raised on the top of the second. And so on. Forest was planted above forest and destroyed, as if Nature were ever repenting, undoing the work she had so industriously done, and burying it.

THE AMERICAN WILDERNESS

Of course this destruction was creation, progress in the march of beauty through death. How quickly these old monuments excite and hold the imagination! We see the old stone stumps budding and blossoming and waving in the wind as magnificent trees, standing shoulder to shoulder, branches interlacing in grand varied round-headed forests; see the sunshine of morning and evening gilding their mossy trunks, and at high noon spangling on the thick glossy leaves of the magnolia, filtering through translucent canopies of linden and ash, and falling in mellow patches on the ferny floor; see the shining after rain, breathe the exhaling fragrance, and hear the winds and birds and the murmur of brooks and insects. We watch them from season to season; see the swelling buds when the sap begins to flow in the spring, the opening leaves and blossoms, the ripening of summer fruits, the colors of autumn, and the maze of leafless branches and sprays in winter; and we see the sudden oncome of the storms that overwhelmed them.

One calm morning at sunrise I saw the oaks and pines in Yosemite Valley shaken by an earthquake, their tops swishing back and forth, and every branch and needle shuddering as if in distress like the frightened screaming birds. One may imagine the trembling, rocking, tumultuous waving of those ancient Yellowstone woods, and the terror of their inhabitants when the first foreboding shocks were felt, the sky grew dark, and rock-laden floods began to roar. But though they were close pressed and buried, cut off from sun and wind, all their happy leaf-fluttering and waving done, other currents coursed through them, fondling and thrilling every fibre, and beautiful wood was replaced by beautiful stone. Now their rocky sepulchres are partly open, and show forth the natural beauty of death.

After the forest times and fire times had passed away, and the volcanic furnaces were banked and held in abeyance, another great change occurred. The glacial winter came on. The sky was again darkened, not with dust and ashes, but with snow which fell in glorious abundance, piling deeper, deeper, slipping from the over-

The Yellowstone National Park

laden heights in booming avalanches, compacting into glaciers, that flowed over all the landscape, wiping off forests, grinding, sculpturing, fashioning the comparatively featureless lava beds into the beautiful rhythm of hill and dale and ranges of mountains we behold today; forming basins for lakes, channels for streams, new soils for forests, gardens, and meadows. While this ice-work was going on, the slumbering volcanic fires were boiling the subterranean waters, and with curious chemistry decomposing the rocks, making beauty in the darkness; these forces, seemingly antagonistic, working harmoniously together. How wild their meetings on the surface were we may imagine. When the glacier period began, geysers and hot springs were playing in grander volume, it may be, than those of today. The glaciers flowed over them while they spouted and thundered, carrying away their fine sinter and travertine structures, and shortening their mysterious channels.

The soils made in the down-grinding required to bring the present features of the landscape into relief are possibly no better than were some of the old volcanic soils that were carried away, and which, as we have seen, nourished magnificent forests, but the glacial landscapes are incomparably more beautiful than the old volcanic ones were. The glacial winter has passed away, like the ancient summers and fire periods, though in the chronology of the geologist all these times are recent. Only small residual glaciers on the cool northern slopes of the highest mountains are left of the vast all-embracing ice-mantle, as solfataras and geysers are all that are left of the ancient volcanoes.

Now the post-glacial agents are at work on the grand old palimpsest of the park region, inscribing new characters; but still in its main telling features it remains distinctly glacial. The moraine soils are being leveled, sorted, refined, re-formed, and covered with vegetation; the polished pavements and scoring and other superficial glacial inscriptions on the crumbling lavas are being rapidly obliterated; gorges are being cut in the decomposed rhyolites and loose

43

conglomerates, and turrets and pinnacles seem to be springing up like growing trees; while the geysers are depositing miles of sinter and travertine. Nevertheless, the ice-work is scarce blurred as yet. These later effects are only spots and wrinkles on the grand glacial countenance of the park.

Perhaps you have already said that you have seen enough for a lifetime. But before you go away you should spend at least one day and a night on a mountain top, for a last general, calming, settling view. Mount Washburn is a good one for the purpose, because it stands in the middle of the park, is unencumbered with other peaks, and is so easy of access that the climb to its summit is only a saunter. First your eye goes roving around the mountain rim amid the hundreds of peaks: some with plain flowing skirts, others abruptly precipitous and defended by sheer battlemented escarpments; flat-topped or round; heaving like sea-waves or spired and turreted like Gothic cathedrals; streaked with snow in the ravines, and darkened with files of adventurous trees climbing the ridges. The nearer peaks are perchance clad in sapphire blue, others far off in creamy white. In the broad glare of noon they seem to shrink and crouch to less than half their real stature, and grow dull and uncommunicative— mere dead, draggled heaps of waste ashes and stone, giving no hint of the multitude of animals enjoying life in their fastnesses, or of the bright bloom-bordered streams and lakes. But when storms blow they awake and arise, wearing robes of cloud and mist in majestic speaking attitudes like gods. In the color glory of morning and evening they become still more impressive; steeped in the divine light of the alpenglow their earthiness disappears, and, blending with the heavens, they seem neither high nor low.

Over all the central plateau, which from here seems level, and over the foothills and lower slopes of the mountains, the forest extends like a black uniform bed of weeds, interrupted only by lakes and meadows and small burned spots called parks—all of them, except the Yellowstone Lake, being mere dots and spangles in general views, made conspicuous by their color and brightness. About eighty-five per cent of the entire area of the park is covered with trees, mostly the indomitable lodge-pole pine (*Pinus contorta,* var. *Murrayana*), with a few patches and sprinklings of Douglas spruce, Engelmann spruce, silver fir (*Abies lasiocarpa*), Pinus flexilis, and a few alders, aspens, and birches. The Douglas spruce is found only on the lowest portions, the silver fir on the highest, and the Engelmann spruce on the dampest places, best defended from fire. Some fine specimens of the flexilis pine are growing on the margins of openings—wide-branching, sturdy trees, as broad as high, with trunks five feet in diameter, leafy and shady, laden with purple cones and rose-colored flowers. The Engelmann spruce and sub-alpine silver fir are beautiful and notable trees—tall, spiry, hardy, frost and snow defying, and widely distributed over the West, wherever there is a mountain to climb or a cold moraine slope to cover. But neither of these is a good fire-fighter. With rather thin bark, and scattering their seeds every year as soon as they are ripe, they are quickly driven out of fire-swept regions. When the glaciers were melting, these hardy mountaineering trees were probably among the first to arrive on the new moraine soil beds; but as the plateau became drier and fires began to run, they were driven up the mountains, and into the wet spots and islands where we now find them, leaving nearly all the park to the lodge-pole pine, which, though as thin-skinned as they and as easily killed by fire, takes pains to store up its seeds in firmly closed cones, and holds them from three to nine years, so that, let the fire come when it may, it is ready to die and ready to live again in a new generation. For when the killing fires have devoured the leaves and thin resinous bark, many of the cones, only scorched, open as soon as the smoke clears away; the hoarded store of seeds is sown broadcast on the cleared ground, and a new growth immediately springs up triumphant out of the ashes. Therefore, this tree not only holds its ground, but extends its conquests farther after every fire. Thus the evenness and closeness of its growth are accounted for. In one part of the forest that I examined, the growth was about as close as a cane-brake. The trees were from four to eight inches in diameter, one hundred feet high, and one hundred and seventy-five years old. The lower limbs die young and drop off for want of light. Life with these close-planted trees is a race for light, more light, and so they push straight for the sky. Mowing off ten feet from the top of the forest would make it look like a crowded mass of telegraph-poles; for only the sunny tops are leafy. A sapling ten years old, growing in the sunshine, has as many leaves as a crowded tree one or two hundred years old. As fires are multiplied and the mountains become drier, this wonderful lodge-pole pine bids fair to obtain possession of nearly all the forest ground in the West.

How still the woods seem from here, yet how lively a stir the hidden animals are making; digging, gnawing, biting, eyes shining, at work and play, getting food, rearing young, roving through the underbrush, climbing the rocks, wading solitary marshes, tracing the banks of the lakes and streams! Insect swarms are dancing in the sunbeams, burrowing in the ground, diving, swimming—a cloud of witnesses telling Nature's joy. The plants are as busy as the animals, every cell in a swirl of enjoyment, humming like a hive, singing the old new song of creation. A few columns and puffs of steam are seen rising above the treetops, some near, but most of them far off, indicating geysers and hot springs, gentle-looking and noiseless as downy clouds, softly hinting the reaction going on between the surface and the hot interior. From here you see them better than when you are standing beside them, frightened and confused, regarding them as lawless cataclysms. The shocks and outbursts of earthquakes, volcanoes, geysers, storms, the pounding of waves, the uprush of sap in plants, each and all tell the orderly love-beats of Nature's heart.

Turning to the eastward, you have the Grand Cañon and reaches of the river in full view; and yonder to the southward lies the great lake, the largest and most important of all the high fountains of the Missouri-Mississippi, and the last to be discovered.

In the year 1541, when De Soto, with a romantic band of adventurers, was seeking gold and glory and the fountain of youth, he found the Mississippi a few hundred miles above its mouth, and made his grave beneath its floods. La Salle, in 1682, after discovering the Ohio, one of the largest and most beautiful branches of the Mississippi, traced the latter to the sea from the mouth of the Illinois, through adventures and privations not easily realized now. About the same time Joliet and Father Marquette reached the "Father of Waters" by way of the Wisconsin, but more than a century passed ere its highest sources in these mountains were seen. The advancing stream of civilization has ever followed its guidance toward the west, but none of the thousand tribes of Indians living on its banks could tell the explorer whence it came. From those romantic De Soto and La Salle days to these times of locomotives and tourists, how much has the great river seen and done! Great as it now is, and still growing longer through the ground of its delta and the basins of receding glaciers at its head, it was immensely broader toward the close of the glacial period, when the ice-mantle of the mountains was melting: then with its three hundred thousand miles of branches outspread over the plains and valleys of the continent, laden with fertile mud, it made the biggest and most generous bed of soil in the world.

Think of this mighty stream springing in the first place in vapor from the sea, flying on the wind, alighting on the mountains in hail and snow and rain, lingering in many a fountain feeding the trees and grass; then gathering its scattered waters, gliding from its noble lake, and going back home to the sea, singing all the way! On it sweeps, through the gates of the mountains, across the vast prairies and plains, through many a wild, gloomy forest, cane-brake, and sunny savanna; from glaciers and snowbanks and pine woods to warm groves of magnolia and palm; geysers dancing at its head keeping time with the sea-waves at its mouth; roaring and gray in rapids, booming in broad, bossy falls, murmuring, gleaming in long, silvery reaches, swaying now hither, now thither, whirling, bending in huge doubling, eddying folds, serene, majestic, ungovernable, overflowing all its metes and bounds, frightening the dwellers upon its banks; building, wasting, uprooting, planting; engulfing old islands and making new ones, taking away fields and towns as if in sport, carrying canoes and ships of commerce in the midst of its spoils and drift, fertilizing the continent as one vast farm. Then, its work done, it gladly vanishes in its ocean home, welcomed by the waiting waves.

Thus naturally, standing here in the midst of its fountains, we trace the fortunes of the great river. And how much more comes to mind as we overlook this wonderful wilderness! Fountains of the Columbia and Colorado lie before us, interlaced with those of the Yellowstone and Missouri, and fine it would be to go with them to the Pacific; but the sun is already in the west, and soon our day will be done.

Yonder is Amethyst Mountain, and other mountains hardly less rich in old forests, which now seem to spring up again in their glory; and you see the storms that buried them—the ashes and torrents laden with boulders and mud, the centuries of sunshine, and the dark, lurid nights. You see again the vast floods of lava, red-hot and white-hot, pouring out from gigantic geysers, usurping the basins of lakes and streams, absorbing or driving away their hissing, screaming waters, flowing around hills and ridges, submerging every subordinate feature. Then you see the snow and glaciers taking possession of the land, making new landscapes. How admirable it is that, after passing through so many vicissitudes of frost and fire and flood, the physiognomy and even the complexion of the landscape should still be so divinely fine!

Thus reviewing the eventful past, we see Nature working with enthusiasm like a man, blowing her volcanic forges like a blacksmith blowing his smithy fires, shoving glaciers over the landscapes like a

The Yellowstone National Park

carpenter shoving his planes, clearing, ploughing, harrowing, irrigating, planting, and sowing broadcast like a farmer and gardener, doing rough work and fine work, planting sequoias and pines, rosebushes and daisies; working in gems, filling every crack and hollow with them; distilling fine essences; painting plants and shells, clouds, mountains, all the earth and heavens, like an artist—ever working toward beauty higher and higher. Where may the mind find more stimulating, quickening pasturage? A thousand Yellowstone wonders are calling, "Look up and down and round about you!" And a multitude of still, small voices may be heard directing you to look through all this transient, shifting show of things called "substantial" into the truly substantial, spiritual world whose forms flesh and wood, rock and water, air and sunshine, only veil and conceal, and to learn that here is heaven and the dwelling-place of the angels.

The sun is setting; long, violet shadows are growing out over the woods from the mountains along the western rim of the park; the Absaroka range is baptized in the divine light of the alpenglow, and its rocks and trees are transfigured. Next to the light of the dawn on high mountain tops, the alpenglow is the most impressive of all the terrestrial manifestations of God.

Now comes the gloaming. The alpenglow is fading into earthy, murky gloom, but do not let your town habits draw you away to the hotel. Stay on this good fire-mountain and spend the night among the stars. Watch their glorious bloom until the dawn, and get one more baptism of light. Then, with fresh heart, go down to your work, and whatever your fate, under whatever ignorance or knowledge you may afterward chance to suffer, you will remember these fine, wild views, and look back with joy to your wanderings in the blessed old Yellowstone Wonderland.

49

Yellowstone National Park, Wyoming

Yellowstone National Park, Wyoming

Yellowstone Terrace, Yellowstone National Park, Wyoming

Old Faithful, Yellowstone National Park, Wyoming

Old Faithful, Yellowstone National Park, Wyoming

Middle Fork, Kings Canyon National Park, California

Winchell Mountain, Kings Canyon National Park, California

Boaring River, Kings Canyon National Park, California

Half Dome, Apple Orchard, Yosemite National Park, California

Glacier National Park, Montana

Zion National Park, Utah

Rocks, Zion National Park, Utah

Grand Canyon from South Rim (1941),
Grand Canyon National Park, Arizona

Grand Canyon National Park, Arizona

Grand Canyon National Park, Arizona

Grand Canyon from North Rim (1941),
Grand Canyon National Park, Arizona

The Sequoia
and General Grant
National Parks

The Big Tree (*Sequoia gigantea*) is Nature's forest masterpiece, and, so far as I know, the greatest of living things. It belongs to an ancient stock, as its remains in old rocks show, and has a strange air of other days about it, a thoroughbred look inherited from the long ago—the auld lang syne of trees. Once the genus was common, and with many species flourished in the now desolate Arctic regions, in the interior of North America, and in Europe, but in long, eventful wanderings from climate to climate only two species have survived the hardships they had to encounter, the gigantea and sempervirens, the former now restricted to the western slopes of the Sierra, the other to the Coast Mountains, and both to California, excepting a few groves of Redwood which extend into Oregon. The Pacific Coast in general is the paradise of conifers. Here nearly all of them are giants, and display a beauty and magnificence unknown elsewhere. The climate is mild, the ground never freezes, and moisture and sunshine abound all the year. Nevertheless it is not easy to account for the colossal size of the Sequoias. The largest are about three hundred feet high and thirty feet in diameter. Who of all the dwellers of the plains and prairies and fertile home forests of round-headed oak and maple, hickory and elm, ever dreamed that earth could bear such growths—trees that the familiar pines and firs seem to know nothing about, lonely, silent, serene, with a physiognomy almost godlike; and so old, thousands of them still living had already counted their years by tens of centuries when Columbus set sail from Spain and were in the vigor of youth or middle age when the star led the Chaldean sages to the infant Saviour's cradle! As far as man is concerned they are the same yesterday, to-day, and forever, emblems of permanence.

No description can give any adequate idea of their singular majesty, much less of their beauty. Excepting the sugar-pine, most of their neighbors with pointed tops seem to be forever shouting Excelsior, while the Big Tree, though soaring above them all, seems satisfied, its rounded head, poised lightly as a cloud, giving no impression of trying to go higher. Only in youth does it show like other conifers a heavenward yearning, keenly aspiring with a long quickgrowing top. Indeed the whole tree for the first century or two, or until a hundred to a hundred and fifty feet high, is arrowhead in form, and, compared with the solemn rigidity of age, is as sensitive to the wind as a squirrel tail. The lower branches are gradually dropped as it grows older, and the upper ones thinned out until comparatively few are left. These, however, are developed to great size, divide again and again, and terminate in bossy rounded masses of leafy branchlets, while the head becomes dome-shaped. Then poised in fullness of strength and beauty, stern and solemn in mien, it glows with eager, enthusiastic life, quivering to the tip of every leaf and branch and far-reaching root, calm as a granite dome, the first to feel the touch of the rosy beams of the morning, the last to bid the sun good-night.

Perfect specimens, unhurt by running fires or lightning, are singularly regular and symmetrical in general form, though not at all conventional, showing infinite variety in sure unity and harmony of plan. The immensely strong, stately shafts, with rich purplish brown bark, are free of limbs for a hundred and fifty feet or so, though dense tufts of sprays occur here and there, producing an ornamental effect, while long parallel furrows give a fluted columnar appearance.

The Sequoia and General Grant

It shoots forth its limbs with equal boldness in every direction, showing no weather side. On the old trees the main branches are crooked and rugged, and strike rigidly outward mostly at right angles from the trunk, but there is always a certain measured restraint in their reach which keeps them within bounds. No other Sierra tree has foliage so densely massed or outline so finely, firmly drawn and so obediently subordinate to an ideal type. A particularly knotty, angular, ungovernable-looking branch, five to eight feet in diameter and perhaps a thousand years old, may occasionally be seen pushing out from the trunk as if determined to break across the bounds of the regular curve, but like all the others, as soon as the general outline is approached the huge limb dissolves into massy bosses of branchlets and sprays, as if the tree were growing beneath an invisible bell glass against the sides of which the branches were moulded, while many small, varied departures from the ideal form give the impression of freedom to grow as they like.

Except in picturesque old age, after being struck by lightning and broken by a thousand snowstorms, this regularity of form is one of the Big Tree's most distinguishing characteristics. Another is the simple sculptural beauty of the trunk and its great thickness as compared with its height and the width of the branches, many of them being from eight to ten feet in diameter at a height of two hundred feet from the ground, and seeming more like finely modeled and sculptured architectural columns than the stems of trees, while the great strong limbs are like rafters supporting the magnificent dome head.

The root system corresponds in magnitude with the other dimensions of the tree, forming a flat far-reaching spongy network two hundred feet or more in width without any taproot, and the instep is so grand and fine, so suggestive of endless strength, it is long ere the eye is released to look above it. The natural swell of the roots, though at first sight excessive, gives rise to buttresses no greater than are required for beauty as well as strength, as at once appears when you stand back far enough to see the whole tree in its true proportions. The fineness of the taper of the trunk is shown by its thickness at great heights—a diameter of ten feet at a height of two hundred being, as we have seen, not uncommon. Indeed the boles of but few trees hold their thickness as well as Sequoia. Resolute, consummate, determined in form, always beheld with wondering admiration, the Big Tree always seems unfamiliar, standing alone, unrelated, with peculiar physiognomy, awfully solemn and earnest. Nevertheless, there is nothing alien in its looks. The madroña, clad in thin, smooth, red and yellow bark and big glossy leaves, seems, in the dark coniferous forests of Washington and Vancouver Island, like some lost wanderer from the magnolia groves of the South, while the Sequoia, with all its strangeness, seems more at home than any of its neighbors, holding the best right to the ground as the oldest, strongest inhabitant. One soon becomes acquainted with new species of pine and fir and spruce as with friendly people, shaking their outstretched branches like shaking hands, and fondling their beautiful little ones; while the venerable aboriginal Sequoia, ancient of other days, keeps you at a distance, taking no notice of you, speaking only to the winds, thinking only of the sky, looking as strange in aspect and behavior among the neighboring trees as would the mastodon or hairy elephant among the homely bears and deer. Only the Sierra juniper is at all like it, standing rigid and unconquerable on glacial pavements for thousands of years, grim, rusty, silent, uncommunicative, with an air of antiquity about as pronounced as that so characteristic of Sequoia.

The bark of full grown trees is from one to two feet thick, rich cinnamon brown, purplish on young trees and shady parts of the old, forming magnificent masses of color with the underbrush and beds of flowers. Toward the end of winter the trees themselves bloom while the snow is still eight or ten feet deep. The pistillate flowers are about three eighths of an inch long, pale green, and grow in countless thousands on the ends of the sprays. The staminate are still more abundant, pale yellow, a fourth of an inch long; and when the golden pollen is ripe they color the whole tree and dust the air and the ground far and near.

The cones are bright grass-green in color, about two and a half inches long, one and a half wide, and are made up of thirty or forty strong, closely packed, rhomboidal scales with four to eight seeds at the base of each. The seeds are extremely small and light, being only from an eighth to a fourth of an inch long and wide, including a filmy surrounding wing, which causes them to glint and waver in falling and enables the wind to carry them considerable distances from the tree.

The faint lisp of snowflakes as they alight is one of the smallest sounds mortal can hear. The sound of falling Sequoia seeds, even when they happen to strike on flat leaves or flakes of bark, is about as faint. Very different is the bumping and thudding of the falling cones. Most of them are cut off by the Douglas squirrel and stored for the sake of the seeds, small as they are. In the calm Indian summer these busy harvesters with ivory sickles go to work early in the morning, as soon as breakfast is over, and nearly all day the ripe cones fall in a steady pattering, bumping shower. Unless harvested in this way they discharge their seeds and remain on the trees for many years. In fruitful seasons the trees are fairly laden. On two small specimen branches one and a half and two inches in diameter I counted four hundred and eighty cones. No other California conifer produces nearly so many seeds, excepting perhaps its relative, the redwood of the Coast Mountains. Millions are ripened annually by a single tree, and the product of one of the main groves in a fruitful year would suffice to plant all the mountain ranges of the world.

The dense tufted sprays make snug nesting places for birds, and in some of the loftiest, leafiest towers of verdure thousands of generations have been reared, the great solemn trees shedding off flocks of merry singers every year from nests, like the flocks of winged seeds from the cones.

The Big Tree keeps its youth far longer than any of its neighbors. Most silver firs are old in their second or third century, pines in their fourth or fifth, while the Big Tree growing beside them is still in the bloom of its youth, juvenile in every feature at the age of old pines, and cannot be said to attain anything like prime size and beauty before its fifteen hundredth year, or under favorable circumstances become old before its three thousandth. On one of the Kings River giants, thirty-five feet and eight inches in diameter exclusive of bark, I counted upwards of four thousand annual wood-rings, in which there was no trace of decay after all these centuries of mountain weather. There is no absolute limit to the existence of any tree. Their death is due to accidents, not, as of animals, to the wearing out of organs. Only the leaves die of old age, their fall is foretold in their structure; but the leaves are renewed every year and so also are the other essential organs—wood, roots, bark, buds. Most of the Sierra trees die of disease. Thus the magnificent silver firs are devoured by fungi, and comparatively few of them live to see their three hundredth birth year. But nothing hurts the Big Tree. I never saw one that was sick or showed the slightest sign of decay. It lives on through indefinite thousands of years until burned, blown down, undermined, or shattered by some tremendous lightning stroke. No ordinary bolt ever seriously hurts Sequoia. In all my walks I have seen only one that was thus killed outright. Lightning, though rare in the California lowlands, is common on the Sierra. Almost every day in June and July small thunderstorms refresh the main forest belt. Clouds like snowy mountains of marvelous beauty grow rapidly in the calm sky about midday and cast cooling shadows and showers that seldom last more than an hour. Nevertheless, these brief, kind storms wound or kill a good many trees. I have seen silver firs two hundred feet high split into long peeled rails and slivers down to the roots, leaving not even a stump, the rails radiating like the spokes of a wheel from a hole in the ground where the tree stood. But the Sequoia, instead of being split and slivered, usually has forty or fifty

The Sequoia and General Grant

feet of its brash knotty top smashed off in short chunks about the size of cord-wood, the beautiful rosy red ruins covering the ground in a circle a hundred feet wide or more. I never saw any that had been cut down to the ground or even to below the branches except one in the Stanislaus Grove, about twelve feet in diameter, the greater part of which was smashed to fragments, leaving only a leafless stump about seventy-five feet high. It is a curious fact that all the very old Sequoias have lost their heads by lightning. "All things come to him who waits." But of all living things Sequoia is perhaps the only one able to wait long enough to make sure of being struck by lightning. Thousands of years it stands ready and waiting, offering its head to every passing cloud as if inviting its fate, praying for heaven's fire as a blessing; and when at last the old head is off, another of the same shape immediately begins to grow on. Every bud and branch seems excited, like bees that have lost their queen, and tries hard to repair the damage. Branches that for many centuries have been growing out horizontally at once turn upward and all their branchlets arrange themselves with reference to a new top of the same peculiar curve as the old one. Even the small subordinate branches halfway down the trunk do their best to push up to the top and help in this curious head-making.

The great age of these noble trees is even more wonderful than their huge size, standing bravely up, millennium in, millennium out, to all that fortune may bring them, triumphant over tempest and fire and time, fruitful and beautiful, giving food and shelter to multitudes of small fleeting creatures dependent on their bounty. Other trees may claim to be about as large or as old: Australian gums, Senegal baobabs, Mexican taxodiums, English yews, and venerable Lebanon cedars, trees of renown, some of which are from ten to thirty feet in diameter. We read of oaks that are supposed to have existed ever since the creation, but strange to say I can find no definite accounts of the age of any of these trees, but only estimates based on tradition and assumed average rates of growth. No other known tree approaches the Sequoia in grandeur, height and thickness being considered, and none as far as I know has looked down on so many centuries or opens such impressive and suggestive views into history. The majestic monument of the Kings River forest is, as we have seen, fully four thousand years old, and measuring the rings of annual growth we find it was no less than twenty-seven feet in diameter at the beginning of the Christian era, while many observations lead me to expect the discovery of others ten or twenty centuries older. As to those of moderate age, there are thousands, mere youths as yet, that

> Saw the light that shone
>   On Mahomet's uplifted crescent,
> On many a royal gilded throne
>   And deed forgotten in the present,
>   . . . saw the age of sacred trees
>   And Druid groves and mystic larches,
> And saw from forest domes like these
>   The builder bring his Gothic arches.

Great trees and groves used to be venerated as sacred monuments and halls of council and worship. But soon after the discovery of the Calaveras Grove one of the grandest trees was cut down for the sake of a stump! The laborious vandals had seen "the biggest tree in the world," then, forsooth, they must try to see the biggest stump and dance on it.

The growth in height for the first two centuries is usually at the rate of eight to ten inches a year. Of course all very large trees are old, but those equal in size may vary greatly in age on account of variations in soil, closeness or openness of growth, etc. Thus a tree about ten feet in diameter that grew on the side of a meadow was, according to my own count of the wood-rings, only two hundred and fifty-nine years old at the time it was felled, while another in the

The Sequoia and General Grant

same grove, of almost exactly the same size but less favorably situated, was fourteen hundred and forty years old. The Calaveras tree cut for a dance floor was twenty-four feet in diameter and only thirteen hundred years old, another about the same size was a thousand years older.

The following Sequoia notes and measurements are copied from my notebooks:—

| Diameter | | Height in | Age. |
Feet.	Inches.	Feet.	Years.
0	1 ¾	10	7
0	5	24	20
0	5	25	41
0	6	25	66
0	6	28 ½	39
0	8	25	29
0	11	45	71
1	0	60	71
3	2	156	260
6	0	192	240
7	3	195	339
7	3	255	506
7	6	240	493
7	7	207	424
9	0	243	259
9	3	222	280
10	6		1440
12			1825[1]
15			2150[2]
24			1300
25			2300
35	8 inside bark		over 4000

1. 6 feet in diameter at height of 200 feet.
2. 7 feet in diameter at height of 200 feet.

THE AMERICAN WILDERNESS

Little, however, is to be learned in confused, hurried tourist trips, spending only a poor noisy hour in a branded grove with a guide. You should go looking and listening alone on long walks through the wild forests and groves in all the seasons of the year. In the spring the winds are balmy and sweet, blowing up and down over great beds of chaparral and through the woods now rich in softening balsam and rosin and the scent of steaming earth. The sky is mostly sunshine, oftentimes tempered by magnificent clouds, the breath of the sea built up into new mountain ranges, warm during the day, cool at night, good flower-opening weather. The young cones of the Big Trees are showing in clusters, their flower time already past, and here and there you may see the sprouting of their tiny seeds of the previous autumn, taking their first feeble hold of the ground and unpacking their tender whorls of cotyledon leaves. Then you will naturally be led on to consider their wonderful growth up and up through the mountain weather, now buried in snow bent and crinkled, now straightening in summer sunshine like uncoiling ferns, shooting eagerly aloft in youth's joyful prime, and towering serene and satisfied through countless years of calm and storm, the greatest of plants and all but immortal.

Under the huge trees up come the small plant people, putting forth fresh leaves and blossoming in such profusion that the hills and valleys would still seem gloriously rich and glad were all the grand trees away. By the side of melting snowbanks rise the crimson sarcodes, round-topped and massive as the Sequoias themselves, and beds of blue violets and larger yellow ones with leaves curiously lobed; azalea and saxifrage, daisies and lilies on the mossy banks of the streams; and a little way back of them, beneath the trees and on sunny spots on the hills around the groves, wild rose and rubus, spiraea and ribes, mitella, tiarella, campanula, monardella, forget-me-not, etc., many of them as worthy of lore immortality as the famous Scotch daisy, wanting only a Burns to sing them home to all hearts.

The Sequoia and General Grant

In the midst of this glad plant work the birds are busy nesting, some singing at their work, some silent, others, especially the big pileated woodpeckers, about as noisy as backwoodsmen building their cabins. Then every bower in the groves is a bridal bower, the winds murmur softly overhead, the streams sing with the birds, while from far-off waterfalls and thunder-clouds come deep rolling organ notes.

In summer the days go by in almost constant brightness, cloudless sunshine pouring over the forest roof, while in the shady depths there is the subdued light of perpetual morning. The new leaves and cones are growing fast and make a grand show, seeds are ripening, young birds learning to fly, and with myriads of insects glad as birds keep the air whirling, joy in every wingbeat, their humming and singing blending with the gentle ah-ing of the winds; while at evening every thicket and grove is enchanted by the tranquil chirping of the blessed hylas, the sweetest and most peaceful of sounds, telling the very heart-joy of earth as it rolls through the heavens.

In the autumn the sighing of the winds is softer than ever, the gentle ah-ah-ing filling the sky with a fine universal mist of music, the birds have little to say, and there is no appreciable stir or rustling among the trees save that caused by the harvesting squirrels. Most of the seeds are ripe and away, those of the trees mottling the sunny air, glinting, glancing through the midst of the merry insect people, rocks and trees, everything alike drenched in gold light, heaven's colors coming down to the meadows and groves, making every leaf a romance, air, earth, and water in peace beyond thought, the great brooding days opening and closing in divine psalms of color.

Winter comes suddenly, arrayed in storms, though to mountaineers silky streamers on the peaks and the tones of the wind give sufficient warning. You hear strange whisperings among the tree-tops, as if the giants were taking counsel together. One after another, nodding and swaying, calling and replying, spreads the news, until all with one accord break forth into glorious song, welcoming the first grand snowstorm of the year, and looming up in the dim clouds and snowdrifts like lighthouse towers in flying scud and spray. Studying the behavior of the giants from some friendly shelter, you will see that even in the glow of their wildest enthusiasm, when the storm roars loudest, they never lose their god-like composure, never toss their arms or bow or wave like the pines, but only slowly, solemnly nod and sway, standing erect, making no sign of strife, none of rest, neither in alliance nor at war with the winds, too calmly, unconsciously noble and strong to strive with or bid defiance to anything. Owing to the density of the leafy branchlets and great breadth of head the Big Tree carries a much heavier load of snow than any of its neighbors, and after a storm, when the sky clears, the laden trees are a glorious spectacle, worth any amount of cold camping to see. Every bossy limb and crown is solid white, and the immense height of the giants becomes visible as the eye travels the white steps of the colossal tower, each relieved by a mass of blue shadow.

In midwinter the forest depths are as fresh and pure as the crevasses and caves of glaciers. Grouse, nuthatches, a few woodpeckers, and other hardy birds dwell in the groves all winter, and the squirrels may be seen every clear day frisking about, lively as ever, tunneling to their stores, never coming up empty-mouthed, diving in the loose snow about as quickly as ducks in water, while storms and sunshine sing to each other.

One of the noblest and most beautiful of the late winter sights is the blossoming of the Big Tree like gigantic goldenrods and the sowing of their pollen over all the forest and the snow-covered ground—a most glorious view of Nature's immortal virility and flower-love.

One of my own best excursions among the Sequoias was made in the autumn of 1875, when I explored the then unknown or little known Sequoia region south of the Mariposa Grove for comprehensive views of the belt, and to learn what I could of the peculiar distribution of the species and its history in general. In particular I was anxious to try to find out whether it had ever been more widely distributed since the glacial period; what conditions favorable or otherwise were affecting it; what were its relations to climate, topography, soil, and the other trees growing with it, etc.; and whether, as was generally supposed, the species was nearing extinction. I was already acquainted in a general way with the northern groves, but excepting some passing glimpses gained on excursions into the high Sierra about the head-waters of Kings and Kern rivers I had seen nothing of the south end of the belt.

Nearly all my mountaineering has been done on foot, carrying as little as possible, depending on camp-fires for warmth, so that I might be light and free to go wherever my studies might lead. On this Sequoia trip, which promised to be long, I was persuaded to take a small wild mule with me to carry provisions and a pair of blankets. The friendly owner of the animal, having noticed that I sometimes looked tired when I came down from the peaks to replenish my bread sack, assured me that his "little Brownie mule" was just what I wanted, tough as a knot, perfectly untirable, low and narrow, just right for squeezing through brush, able to climb like a chipmunk, jump from boulder to boulder like a wild sheep, and go anywhere a man could go. But tough as he was and accomplished as a climber, many a time in the course of our journey when he was jaded and hungry, wedged fast in rocks or struggling in chaparral like a fly in a spiderweb, his troubles were sad to see, and I wished he would leave me and find his way home alone.

We set out from Yosemite about the end of August, and our first camp was made in the well-known Mariposa Grove. Here and in the adjacent pine woods I spent nearly a week, carefully examining the boundaries of the grove for traces of its greater extension without finding any. Then I struck out into the majestic trackless forest to the southeastward, hoping to find new groves or traces of old ones in the dense silver fir and pine woods about the head of Big Creek, where soil and climate seemed most favorable to their growth, but not a single tree or old monument of any sort came to light until I climbed the high rock called Wamellow by the Indians. Here I obtained telling views of the fertile forest-filled basin of the upper Fresno. Innumerable spires of the noble yellow pine were displayed rising above one another on the braided slopes, and yet nobler sugar pines with superb arms outstretched in the rich autumn light, while away toward the southwest, on the verge of the glowing horizon, I discovered the majestic dome-like crowns of Big Trees towering high over all, singly and in close grove congregations. There is something wonderfully attractive in this king tree, even when beheld from afar, that draws us to it with indescribable enthusiasm; its superior height and massive smoothly rounded outlines proclaiming its character in any company; and when one of the oldest attains full stature on some commanding ridge it seems the very god of the woods. I ran back to camp, packed Brownie, steered over the divide and down into the heart of the Fresno Grove. Then choosing a camp on the side of a brook where the grass was good, I made a cup of tea, and set off free among the brown giants, glorying in the abundance of new work about me. One of the first special things that caught my attention was an extensive landslip. The ground on the side of a stream had given way to a depth of about fifty feet and with all its trees had been launched into the bottom of the stream ravine. Most of the trees—pines, firs, incense cedar, and Sequoia—were still standing erect and uninjured, as if unconscious that anything out of the common had happened. Tracing the ravine alongside the avalanche, I saw many trees whose roots had been laid bare, and in one instance discovered a Sequoia about fifteen feet in diameter growing above an old prostrate trunk that seemed to belong to a former generation. This slip had occurred seven or eight years ago, and I was glad to find that not only were most of the Big Trees uninjured, but that many companies of hopeful seedlings and saplings were growing confidently on the fresh soil along the broken front of the avalanche. These young trees were already eight or ten feet high, and were shooting up vigorously, as if sure of eternal life, though young pines, firs, and libocedrus were running a race with them for the sunshine with an even start. Farther down the ravine I counted five hundred and thirty-six promising young Sequoias on a bed of rough bouldery soil not exceeding two acres in extent.

The Fresno Big Trees covered an area of about four square miles, and while wandering about surveying the boundaries of the grove, anxious to see every tree, I came suddenly on a handsome log cabin, richly embowered and so fresh and unweathered it was still redolent of gum and balsam like a newly felled tree. Strolling forward, wondering who could have built it, I found an old, weary-eyed, speculative, gray-haired man on a bark stool by the door, reading a book. The discovery of his hermitage by a stranger seemed to surprise him, but when I explained that I was only a tree-lover sauntering along the mountains to study Sequoia, he bade me welcome, made me bring my mule down to a little slanting meadow before his door and camp with him, promising to show me his pet trees and many curious things bearing on my studies.

After supper, as the evening shadows were falling, the good hermit sketched his life in the mines, which in the main was like that of most other pioneer gold-hunters—a succession of intense experiences full of big ups and downs like the mountain topography. Since " '49" he had wandered over most of the Sierra, sinking innumerable prospect holes like a sailor making soundings, digging new channels for streams, sifting gold-sprinkled boulder and gravel beds with unquenchable energy, life's noon the meanwhile passing unnoticed into late afternoon shadows. Then, health and gold gone, the game played and lost, like a wounded deer creeping into this forest solitude, he awaits the sundown call. How sad the undertones of many a life here, now the noise of the first big gold battles has died away! How many interesting wrecks lie drifted and stranded in hidden nooks of the gold region! Perhaps no other range contains the remains of so many rare and interesting men. The name of my hermit friend is John A. Nelder, a fine kind man, who in going into the woods has at last gone home; for he loves nature truly, and realizes that these last shadowy days with scarce a glint of gold in them are the best of all. Birds, squirrels, plants get loving, natural recognition, and delightful it was to see how sensitively he responds to the silent influences of the woods. His eyes brightened as he gazed on the trees that stand guard around his little home; squirrels and mountain quail came to his call to be fed, and he tenderly stroked the little snowbent sapling Sequoias, hoping they yet might grow straight to the sky and rule the grove. One of the greatest of his trees stands a little way back of his cabin, and he proudly led me to it, bidding me admire its colossal proportions and measure it to see if in all the forest there could be another so grand. It proved to be only twenty-six feet in diameter, and he seemed distressed to learn that the Mariposa Grizzly Giant was larger. I tried to comfort him by observing that his was the taller, finer formed, and perhaps the more favorably situated. Then he led me to some noble ruins, remnants of gigantic trunks of trees that he supposed must have been larger than any now standing, and though they had lain on the damp ground exposed to fire and the weather for centuries, the wood was perfectly sound. Sequoia timber is not only beautiful in color, rose red when fresh, and as easily worked as pine, but it is almost absolutely unperishable. Build a house of Big Tree logs on granite and that house will last about as long as its foundation. Indeed fire seems to be the only agent that has any appreciable effect on it. From one of these ancient trunk remnants I cut a specimen of the wood, which neither in color, strength, nor soundness could be distinguished from specimens cut from living trees, although it had certainly lain on the damp forest floor for more than three hundred and eighty years, probably more than thrice as long. The time in this instance was determined as follows: When the tree from which the specimen was derived fell it sunk itself into the ground, making a ditch about two

66

The Sequoia and General Grant

hundred feet long and five or six feet deep; and in the middle of this ditch, where a part of the fallen trunk had been burned, a silver fir four feet in diameter and three hundred and eighty years old was growing, showing that the Sequoia trunk had lain on the ground three hundred and eighty years plus the unknown time that it lay before the part whose place had been taken by the fir was burned out of the way, and that which had elapsed ere the seed from which the monumental fir sprang fell into the prepared soil and took root. Now because Sequoia trunks are never wholly consumed in one forest fire and these fires recur only at considerable intervals, and because Sequoia ditches, after being cleared, are often left unplanted for centuries, it becomes evident that the trunk remnant in question may have been on the ground a thousand years or more. Similar vestiges are common, and together with the root-bowls and long straight ditches of the fallen monarchs, throw a sure light back on the post-glacial history of the species, bearing on its distribution. One of the most interesting features of this grove is the apparent ease and strength and comfortable independence in which the trees occupy their place in the general forest. Seedlings, saplings, young and middle-aged trees are grouped promisingly around the old patriarchs, betraying no sign of approach to extinction. On the contrary, all seem to be saying, "Everything is to our mind and we mean to live forever." But, sad to tell, a lumber company was building a large mill and flume near by, assuring widespread destruction.

In the cones and sometimes in the lower portion of the trunk and roots there is a dark gritty substance which dissolves readily in water and yields a magnificent purple color. It is a strong astringent, and is said to be used by the Indians as a big medicine. Mr. Nelder showed me specimens of ink he had made from it, which I tried and found good, flowing freely and holding its color well. Indeed everything about the tree seems constant. With these interesting trees, forming the largest of the northern groves, I stopped only a week, for I had far to go before the fall of the snow. The hermit seemed to cling to

67

me and tried to make me promise to winter with him after the
season's work was done. Brownie had to be got home, however, and
other work awaited me, therefore I could only promise to stop a day
or two on my way back to Yosemite and give him the forest news.

The next two weeks were spent in the wide basin of the San Joaquin, climbing innumerable ridges and surveying the far-extending
sea of pines and firs. But not a single Sequoia crown appeared
among them all, nor any trace of a fallen trunk, until I had crossed
the south divide of the basin, opposite Dinky Creek, one of the
northmost tributaries of Kings River. On this stream there is a small
grove, said to have been discovered a few years before my visit by
two hunters in pursuit of a wounded bear. Just as I was fording one
of the branches of Dinky Creek I met a shepherd, and when I asked
him whether he knew anything about the Big Trees of the neighborhood he replied, "I know all about them, for I visited them only a
few days ago and pastured my sheep in the grove." He was fresh
from the East, and as this was his first summer in the Sierra I was
curious to learn what impression the Sequoias had made on him.
When I asked whether it was true that the Big Trees were really so
big as people say, he warmly replied, "Oh, yes sir, you bet. They're
whales. I never used to believe half I heard about the awful size of
California trees, but they're monsters and no mistake. One of them
over here, they tell me, is the biggest tree in the whole world, and I
guess it is, for it's forty foot through and as many good long paces
around." He was very earnest, and in fullness of faith offered to
guide me to the grove that I might not miss seeing this biggest tree.
A fair measurement four feet from the ground, above the main swell
of the roots, showed a diameter of only thirty-two feet, much to the
young man's disgust. "Only thirty-two feet," he lamented, "only
thirty-two, and I always thought it was forty!" Then with a sigh of
relief, "No matter, that's a big tree, anyway; no fool of a tree, sir, that
you can cut a plank out of thirty feet broad, straight-edged, no bark,
all good wood, sound and solid. It would make the brag white pine

The Sequoia and General Grant

planks from old Maine look like laths." A good many other fine specimens are distributed along three small branches of the creek, and I noticed several thrifty moderate-sized Sequoias growing on a granite ledge, apparently as independent of deep soil as the pines and firs, clinging to seams and fissures and sending their roots far abroad in search of moisture.

The creek is very clear and beautiful, gliding through tangles of shrubs and flower beds, gay bee and butterfly pastures, the grove's own stream, pure Sequoia water, flowing all the year, every drop filtered through moss and leaves and the myriad spongy rootlets of the giant trees. One of the most interesting features of the grove is a small waterfall with a flowery, ferny, clear brimming pool at the foot of it. How cheerily it sings the songs of the wilderness, and how sweet its tones! You seem to taste as well as hear them, while only the subdued roar of the river in the deep cañon reaches up into the grove, sounding like the sea and the winds. So charming a fall and pool in the heart of so glorious a forest good pagans would have consecrated to some lovely nymph.

Hence down into the main Kings River cañon, a mile deep, I led and dragged and shoved my patient, much-enduring mule through miles and miles of gardens and brush, fording innumerable streams, crossing savage rock slopes and taluses, scrambling, sliding through gulches and gorges, then up into the grand Sequoia forests of the south side, cheered by the royal crowns displayed on the narrow horizon. In a day and a half we reached the Sequoia woods in the neighborhood of the old Thomas' Mill Flat. Thence striking off northeastward I found a magnificent forest nearly six miles long by two in width, composed mostly of Big Trees, with outlying groves as far east as Boulder Creek. Here five or six days were spent, and it was delightful to learn from countless trees, old and young, how comfortably they were settled down in concordance with climate and soil and their noble neighbors.

Imbedded in these majestic woods there are numerous meadows, around the sides of which the Big Trees press close together in beautiful lines, showing their grandeur openly from the ground to their domed heads in the sky. The young trees are still more numerous and exuberant than in the Fresno and Dinky groves, standing apart in beautiful family groups, or crowding around the old giants. For every venerable lightning-stricken tree, there is one or more in all the glory of prime, and for each of these, many young trees and crowds of saplings. The young trees express the grandeur of their race in a way indefinable by any words at my command. When they are five or six feet in diameter and a hundred and fifty feet high, they seem like mere baby saplings as many inches in diameter, their juvenile habit and gestures completely veiling their real size, even to those who, from long experience, are able to make fair approximation in their measurements of common trees. One morning I noticed three airy, spiry, quick-growing babies on the side of a meadow, the largest of which I took to be about eight inches in diameter. On measuring it, I found to my astonishment it was five feet six inches in diameter, and about a hundred and forty feet high.

On a bed of sandy ground fifteen yards square, which had been occupied by four sugar pines, I counted ninety-four promising seedlings, an instance of Sequoia gaining ground from its neighbors. Here also I noted eighty-six young Sequoias from one to fifty feet high on less than half an acre of ground that had been cleared and prepared for their reception by fire. This was a small bay burned into dense chaparral, showing that fire, the great destroyer of tree life, is sometimes followed by conditions favorable for new growths. Sufficient fresh soil, however, is furnished for the constant renewal of the forest by the fall of old trees without the help of any other agent—burrowing animals, fire, flood, landslip, etc.—for the ground is thus turned and stirred as well as cleared, and in every roomy, shady hollow beside the walls of upturned roots many hopeful seedlings spring up.

The largest, and as far as I know the oldest, of all the Kings River

The Sequoia and General Grant

trees that I saw is the majestic stump, already referred to, about a hundred and forty feet high, which above the swell of the roots is thirty-five feet and eight inches inside the bark, and over four thousand years old. It was burned nearly half through at the base, and I spent a day in chopping off the charred surface, cutting into the heart, and counting the wood-rings with the aid of a lens. I made out a little over four thousand without difficulty or doubt, but I was unable to get a complete count, owing to confusion in the rings where wounds had been healed over. Judging by what is left of it, this was a fine, tall, symmetrical tree nearly forty feet in diameter before it lost its bark. In the last sixteen hundred and seventy-two years the increase in diameter was ten feet. A short distance south of this forest lies a beautiful grove, now mostly included in the General Grant National Park. I found many shakemakers at work in it, access to these magnificent woods having been made easy by the old mill wagon road. The Park is only two miles square, and the largest of its many fine trees is the General Grant, so named before the date of my first visit, twenty-eight years ago, and said to be the largest tree in the world, though above the craggy bulging base the diameter is less than thirty feet. The Sanger Lumber Company owns nearly all the Kings River groves outside the Park, and for many years the mills have been spreading desolation without any advantage.

One of the shake-makers directed me to an "old snag biggeren Grant." It proved to be a huge black charred stump thirty-two feet in diameter, the next in size to the grand monument mentioned above.

I found a scattered growth of Big Trees extending across the main divide to within a short distance of Hyde's Mill, on a tributary of Dry Creek. The mountain ridge on the south side of the stream was covered from base to summit with a most superb growth of Big Trees. What a picture it made! In all my wide forest wanderings I had seen none so sublime. Every tree of all the mighty host seemed perfect in beauty and strength, and their majestic domed heads, rising above one another on the mountain slope, were most imposingly displayed, like a range of bossy upswelling cumulus clouds on a calm sky.

In this glorious forest the mill was busy, forming a sore, sad centre of destruction, though small as yet, so immensely heavy was the growth. Only the smaller and most accessible of the trees were being cut. The logs, from three to ten or twelve feet in diameter, were dragged or rolled with long strings of oxen into a chute and sent flying down the steep mountain side to the mill flat, where the largest of them were blasted into manageable dimensions for the saws. And as the timber is very brash, by this blasting and careless felling on uneven ground, half or three fourths of the timber was wasted.

I spent several days exploring the ridge and counting the annual wood-rings on a large number of stumps in the clearings, then replenished my bread sack and pushed on southward. All the way across the broad rough basins of the Kaweah and Tule rivers Sequoia ruled supreme, forming an almost continuous belt for sixty or seventy miles, waving up and down in huge massy mountain billows in compliance with the grand glacier-ploughed topography.

Day after day, from grove to grove, cañon to cañon, I made a long, wavering way, terribly rough in some places for Brownie, but cheery for me, for Big Trees were seldom out of sight. We crossed the rugged, picturesque basins of Redwood Creek, the North Fork of the Kaweah, and Marble Fork gloriously forested, and full of beautiful cascades and falls, sheer and slanting, infinitely varied with broad curly foam fleeces and strips of embroidery in which the sunbeams revel. Thence we climbed into the noble forest on the Marble and Middle Fork Divide. After a general exploration of the Kaweah basin, this part of the Sequoia belt seemed to me the finest, and I then named it "the Giant Forest." It extends, a magnificent growth of giants grouped in pure temple groves, ranged in colonnades along the sides of meadows, or scattered among the other trees, from the

The Sequoia and General Grant

granite headlands overlooking the hot foothills and plains of the San Joaquin back to within a few miles of the old glacier fountains at an elevation of 5000 to 8400 feet above the sea.

When I entered this sublime wilderness the day was nearly done, the trees with rosy, glowing countenances seemed to be hushed and thoughtful, as if waiting in conscious religious dependence on the sun, and one naturally walked softly and awe-stricken among them. I wandered on, meeting nobler trees where all are noble, subdued in the general calm, as if in some vast hall pervaded by the deepest sanctities and solemnities that sway human souls. At sundown the trees seemed to cease their worship and breathe free. I heard the birds going home. I too sought a home for the night on the edge of a level meadow where there is a long, open view between the evenly ranked trees standing guard along its sides. Then after a good place was found for poor Brownie, who had had a hard, weary day sliding and scrambling across the Marble Cañon, I made my bed and supper and lay on my back looking up to the stars through pillared arches finer far than the pious heart of man, telling its love, ever reared. Then I took a walk up the meadow to see the trees in the pale light. They seemed still more marvelously massive and tall than by day, heaving their colossal heads into the depths of the sky, among the stars, some of which appeared to be sparkling on their branches like flowers. I built a big fire that vividly illuminated the huge brown boles of the nearest trees and the little plants and cones and fallen leaves at their feet, keeping up the show until I fell asleep to dream of boundless forests and trail-building for Brownie.

Joyous birds welcomed the dawn; and the squirrels, now their food cones were ripe and had to be quickly gathered and stored for winter, began their work before sunrise. My tea-and-bread-crumb breakfast was soon done, and leaving jaded Brownie to feed and rest I sauntered forth to my studies. In every direction Sequoia ruled the woods. Most of the other big conifers were present here and there, but not as rivals or companions. They only served to thicken and

73

enrich the general wilderness. Trees of every age cover craggy ridges as well as the deep moraine-soiled slopes, and plant their magnificent shafts along every brookside and meadow. Bogs and meadows are rare or entirely wanting in the isolated groves north of Kings River; here there is a beautiful series of them lying on the broad top of the main dividing ridge, imbedded in the very heart of the mammoth woods as if for ornament, their smooth, plushy bosoms kept bright and fertile by streams and sunshine.

Resting awhile on one of the most beautiful of them when the sun was high, it seemed impossible that any other forest picture in the world could rival it. There lay the grassy, flowery lawn, three fourths of a mile long, smoothly outspread, basking in mellow autumn light, colored brown and yellow and purple, streaked with lines of green along the streams, and ruffled here and there with patches of ledum and scarlet vaccinium. Around the margin there is first a fringe of azalea and willow bushes, colored orange yellow, enlivened with vivid dashes of red cornel, as if painted. Then up spring the mighty walls of verdure three hundred feet high, the brown fluted pillars so thick and tall and strong they seem fit to uphold the sky; the dense foliage, swelling forward in rounded bosses on the upper half, variously shaded and tinted, that of the young trees dark green, of the old yellowish. An aged lightning-smitten patriarch standing a little forward beyond the general line with knotty arms outspread was covered with gray and yellow lichens and surrounded by a group of saplings whose slender spires seemed to lack not a single leaf or spray in their wondrous perfection. Such was the Kaweah meadow picture that golden afternoon, and as I gazed every color seemed to deepen and glow as if the progress of the fresh sun-work were visible from hour to hour, while every tree seemed religious and conscious of the presence of God. A free man revels in a scene like this and time goes by unmeasured. I stood fixed in silent wonder or sauntered about shifting my points of view, studying the physiognomy of separate trees, and going out to the different color patches to see

The Sequoia and General Grant

how they were put on and what they were made of, giving free expression to my joy, exulting in Nature's wild immortal vigor and beauty, never dreaming any other human being was near. Suddenly the spell was broken by dull bumping, thudding sounds, and a man and horse came in sight at the farther end of the meadow, where they seemed sadly out of place. A good big bear or mastodon or megatherium would have been more in keeping with the old mammoth forest. Nevertheless, it is always pleasant to meet one of our own species after solitary rambles, and I stepped out where I could be seen and shouted, when the rider reined in his galloping mustang and waited my approach. He seemed too much surprised to speak until, laughing in his puzzled face, I said I was glad to meet a fellow mountaineer in so lonely a place. Then he abruptly asked, "What are you doing? How did you get here?" I explained that I came across the cañons from Yosemite and was only looking at the trees. "Oh then, I know," he said, greatly to my surprise, "you must be John Muir." He was herding a band of horses that had been driven up a rough trail from the lowlands to feed on these forest meadows. A few handfuls of crumb detritus was all that was left in my bread sack, so I told him that I was nearly out of provision and asked whether he could spare me a little flour. "Oh yes, of course you can have anything I've got," he said. "Just take my track and it will lead you to my camp in a big hollow log on the side of a meadow two or three miles from here. I must ride after some strayed horses, but I'll be back before night; in the mean time make yourself at home." He galloped away to the northward, I returned to my own camp, saddled Brownie, and by the middle of the afternoon discovered his noble den in a fallen Sequoia hollowed by fire—a spacious loghouse of one log, carbon-lined, centuries old yet sweet and fresh, weather proof, earthquake proof, likely to outlast the most durable stone castle, and commanding views of garden and grove grander far than the richest king ever enjoyed. Brownie found plenty of grass and I found bread, which I ate with views from the big round, ever-open door. Soon the Good Samaritan mountaineer came in, and I enjoyed a famous rest listening to his observations on trees, animals, adventures, etc., while he was busily preparing supper. In answer to inquiries concerning the distribution of the Big Trees he gave a good deal of particular information of the forest we were in, and he had heard that the species extended a long way south, he knew not how far. I wandered about for several days within a radius of six or seven miles of the camp, surveying boundaries, measuring trees, and climbing the highest points for general views. From the south side of the divide I saw telling ranks of Sequoia-crowned headlands stretching far into the hazy distance, and plunging vaguely down into profound cañon depths foreshadowing weeks of good work. I had now been out on the trip more than a month, and I began to fear my studies would be interrupted by snow, for winter was drawing nigh. "Where there isn't a way make a way," is easily said when no way at the time is needed, but to the Sierra explorer with a mule traveling across the cañon lines of drainage the brave old phrase becomes heavy with meaning. There are ways across the Sierra graded by glaciers, well marked, and followed by men and beasts and birds, and one of them even by locomotives; but none natural or artificial along the range, and the explorer who would thus travel at right angles to the glacial ways must traverse cañons and ridges extending side by side in endless succession, roughened by side gorges and gulches and stubborn chaparral, and defended by innumerable sheer-fronted precipices. My own ways are easily made in any direction, but Brownie, though one of the toughest and most skillful of his race, was oftentimes discouraged for want of hands, and caused endless work. Wild at first, he was tame enough now; and when turned loose he not only refused to run away, but as his troubles increased came to depend on me in such a pitiful, touching way, I became attached to him and helped him as if he were a good-natured boy in distress, and then the labor grew lighter. Bidding good-by to the kind Sequoia cave-

The Sequoia and General Grant

dweller, we vanished again in the wilderness, drifting slowly southward, Sequoias on every ridge-top beckoning and pointing the way.

In the forest between the Middle and East forks of the Kaweah, I met a great fire, and as fire is the master scourge and controller of the distribution of trees, I stopped to watch it and learn what I could of its works and ways with the giants. It came racing up the steep chaparral-covered slopes of the East Fork cañon with passionate enthusiasm in a broad cataract of flames, now bending down low to feed on the green bushes, devouring acres of them at a breath, now towering high in the air as if looking abroad to choose a way, then stooping to feed again, the lurid flapping surges and the smoke and terrible rushing and roaring hiding all that is gentle and orderly in the work. But as soon as the deep forest was reached the ungovernable flood became calm like a torrent entering a lake, creeping and spreading beneath the trees where the ground was level or sloped gently, slowly nibbling the cake of compressed needles and scales with flames an inch high, rising here and there to a foot or two on dry twigs and clumps of small bushes and brome grass. Only at considerable intervals were fierce bonfires lighted, where heavy branches broken off by snow had accumulated, or around some venerable giant whose head had been stricken off by lightning.

I tethered Brownie on the edge of a little meadow beside a stream a good safe way off, and then cautiously chose a camp for myself in a big stout hollow trunk not likely to be crushed by the fall of burning trees, and made a bed of ferns and boughs in it. The night, however, and the strange wild fireworks were too beautiful and exciting to allow much sleep. There was no danger of being chased and hemmed in, for in the main forest belt of the Sierra, even when swift winds are blowing, fires seldom or never sweep over the trees in broad all-embracing sheets as they do in the dense Rocky Mountain woods and in those of the Cascade Mountains of Oregon and Washington. Here they creep from tree to tree with tranquil deliberation, allowing close observation, though caution is required in venturing around the burning giants to avoid falling limbs and knots and fragments from dead shattered tops. Though the day was best for study, I sauntered about night after night, learning what I could and admiring the wonderful show vividly displayed in the lonely darkness, the ground-fire advancing in long crooked lines gently grazing and smoking on the close-pressed leaves, springing up in thousands of little jets of pure flame on dry tassels and twigs, and tall spires and flat sheets with jagged flapping edges dancing here and there on grass tufts and bushes, big bonfires blazing in perfect storms of energy where heavy branches mixed with small ones lay smashed together in hundred cord piles, big red arches between spreading root-swells and trees growing close together, huge fire-mantled trunks on the hill slopes glowing like bars of hot iron, violet-colored fire running up the tall trees, tracing the furrows of the bark in quick quivering rills, and lighting magnificent torches on dry shattered tops, and ever and anon, with a tremendous roar and burst of light, young trees clad in low-descending feathery branches vanishing in one flame two or three hundred feet high.

One of the most impressive and beautiful sights was made by the great fallen trunks lying on the hillsides all red and glowing like colossal iron bars fresh from a furnace, two hundred feet long some of them, and ten to twenty feet thick. After repeated burnings have consumed the bark and sapwood, the sound charred surface, being full of cracks and sprinkled with leaves, is quickly overspread with a pure, rich, furred, ruby glow almost flameless and smokeless, producing a marvelous effect in the night. Another grand and interesting sight are the fires on the tops of the largest living trees flaming above the green branches at a height of perhaps two hundred feet, entirely cut off from the ground-fires, and looking like signal beacons on watch towers. From one standpoint I sometimes saw a dozen or more, those in the distance looking like great stars above the forest roof. At first I could not imagine how these Sequoia lamps were lighted, but the very first night, strolling about waiting and

The Sequoia and General Grant

watching, I saw the thing done again and again. The thick, fibrous bark of old trees is divided by deep, nearly continuous furrows, the sides of which are bearded with the bristling ends of fibres broken by the growth swelling of the trunk, and when the fire comes creeping around the feet of the trees, it runs up these bristly furrows in lovely pale blue quivering, bickering rills of flame with a low, earnest whispering sound to the lightning-shattered top of the trunk, which, in the dry Indian summer, with perhaps leaves and twigs and squirrel-gnawed cone-scales and seed-wings lodged in it, is readily ignited. These lamp-lighting rills, the most beautiful fire streams I ever saw, last only a minute or two, but the big lamps burn with varying brightness for days and weeks, throwing off sparks like the spray of a fountain, while ever and anon a shower of red coals comes sifting down through the branches, followed at times with startling effect by a big burned-off chunk weighing perhaps half a ton.

The immense bonfires where fifty or a hundred cords of peeled, split, smashed wood has been piled around some old giant by a single stroke of lightning is another grand sight in the night. The light is so great I found I could read common print three hundred yards from them, and the illumination of the circle of onlooking trees is indescribably impressive. Other big fires, roaring and booming like waterfalls, were blazing on the upper sides of trees on hillslopes, against which limbs broken off by heavy snow had rolled, while branches high overhead, tossed and shaken by the ascending air current, seemed to be writhing in pain. Perhaps the most startling phenomenon of all was the quick death of childlike Sequoias only a century or two of age. In the midst of the other comparatively slow and steady fire work one of these tall, beautiful saplings, leafy and branchy, would be seen blazing up suddenly, all in one heaving, booming, passionate flame reaching from the ground to the top of the tree and fifty to a hundred feet or more above it, with a smoke column bending forward and streaming away on the upper, free-flowing wind. To burn these green trees a strong fire of dry wood beneath them is required, to send up a current of air hot enough to distill inflammable gases from the leaves and sprays; then instead of the lower limbs gradually catching fire and igniting the next and next in succession, the whole tree seems to explode almost simultaneously, and with awful roaring and throbbing a round, tapering flame shoots up two or three hundred feet, and in a second or two is quenched, leaving the green spire a black, dead mast, bristled and roughened with down-curling boughs. Nearly all the trees that have been burned down are lying with their heads uphill, because they are burned far more deeply on the upper side, on account of broken limbs rolling down against them to make hot fires, while only leaves and twigs accumulate on the lower side and are quickly consumed without injury to the tree. But green, resinless Sequoia wood burns very slowly, and many successive fires are required to burn down a large tree. Fires can run only at intervals of several years, and when the ordinary amount of firewood that has rolled against the gigantic trunk is consumed, only a shallow scar is made, which is slowly deepened by recurring fires until far beyond the centre of gravity, and when at last the tree falls, it of course falls uphill. The healing folds of wood layers on some of the deeply burned trees show that centuries have elapsed since the last wounds were made.

When a great Sequoia falls, its head is smashed into fragments about as small as those made by lightning, which are mostly devoured by the first running, hunting fire that finds them, while the trunk is slowly wasted away by centuries of fire and weather. One of the most interesting fire actions on the trunk is the boring of those great tunnel-like hollows through which horsemen may gallop. All of these famous hollows are burned out of the solid wood, for no Sequoia is ever hollowed by decay. When the tree falls the brash trunk is often broken straight across into sections as if sawed; into these joints the fire creeps, and, on account of the great size of the broken ends, burns for weeks or even months without being much influenced by the weather. After the great glowing ends fronting each other have burned so far apart that their rims cease to burn, the fire continues to work on in the centres, and the ends become deeply concave. Then heat being radiated from side to side, the burning goes on in each section of the trunk independent of the other, until the diameter of the bore is so great that the heat radiated across from side to side is not sufficient to keep them burning. It appears, therefore, that only very large trees can receive the fire-auger and have any shell rim left.

Fire attacks the large trees only at the ground, consuming the fallen leaves and humus at their feet, doing them but little harm unless considerable quantities of fallen limbs happen to be piled about them, their thick mail of spongy, unpitchy, almost unburnable bark affording strong protection. Therefore the oldest and most perfect unscarred trees are found on ground that is nearly level, while those growing on hillsides, against which falling branches roll, are always deeply scarred on the upper side, and as we have seen are sometimes burned down. The saddest thing of all was to see the hopeful seedlings, many of them crinkled and bent with the pressure of winter snow, yet bravely aspiring at the top, helplessly perishing, and young trees, perfect spires of verdure and naturally immortal, suddenly changed to dead masts. Yet the sun looked cheerily down the openings in the forest roof, turning the black smoke to a beautiful brown, as if all was for the best.

Beneath the smoke-clouds of the suffering forest we again pushed southward, descending a side-gorge of the East Fork cañon and climbing another into new forests and groves not a whit less noble. Brownie, the meanwhile, had been resting, while I was weary and sleepy with almost ceaseless wanderings, giving only an hour or two each night or day to sleep in my log home. Waymaking here seemed to become more and more difficult, "impossible," in common phrase, for four-legged travelers. Two or three miles was all the day's work as far as distance was concerned. Nevertheless, just before sundown we found a charming camp ground with plenty of grass, and a forest to study that had felt no fire for many a year. The camp hollow was evidently a favorite home of bears. On many of the trees, at a height of six or eight feet, their autographs were inscribed in strong, free, flowing strokes on the soft bark where they had stood up like cats to stretch their limbs. Using both hands, every claw a pen, the handsome curved lines of their writing take the form of remarkably regular interlacing pointed arches, producing a truly ornamental effect. I looked and listened, half expecting to see some of the writers alarmed and withdrawing from the unwonted disturbance. Brownie also looked and listened, for mules fear bears instinctively and have a very keen nose for them. When I turned him loose, instead of going to the best grass, he kept cautiously near the camp-fire for protection, but was careful not to step on me. The great starry night passed away in deep peace and the rosy morning sunbeams were searching the grove ere I awoke from a long, blessed sleep.

The breadth of the Sequoia belt here is about the same as on the north side of the river, extending, rather thin and scattered in some places, among the noble pines from near the main forest belt of the range well back towards the frosty-peaks, where most of the trees are growing on moraines but little changed as yet.

Two days' scramble above Bear Hollow I enjoyed an interesting interview with deer. Soon after sunrise a little company of four came to my camp in a wild garden imbedded in chaparral, and after much cautious observation quietly began to eat breakfast with me. Keeping perfectly still I soon had their confidence, and they came so near I found no difficulty, while admiring their graceful manners and gestures, in determining what plants they were eating, thus gaining a far finer knowledge and sympathy than comes by killing and hunting.

Indian summer gold with scarce a whisper of winter in it was painting the glad wilderness in richer and yet richer colors as we scrambled across the South cañon into the basin of the Tule. Here the Big Tree forests are still more extensive, and furnished abun-

The Sequoia and General Grant

dance of work in tracing boundaries and gloriously crowned ridges up and down, back and forth, exploring, studying, admiring, while the great measureless days passed on and away uncounted. But in the calm of the camp-fire the end of the season seemed near. Brownie too often brought snow-storms to mind. He became doubly jaded, though I never rode him, and always left him in camp to feed and rest while I explored. The invincible bread business also troubled me again; the last mealy crumbs were consumed, and grass was becoming scarce even in the roughest rock-piles, naturally inaccessible to sheep. One afternoon, as I gazed over the rolling bossy Sequoia billows stretching interminably southward, seeking a way and counting how far I might go without food, a rifle shot rang out sharp and clear. Marking the direction I pushed gladly on, hoping to find some hunter who could spare a little food. Within a few hundred rods I struck the track of a shod horse, which led to the camp of two Indian shepherds. One of them was cooking supper when I arrived. Glancing curiously at me he saw that I was hungry, and gave me some mutton and bread, and said encouragingly as he pointed to the west, "Putty soon Indian come, heap speak English." Toward sundown two thousand sheep beneath a cloud of dust came streaming through the grand Sequoias to a meadow below the camp, and presently the English-speaking shepherd came in, to whom I explained my wants and what I was doing. Like most white men, he could not conceive how anything other than gold could be the object of such rambles as mine, and asked repeatedly whether I had discovered any mines. I tried to make him talk about trees and the wild animals, but unfortunately he proved to be a tame Indian from the Tule Reservation, had been to school, claimed to be civilized, and spoke contemptuously of "wild Indians," and so of course his inherited instincts were blurred or lost. The Big Trees, he said, grew far south, for he had seen them in crossing the mountains from Porterville to Lone Pine. In the morning he kindly gave me a few pounds of flour, and assured me that I would get plenty more at a sawmill on the South Fork if I reached it before it was shut down for the season.

Of all the Tule basin forest the section on the North Fork seemed the finest, surpassing, I think, even the Giant Forest of the Kaweah. Southward from here, though the width and general continuity of the belt is well sustained, I thought I could detect a slight falling off in the height of the trees and in closeness of growth. All the basin was swept by swarms of hoofed locusts, the southern part over and over again, until not a leaf within reach was left on the wettest bogs, the outer edges of the thorniest chaparral beds, or even on the young conifers, which, unless under the stress of dire famine, sheep never touch. Of course Brownie suffered, though I made diligent search for grassy sheep-proof spots. Turning him loose one evening on the side of a carex bog, he dolefully prospected the desolate neighborhood without finding anything that even a starving mule could eat. Then, utterly discouraged, he stole up behind me while I was bent over on my knees making a fire for tea, and in a pitiful mixture of bray and neigh, begged for help. It was a mighty touching prayer, and I answered it as well as I could with half of what was left of a cake made from the last of the flour given me by the Indians, hastily passing it over my shoulder, and saying, "Yes, poor fellow, I know, but soon you'll have plenty. Tomorrow down we go to alfalfa and barley," speaking to him as if he were human, as through stress of trouble plainly he was. After eating his portion of bread he seemed content, for he said no more, but patiently turned away to gnaw leafless ceanothus stubs. Such clinging, confiding dependence after all our scrambles and adventures together was very touching, and I felt conscience-stricken for having led him so far in so rough and desolate a country. "Man," says Lord Bacon, "is the god of the dog." So, also, he is of the mule and many other dependent fellow mortals.

Next morning I turned westward, determined to force a way straight to pasture, letting Sequoia wait. Fortunately ere we had struggled down through half a mile of chaparral we heard a mill

The Sequoia and General Grant

whistle, for which we gladly made a bee line. At the sawmill we both got a good meal, then taking the dusty lumber road pursued our way to the lowlands. The nearest good pasture I counted might be thirty or forty miles away. But scarcely had we gone ten when I noticed a little log cabin a hundred yards or so back from the road, and a tall man straight as a pine standing in front of it observing us as we came plodding down through the dust. Seeing no sign of grass or hay, I was going past without stopping, when he shouted, "Travelin'?" Then drawing nearer, "Where have you come from? I didn't notice you go up." I replied I had come through the woods from the north, looking at the trees. "Oh, then, you must be John Muir. Halt, you're tired; come and rest and I'll cook for you." Then I explained that I was tracing the Sequoia belt, that on account of sheep my mule was starving, and therefore must push on to the lowlands. "No, no," he said, "that corral over there is full of hay and grain. Turn your mule into it. I don't own it, but the fellow who does is hauling lumber, and it will be all right. He's a white man. Come and rest. How tired you must be! The Big Trees don't go much farther south, nohow. I know the country up there, have hunted all over it. Come and rest, and let your little doggone rat of a mule rest. How in heavens did you get him across the cañons—roll him? or carry him? He's poor, but he'll get fat, and I'll give you a horse and go with you up the mountains, and while you're looking at the trees I'll go hunting. It will be a short job, for the end of the Big Trees is not far." Of course I stopped. No true invitation is ever declined. He had been hungry and tired himself many a time in the Rocky Mountains as well as in the Sierra. Now he owned a band of cattle and lived alone. His cabin was about eight by ten feet, the door at one end, a fireplace at the other, and a bed on one side fastened to the logs. Leading me in without a word of mean apology, he made me lie down on the bed, then reached under it, brought forth a sack of apples and advised me to keep "chawing" at them until he got supper ready.

Finer, braver hospitality I never found in all this good world so often called selfish.

Next day with hearty, easy alacrity the mountaineer procured horses, prepared and packed provisions, and got everything ready for an early start the following morning. Well mounted, we pushed rapidly up the South Fork of the river and soon after noon were among the giants once more. On the divide between the Tule and Deer Creek a central camp was made, and the mountaineer spent his time in deer-hunting, while with provisions for two or three days I explored the woods, and in accordance with what I had been told soon reached the southern extremity of the belt on the South Fork of Deer Creek. To make sure, I searched the woods a considerable distance south of the last Deer Creek grove, passed over into the basin of the Kern, and climbed several high points commanding extensive views over the sugar-pine woods, without seeing a single Sequoia crown in all the wide expanse to the southward. On the way back to camp, however, I was greatly interested in a grove I discovered on the east side of the Kern River divide, opposite the North Fork of Deer Creek. The height of the pass where the species crossed over is about 7000 feet, and I heard of still another grove whose waters drain into the upper Kern opposite the Middle Fork of the Tule.

It appears, therefore, that though the Sequoia belt is two hundred and sixty miles long, most of the trees are on a section to the south of Kings River only about seventy miles in length. But though the area occupied by the species increases so much to the southward, there is but little difference in the size of the trees. A diameter of twenty feet and height of two hundred and seventy-five is perhaps about the average for anything like mature and favorably situated trees. Specimens twenty-five feet in diameter are not rare, and a good many approach a height of three hundred feet. Occasionally one meets a specimen thirty feet in diameter, and rarely one that is larger. The majestic stump on Kings River is the largest I saw and measured on the entire trip. Careful search around the boundaries of the forests and groves and in the gaps of the belt failed to discover any trace of the former existence of the species beyond its present limits. On the contrary, it seems to be slightly extending its boundaries; for the outstanding stragglers, occasionally met a mile or two from the main bodies, are young instead of old monumental trees. Ancient ruins and the ditches and root-bowls the big trunks make in falling were found in all the groves, but none outside of them. We may therefore conclude that the area covered by the species has not been diminished during the last eight or ten thousand years, and probably not at all in post-glacial times. For admitting that upon those areas supposed to have been once covered by Sequoia every tree may have fallen, and that fire and the weather had left not a vestige of them, many of the ditches made by the fall of the ponderous trunks, weighing five hundred to nearly a thousand tons, and the bowls made by their upturned roots would remain visible for thousands of years after the last remnants of the trees had vanished. Some of these records would doubtless be effaced in a comparatively short time by the inwashing of sediments, but no inconsiderable part of them would remain enduringly engraved on flat ridge tops, almost wholly free from such action.

In the northern groves, the only ones that at first came under the observation of students, there are but few seedlings and young trees to take the places of the old ones. Therefore the species was regarded as doomed to speedy extinction, as being only an expiring remnant vanquished in the so-called struggle for life, and shoved into its last strongholds in most glens where conditions are exceptionally favorable. But the majestic continuous forests of the south end of the belt create a very different impression. Here, as we have seen, no tree in the forest is more enduringly established. Nevertheless it is oftentimes vaguely said that the Sierra climate is drying out, and that this oncoming, constantly increasing drought will of itself surely extinguish King Sequoia, though sections of wood-rings show that there has been no appreciable change of climate during the last forty centuries. Furthermore, that Sequoia can grow and is growing on as dry ground as any of its neighbors or rivals, we have seen proved over and over again. "Why, then," it will be asked, "are the Big Tree groves always found on well-watered spots?" Simply because Big Trees give rise to streams. It is a mistake to suppose that the water is the cause of the groves being there. On the contrary, the groves are the cause of the water being there. The roots of this immense tree fill the ground, forming a sponge which hoards the bounty of the clouds and sends it forth in clear perennial streams instead of allowing it to rush headlong in short-lived destructive floods. Evaporation is also checked, and the air kept still in the shady Sequoia depths, while thirsty robber winds are shut out.

Since, then, it appears that Sequoia can and does grow on as dry ground as its neighbors and that the greater moisture found with it is an effect rather than a cause of its presence, the notions as to the former greater extension of the species and its near approach to extinction, based on its supposed dependence on greater moisture, are seen to be erroneous. Indeed, all my observations go to show that in case of prolonged drought the sugar pines and firs would die before Sequoia. Again, if the restricted and irregular distribution of the species be interpreted as the result of the desiccation of the range, then, instead of increasing in individuals toward the south, where the rainfall is less, it should diminish.

If, then, its peculiar distribution has not been governed by superior conditions of soil and moisture, by what has it been governed? Several years before I made this trip, I noticed that the northern groves were located on those parts of the Sierra soil-belt that were first laid bare and opened to preëmption when the icesheet began to break up into individual glaciers. And when I was examining the basin of the San Joaquin and trying to account for the absence of Sequoia, when every condition seemed favorable for its growth, it occurred to me that this remarkable gap in the belt is located in the channel of the great ancient glacier of the San Joaquin and Kings

The Sequoia and General Grant

River basins, which poured its frozen floods to the plain, fed by the snows that fell on more than fifty miles of the Summit peaks of the range. Constantly brooding on the question, I next perceived that the great gap in the belt to the northward, forty miles wide, between the Stanislaus and Tuolumne groves, occurs in the channel of the great Stanislaus and Tuolumne glacier, and that the smaller gap between the Merced and Mariposa groves occurs in the channel of the smaller Merced glacier. The wider the ancient glacier, the wider the gap in the Sequoia belt, while the groves and forests attain their greatest development in the Kaweah and Tule River basins, just where, owing to topographical conditions, the region was first cleared and warmed, while protected from the main ice-rivers, that flowed past to right and left down the Kings and Kern valleys. In general, where the ground on the belt was first cleared of ice, there the Sequoia now is, and where at the same elevation and time the ancient glaciers lingered, there the Sequoia is not. What the other conditions may have been which enabled the Sequoia to establish itself upon these oldest and warmest parts of the main soil-belt I cannot say. I might venture to state, however, that since the Sequoia forests present a more and more ancient and long established aspect to the southward, the species was probably distributed from the south toward the close of the glacial period, before the arrival of other trees. About this branch of the question, however, there is at present much fog, but the general relationship we have pointed out between the distribution of the Big Tree and the ancient glacial system is clear. And when we bear in mind that all the existing forests of the Sierra are growing on comparatively fresh moraine soil, and that the range itself has been recently sculptured and brought to light from beneath the ice-mantle of the glacial winter, then many lawless mysteries vanish, and harmonies take their places.

All the observed phenomena bearing on the post-glacial history of this colossal tree point to the conclusion that it never was more widely distributed on the Sierra since the close of the glacial epoch;

89

that its present forests are scarcely past prime; if, indeed, they have reached prime; that the post-glacial day of the species is probably not half done; yet, when from a wider outlook the vast antiquity of the genus is considered, and its ancient richness in species and individuals, comparing our Sierra giant and Sequoia sempervirens of the coast, the only other living species, with the many fossil species already discovered, and described by Heer and Lesquereux, some of which flourished over large areas around the Arctic Circle, and in Europe and our own territories, during tertiary and cretaceous times —then, indeed, it becomes plain that our two surviving species, restricted to narrow belts within the limits of California, are mere remnants of the genus both as to species and individuals, and that they probably are verging to extinction. But the verge of a period beginning in cretaceous times may have a breadth of tens of thousands of years, not to mention the possible existence of conditions calculated to multiply and reëxtend both species and individuals. No unfavorable change of climate, so far as I can see, no disease, but only fire and the axe and the ravages of flocks and herds threaten the existence of these noblest of God's trees. In Nature's keeping they are safe, but through man's agency destruction is making rapid progress, while in the work of protection only a beginning has been made. The Mariposa Grove belongs to and is guarded by the State; the General Grant and Sequoia National Parks, established ten years ago, are efficiently guarded by a troop of cavalry under the direction of the Secretary of the Interior; so also are the small Tuolumne and Merced groves, which are included in the Yosemite National Park, while a few scattered patches and fringes, scarce at all protected, though belonging to the national government, are in the Sierra Forest Reservation.

Perhaps more than half of all the Big Trees have been sold, and are now in the hands of speculators and mill men. Even the beautiful little Calaveras Grove of ninety trees, so historically interesting from

The Sequoia and General Grant

its being the first discovered, is now owned, together with the much larger South or Stanislaus Grove, by a lumber company.

Far the largest and most important section of protected Big Trees is in the grand Sequoia National Park, now easily accessible by stage from Visalia. It contains seven townships and extends across the whole breadth of the magnificent Kaweah basin. But large as it is, it should be made much larger. Its natural eastern boundary is the high Sierra, and the northern and southern boundaries, the Kings and Kern rivers, thus including the sublime scenery on the headwaters of these rivers and perhaps nine tenths of all the Big Trees in existence. Private claims cut and blotch both of the Sequoia parks as well as all the best of the forests, every one of which the government should gradually extinguish by purchase, as it readily may, for none of these holdings are of much value to their owners. Thus as far as possible the grand blunder of selling would be corrected. The value of these forests in storing and dispensing the bounty of the mountain clouds is infinitely greater than lumber or sheep. To the dwellers of the plain, depending on irrigation, the Big Tree, leaving all its higher uses out of the count, is a tree of life, a never-failing spring, sending living water to the lowlands all through the hot, rainless summer. For every grove cut down a stream is dried up. Therefore, all California is crying, "Save the trees of the fountains," nor, judging by the signs of the times, is it likely that the cry will cease until the salvation of all that is left of Sequoia gigantea is sure.

The Approach
to the Valley

When I set out on the long excursion that finally led to California I wandered afoot and alone, from Indiana to the Gulf of Mexico, with a plant-press on my back, holding a generally southward course, like the birds when they are going from summer to winter. From the west coast of Florida I crossed the gulf to Cuba, enjoyed the rich tropical flora there for a few months, intending to go thence to the north end of South America, make my way through the woods to the headwaters of the Amazon, and float down that grand river to the ocean. But I was unable to find a ship bound for South America—fortunately perhaps, for I had incredibly little money for so long a trip and had not yet fully recovered from a fever caught in the Florida swamps. Therefore I decided to visit California for a year or two to see its wonderful flora and the famous Yosemite Valley. All the world was before me and every day was a holiday, so it did not seem important to which one of the world's wildernesses I first should wander.

Arriving by the Panama steamer, I stopped one day in San Francisco and then inquired for the nearest way out of town. "But where do you want to go?" asked the man to whom I had applied for this important information. "To any place that is wild," I said. This reply startled him. He seemed to fear I might be crazy and therefore the sooner I was out of town the better, so he directed me to the Oakland ferry.

So on the first of April, 1868, I set out afoot for Yosemite. It was the bloom-time of the year over the lowlands and coast ranges; the landscapes of the Santa Clara Valley were fairly drenched with sunshine, all the air was quivering with the songs of the meadowlarks, and the hills were so covered with flowers that they seemed to be painted. Slow indeed was my progress through these glorious gardens, the first of the California flora I had seen. Cattle and cultivation were making few scars as yet, and I wandered enchanted in long wavering curves, knowing by my pocket map that Yosemite Valley lay to the east and that I should surely find it.

The Sierra from the West

Looking eastward from the summit of the Pacheco Pass one shining morning, a landscape was displayed that after all my wanderings still appears as the most beautiful I have ever beheld. At my feet lay the Great Central Valley of California, level and flowery, like a lake of pure sunshine, forty or fifty miles wide, five hundred miles long, one rich furred garden of yellow *Compositœ*. And from the eastern boundary of this vast golden flower-bed rose the mighty Sierra, miles in height, and so gloriously colored and so radiant, it seemed not clothed with light, but wholly composed of it, like the wall of some celestial city. Along the top and extending a good way down, was a rich pearl-gray belt of snow; below it a belt of blue and dark purple, marking the extension of the forests; and stretching along the base of the range a broad belt of rose-purple; all these colors, from the blue sky to the yellow valley smoothly blending as they do in a rainbow, making a wall of light ineffably fine. Then it seemed to me that the Sierra should be called, not the Nevada or Snowy Range, but the Range of Light. And after ten years of wandering and wondering in the heart of it, rejoicing in its glorious floods of light, the white beams of the morning streaming through the passes, the noonday radiance on the crystal rocks, the flush of the alpenglow, and the irised spray of countless waterfalls, it still seems above all others the Range of Light.

In general views no mark of man is visible upon it, nor anything to suggest the wonderful depth and grandeur of its sculpture. None of its magnificent forest-crowned ridges seems to rise much above the general level to publish its wealth. No great valley or river is seen, or group of well-marked features of any kind standing out as distinct pictures. Even the summit peaks, marshaled in glorious array so high in the sky, seem comparatively regular in form. Nevertheless the whole range five hundred miles long is furrowed with cañons 2000 to 5000 feet deep, in which once flowed majestic glaciers, and in which now flow and sing the bright rejoicing rivers.

CHARACTERISTICS OF THE CAÑONS

Though of such stupendous depth, these cañons are not gloomy gorges, savage and inaccessible. With rough passages here and there they are flowery pathways conducting to the snowy, ice fountains; mountain streets full of life and light, graded and sculptured by the ancient glaciers, and presenting throughout all their courses a rich variety of novel and attractive scenery—the most attractive that has yet been discovered in the mountain ranges of the world. In many places, especially in the middle region of the western flank, the main cañons widen into spacious valleys or parks diversified like landscape gardens with meadows and groves and thickets of blooming bushes, while the lofty walls, infinitely varied in form, are fringed with ferns, flowering plants, shrubs of many species, and tall evergreens and oaks that find footholds on small benches and tables, all enlivened and made glorious with rejoicing streams that come chanting in chorus over the cliffs and through side cañons in falls of every conceivable form, to join the river that flows in tranquil, shining beauty down the middle of each one of them.

THE INCOMPARABLE YOSEMITE

The most famous and accessible of these cañon valleys, and also the one that presents their most striking and sublime features on the grandest scale, is the Yosemite, situated in the basin of the Merced River at an elevation of 4000 feet above the level of the sea. It is about seven miles long, half a mile to a mile wide, and nearly a mile deep in the solid granite flank of the range. The walls are made up of rocks, mountains in size, partly separated from each other by side cañons, and they are so sheer in front, and so compactly and harmoniously arranged on a level floor, that the Valley, comprehensively seen, looks like an immense hall or temple lighted from above.

But no temple made with hands can compare with Yosemite. Every rock in its walls seems to glow with life. Some lean back in majestic repose; others, absolutely sheer or nearly so for thousands of feet, advance beyond their companions in thoughtful attitudes, giving welcome to storms and calms alike, seemingly aware, yet heedless, of everything going on about them. Awful in stern, immovable majesty, how softly these rocks are adorned, and how fine and reassuring the company they keep: their feet among beautiful groves and meadows, their brows in the sky, a thousand flowers leaning confidingly against their feet, bathed in floods of water, floods of light, while the snow and waterfalls, the winds and avalanches and clouds shine and sing and wreathe about them as the years go by, and myriads of small winged creatures—birds, bees, butterflies—give glad animation and help to make all the air into music. Down through the middle of the Valley flows the crystal Merced, River of Mercy, peacefully quiet, reflecting lilies and trees and the onlooking rocks; things frail and fleeting and types of endurance meeting here and blending in countless forms, as if into this one mountain mansion Nature had gathered her choicest treasures, to draw her lovers into close and confiding communion with her.

THE APPROACH TO THE VALLEY

Sauntering up the foothills to Yosemite by any of the old trails or roads in use before the railway was built from the town of Merced up the river to the boundary of Yosemite Park, richer and wilder become the forests and streams. At an elevation of 6000 feet above the level of the sea the silver firs are 200 feet high, with branches whorled around the colossal shafts in regular order, and every branch beautifully pinnate like a fern frond. The Douglas spruce, the yellow and sugar pines and brown-barked libocedrus here reach their finest developments of beauty and grandeur. The majestic Sequoia is here, too, the king of conifers, the noblest of all the noble race. These colossal trees are as wonderful in fineness of beauty and proportion as in stature—an assemblage of conifers surpassing all that have ever yet been discovered in the forests of the world. Here indeed is the tree-lover's paradise; the woods, dry and wholesome, letting in the light in shimmering masses of half sunshine, half shade; the night air as well as the day air indescribably spicy and exhilarating; plushy fir-boughs for campers' beds, and cascades to sing us to sleep. On the highest ridges, over which these old Yosemite ways passed, the silver fir (*Abies magnifica*) forms the bulk of the woods, pressing forward in glorious array to the very brink of the Valley walls on both sides, and beyond the Valley to a height of from 8000 to 9000 feet above the level of the sea. Thus it appears that Yosemite, presenting such stupendous faces of bare granite, is nevertheless imbedded in magnificent forests, and the main species of pine, fir, spruce and libocedrus are also found in the Valley itself, but there are no "big trees" (*Sequoia gigantea*) in the Valley or about the rim of it. The nearest are about ten and twenty miles beyond the lower end of the valley on small tributaries of the Merced and Tuolumne Rivers.

THE FIRST VIEW: THE BRIDAL VEIL

From the margin of these glorious forests the first general view of the Valley used to be gained—a revelation in landscape affairs that enriches one's life forever. Entering the Valley, gazing overwhelmed with the multitude of grand objects about us, perhaps the first to fix our attention will be the Bridal Veil, a beautiful waterfall on our right. Its brow, where it first leaps free from the cliff, is about 900 feet above us; and as it sways and sings in the wind, clad in gauzy, sun-sifted spray, half falling, half floating, it seems infinitely gentle and fine, but the hymns it sings tell the solemn fateful power hidden beneath its soft clothing.

The Bridal Veil shoots free from the upper edge of the cliff by the velocity the stream has acquired in descending a long slope above the head of the fall. Looking from the top of the rock-avalanche talus on the west side, about one hundred feet above the foot of the fall, the under surface of the water arch is seen to be finely grooved and striated; and the sky is seen through the arch between rock and water, making a novel and beautiful effect.

Under ordinary weather conditions the fall strikes on flat-topped slabs, forming a kind of ledge about two-thirds of the way down from the top, and as the fall sways back and forth with great variety of motions among these flat-topped pillars, kissing and plashing notes as well as thunder-like detonations are produced, like those of the Yosemite Fall, though on a smaller scale.

The rainbows of the Veil, or rather the spray-and-foam-bows, are superb, because the waters are dashed among angular blocks of granite at the foot, producing abundance of spray of the best quality for iris effects, and also for a luxuriant growth of grass and maiden-hair on the side of the talus, which lower down is planted with oak, laurel and willows.

GENERAL FEATURES OF THE VALLEY

On the other side of the Valley, almost immediately opposite the Bridal Veil, there is another fine fall, considerably wider than the Veil when the snow is melting fast and more than 1000 feet in height, measured from the brow of the cliff where it first springs out into the air to the head of the rocky talus on which it strikes and is broken up into ragged cascades. It is called the Ribbon Fall or Virgin's Tears. During the spring floods it is a magnificent object, but the suffocating blasts of spray that fill the recess in the wall which it occupies prevent a near approach. In autumn, however, when its feeble current falls in a shower, it may then pass for tears with the sentimental onlooker fresh from a visit to the Bridal Veil.

Just beyond this glorious flood the El Capitan Rock, regarded by many as the most sublime feature of the Valley, is seen through the pine groves, standing forward beyond the general line of the wall in most imposing grandeur, a type of permanence. It is 3300 feet high, a plain, severely simple, glacier-sculptured face of granite, the end of one of the most compact and enduring of the mountain ridges, unrivaled in height and breadth and flawless strength.

Across the Valley from here, next to the Bridal Veil, are the pictur-esque Cathedral Rocks, nearly 2700 feet high, making a noble display of fine yet massive sculpture. They are closely related to El Capitan, having been eroded from the same mountain ridge by the great Yosemite Glacier when the Valley was in process of formation.

Next to the Cathedral Rocks on the south side towers the Sentinel Rock to a height of more than 3000 feet, a telling monument of the glacial period.

Almost immediately opposite the Sentinel are the Three Brothers, an immense mountain mass with three gables fronting the Valley, one above another, the topmost gable nearly 4000 feet high. They were named for three brothers, sons of old Tenaya, the Yosemite chief, captured here during the Indian War, at the time of the dis-covery of the Valley in 1852.

Sauntering up the Valley through meadow and grove, in the com-pany of these majestic rocks, which seem to follow us as we advance, gazing, admiring, looking for new wonders ahead where all about us is so wonderful, the thunder of the Yosemite Fall is heard, and when we arrive in front of the Sentinel Rock it is revealed in all its glory from base to summit, half a mile in height, and seeming to spring out into the Valley sunshine direct from the sky. But even this fall, perhaps the most wonderful of its kind in the world, cannot at first hold our attention, for now the wide upper portion of the Valley is displayed to view, with the finely modeled North Dome, the Royal

Arches and Washington Column on our left; Glacier Point, with its massive, magnificent sculpture on the right; and in the middle, directly in front, looms Tissiack or Half Dome, the most beautiful and most sublime of all the wonderful Yosemite rocks, rising in serene majesty from flowery groves and meadows to a height of 4750 feet.

THE UPPER CAÑONS

Here the Valley divides into three branches, the Tenaya, Nevada, and Illilouette Cañons, extending back into the fountains of the High Sierra, with scenery every way worthy the relation they bear to Yosemite.

In the south branch, a mile or two from the main Valley, is the Illilouette Fall, 600 feet high, one of the most beautiful of all the Yosemite choir, but to most people inaccessible as yet on account of its rough, steep, boulder-choked cañon. Its principal fountains of ice and snow lie in the beautiful and interesting mountains of the Merced group, while its broad open basin between its fountain mountains and cañon is noted for the beauty of its lakes and forests and magnificent moraines.

Returning to the Valley, and going up the north branch of Tenaya Cañon, we pass between the North Dome and Half Dome, and in less than an hour come to Mirror Lake, the Dome Cascades, and Tenaya Fall. Beyond the Fall, on the north side of the cañon, is the sublime El Capitan-like rock called Mount Watkins; on the south the vast granite wave of Clouds' Rest, a mile in height; and between them the fine Tenaya Cascade with silvery plumes outspread on smooth glacier-polished folds of granite, making a vertical descent in all of about 700 feet.

Just beyond the Dome Cascades, on the shoulder of Mount Watkins, there is an old trail once used by Indians on their way across the range to Mono, but in the cañon above this point there is no trail of any sort. Between Mount Watkins and Clouds' Rest the cañon is accessible only to mountaineers, and it is so dangerous that I hesitate to advise even good climbers, anxious to test their nerve and skill, to attempt to pass through it. Beyond the Cascades no great difficulty will be encountered. A succession of charming lily gardens and meadows occurs in filled-up lake basins among the rock-waves in the bottom of the cañon, and everywhere the surface of the granite has a smooth-wiped appearance, and in many places reflects the sunbeams like glass, a phenomenon due to glacial action, the cañon having been the channel of one of the main tributaries of the ancient Yosemite Glacier.

About ten miles above the Valley we come to the beautiful Tenaya Lake, and here the cañon terminates. A mile or two above the lake stands the grand Sierra Cathedral, a building of one stone, hewn from the living rock, with sides, roof, gable, spire and ornamental pinnacles, fashioned and finished symmetrically like a work of art, and set on a well-graded plateau about 9000 feet high, as if Nature in making so fine a building had also been careful that it should be finely seen. From every direction its peculiar form and graceful, majestic beauty of expression never fail to charm. Its height from its base to the ridge of the roof is about 2500 feet, and among the pinnacles that adorn the front grand views may be gained of the upper basins of the Merced and Tuolumne Rivers.

Passing the Cathedral we descend into the delightful, spacious Tuolumne Valley, from which excursions may be made to Mounts Dana, Lyell, Ritter, Conness, and Mono Lake, and to the many curious peaks that rise above the meadows on the south, and to the Big Tuolumne Cañon, with its glorious abundance of rocks and falling, gliding, tossing water. For all these the beautiful meadows near the Soda Springs form a delightful center.

NATURAL FEATURES
NEAR THE VALLEY

Returning now to Yosemite and ascending the middle or Nevada branch of the Valley, occupied by the main Merced River, we come within a few miles to the Vernal and Nevada Falls, 400 and 600 feet high, pouring their white, rejoicing waters in the midst of the most novel and sublime rock scenery to be found in all the world. Tracing the river beyond the head of the Nevada Fall we are led into the Little Yosemite, a valley like the great Yosemite in form, sculpture and vegetation. It is about three miles long, with walls 1500 to 2000 feet high, cascades coming over them, and the river flowing through the meadows and groves of the level bottom in tranquil, richly-embowered reaches.

Beyond this Little Yosemite in the main cañon, there are three other little yosemites, the highest situated a few miles below the base of Mount Lyell, at an elevation of about 7800 feet above the sea. To describe these, with all their wealth of Yosemite furniture, and the wilderness of lofty peaks above them, the home of the avalanche and treasury of the fountain snow, would take us far beyond the bounds of a single book. Nor can we here consider the formation of these mountain landscapes—how the crystal rocks were brought to light by glaciers made up of crystal snow, making beauty whose influence is so mysterious on every one who sees it.

Of the small glacier lakes so characteristic of these upper regions, there are no fewer than sixty-seven in the basin of the main middle branch, besides countless smaller pools. In the basin of the Illilouette there are sixteen, in the Tenaya basin and its branches thirteen, in the Yosemite Creek basin fourteen, and in the Pohono or Bridal Veil one, making a grand total of one hundred and eleven lakes whose waters come to sing at Yosemite. So glorious is the background of the great Valley, so harmonious its relations to its widespreading fountains.

The same harmony prevails in all the other features of the adjacent landscapes. Climbing out of the Valley by the subordinate cañons, we find the ground rising from the brink of the walls: on the south side to the fountains of the Bridal Veil Creek, the basin of which is noted for the beauty of its meadows and its superb forests of silver fir; on the north side through the basin of the Yosemite Creek to the dividing ridge along the Tuolumne Cañon and the fountains of the Hoffman Range.

DOWN THE YOSEMITE CREEK

In general views the Yosemite Creek basin seems to be paved with domes and smooth, whaleback masses of granite in every stage of development—some showing only their crowns; others rising high and free above the girdling forests, singly or in groups. Others are developed only on one side, forming bold outstanding bosses usually well fringed with shrubs and trees, and presenting the polished surfaces given them by the glacier that brought them into relief. On the upper portion of the basin broad moraine beds have been deposited and on these fine, thrifty forests are growing. Lakes and meadows and small spongy bogs may be found hiding here and there in the woods or back in the fountain recesses of Mount Hoffman, while a thousand gardens are planted along the banks of the streams.

All the wide, fan-shaped upper portion of the basin is covered with a network of small rills that go cheerily on their way to their grand fall in the Valley, now flowing on smooth pavements in sheets thin as glass, now diving under willows and laving their red roots,

The Approach to the Valley

oozing through green, plushy bogs, plashing over small falls and dancing down slanting cascades, calming again, gliding through patches of smooth glacier meadows with sod of alpine agrostis mixed with blue and white violets and daisies, breaking, tossing among rough boulders and fallen trees, resting in calm pools, flowing together until, all united, they go to their fate with stately, tranquil gestures like a full-grown river. At the crossing of the Mono Trail, about two miles above the head of the Yosemite Fall, the stream is nearly forty feet wide, and when the snow is melting rapidly in the spring it is about four feet deep, with a current of two and a half miles an hour. This is about the volume of water that forms the Fall in May and June when there had been much snow the preceding winter; but it varies greatly from month to month. The snow rapidly vanishes from the open portion of the basin, which faces southward, and only a few of the tributaries reach back to perennial snow and ice fountains in the shadowy amphitheaters on the precipitous northern slopes of Mount Hoffman. The total descent made by the stream from its highest sources to its confluence with the Merced in the Valley is about 6000 feet, while the distance is only about ten miles, an average fall of 600 feet per mile. The last mile of its course lies between the sides of sunken domes and swelling folds of the granite that are clustered and pressed together like a mass of bossy cumulus clouds. Through this shining way Yosemite Creek goes to its fate, swaying and swirling with easy, graceful gestures and singing the last of its mountain songs before it reaches the dizzy edge of Yosemite to fall 2600 feet into another world, where climate, vegetation, inhabitants, all are different. Emerging from this last cañon the stream glides, in flat, lace-like folds, down a smooth incline into a small pool where it seems to rest and compose itself before taking the grand plunge. Then calmly, as if leaving a lake, it slips over the polished lip of the pool down another incline and out over the brow of the precipice in a magnificent curve thick-sown with rainbow spray.

THE YOSEMITE FALL

Long ago before I had traced this fine stream to its head back of Mount Hoffman, I was eager to reach the extreme verge to see how it behaved in flying so far through the air; but after enjoying this view and getting safely away I have never advised any one to follow my steps. The last incline down which the stream journeys so gracefully is so steep and smooth one must slip cautiously forward on hands and feet alongside the rushing water, which so near one's head is very exciting. But to gain a perfect view one must go yet farther, over a curving brow to a slight shelf on the extreme brink. This shelf, formed by the flaking off of a fold of granite, is about three inches wide, just wide enough for a safe rest for one's heels. To me it seemed nerve-trying to slip to this narrow foothold and poise on the edge of such a precipice so close to the confusing whirl of the waters; and after casting longing glances over the shining brow of the fall and listening to its sublime psalm, I concluded not to attempt to go nearer, but, nevertheless, against reasonable judgment, I did. Noticing some tufts of artemisia in a cleft of rock, I filled my mouth with the leaves, hoping their bitter taste might help to keep caution keen and prevent giddiness. In spite of myself I reached the little ledge, got my heels well set, and worked sidewise twenty or thirty feet to a point close to the out-plunging current. Here the view is perfectly free down into the heart of the bright irised throng of comet-like streamers into which the whole ponderous volume of the fall separates, two or three hundred feet below the brow. So glorious a display of pure wildness, acting at close range while cut off from all the world beside, is terribly impressive. A less nerve-trying view may be obtained from a fissured portion of the edge of the cliff about forty yards to the eastward of the fall. Seen from this point towards noon, in the spring, the rainbow on its brow seems to be broken up and mingled with the rushing comets until all the fall is stained with iris colors, leaving no white water visible. This is the best of the safe views from above, the huge steadfast rocks, the flying waters, and the rainbow light forming one of the most glorious pictures conceivable.

The Yosemite Fall is separated into an upper and a lower fall with a series of falls and cascades between them, but when viewed in front from the bottom of the Valley they all appear as one.

So grandly does this magnificent fall display itself from the floor of the Valley, few visitors take the trouble to climb the walls to gain nearer views, unable to realize how vastly more impressive it is near by than at a distance of one or two miles.

A WONDERFUL ASCENT

The views developed in a walk up the zigzags of the trail leading to the foot of the Upper Fall are about as varied and impressive as those displayed along the favorite Glacier Point Trail. One rises as if on wings. The groves, meadows, fern-flats and reaches of the river gain new interest, as if never seen before; all the views changing in a most striking manner as we go higher from point to point. The foreground also changes every few rods in the most surprising manner, although the earthquake talus and the level bench on the face of the wall over which the trail passes seem monotonous and commonplace as seen from the bottom of the Valley. Up we climb with glad exhilaration, through shaggy fringes of laurel, ceanothus, glossy-leaved manzanita and live-oak, from shadow to shadow across bars and patches of sunshine, the leafy openings making charming frames for the Valley pictures beheld through them, and for the glimpses of the high peaks that appear in the distance. The higher we go the farther we seem to

107

be from the summit of the vast granite wall. Here we pass a projecting buttress whose grooved and rounded surface tells a plain story of the time when the Valley, now filled with sunshine, was filled with ice, when the grand old Yosemite Glacier, flowing river-like from its distant fountains, swept through it, crushing, grinding, wearing its way ever deeper, developing and fashioning these sublime rocks. Again we cross a white, battered gully, the pathway of rock avalanches or snow avalanches. Farther on we come to a gentle stream slipping down the face of the cliff in lace-like strips, and dropping from ledge to ledge—too small to be called a fall—trickling, dripping, oozing, a pathless wanderer from one of the upland meadows lying a little way back of the Valley rim, seeking a way century after century to the depths of the Valley without any appreciable channel. Every morning after a cool night, evaporation being checked, it gathers strength and sings like a bird, but as the day advances and the sun strikes its thin currents outspread on the heated precipices, most of its waters vanish ere the bottom of the Valley is reached. Many a fine, hanging-garden aloft on breezy inaccessible heights owes to it its freshness and fullness of beauty; ferneries in shady nooks, filled with Adiantum, Woodwardia, Woodsia, Aspidium, Pellaea, and Cheilanthes, rosetted and tufted and ranged in lines, daintily overlapping, thatching the stupendous cliffs with softest beauty, some of the delicate fronds seeming to float on the warm moist air, without any connection with rock or stream. Nor is there any lack of colored plants wherever they can find a place to cling to; lilies and mints, the showy cardinal mimulus, and glowing cushions of the golden bahia, enlivened with butterflies and bees and all the other small, happy humming creatures that belong to them.

After the highest point on the lower division of the trail is gained it leads up into the deep recess occupied by the great fall, the noblest display of falling water to be found in the Valley, or perhaps in the

The Approach to the Valley

world. When it first comes in sight it seems almost within reach of one's hand, so great in the spring is its volume and velocity, yet it is still nearly a third of a mile away and appears to recede as we advance. The sculpture of the walls about it is on a scale of grandeur, according nobly with the fall—plain and massive, though elaborately finished, like all the other cliffs about the Valley.

In the afternoon an immense shadow is cast athwart the plateau in front of the fall, and over the chaparral bushes that clothe the slopes and benches of the walls to the eastward, creeping upward until the fall is wholly overcast, the contrast between the shaded and illumined sections being very striking in these near views.

Under this shadow, during the cool centuries immediately following the breaking-up of the Glacial Period, dwelt a small residual glacier, one of the few that lingered on this sun-beaten side of the Valley after the main trunk glacier had vanished. It sent down a long winding current through the narrow cañon on the west side of the fall, and must have formed a striking feature of the ancient scenery of the Valley; the lofty fall of ice and fall of water side by side, yet separate and distinct.

The coolness of the afternoon shadow and the abundant dewy spray make a fine climate for the plateau ferns and grasses, and for the beautiful azalea bushes that grow here in profusion and bloom in September, long after the warmer thickets down on the floor of the Valley have withered and gone to seed. Even close to the fall, and behind it at the base of the cliff, a few venturesome plants may be found undisturbed by the rock-shaking torrent.

The basin at the foot of the fall into which the current directly pours, when it is not swayed by the wind, is about ten feet deep and fifteen to twenty feet in diameter. That it is not much deeper is surprising, when the great height and force of the fall is considered. But the rock where the water strikes probably suffers less erosion than it would were the descent less than half as great, since the current is outspread, and much of its force is spent ere it reaches the bottom—being received on the air as upon an elastic cushion, and borne outward and dissipated over a surface more than fifty yards wide.

This surface, easily examined when the water is low, is intensely clean and fresh looking. It is the raw, quick flesh of the mountain wholly untouched by the weather. In summer droughts, when the snowfall of the preceding winter has been light, the fall is reduced to a mere shower of separate drops without any obscuring spray. Then we may safely go back of it and view the crystal shower from beneath, each drop wavering and pulsing as it makes its way through the air, and flashing off jets of colored light of ravishing beauty. But all this is invisible from the bottom of the Valley, like a thousand other interesting things. One must labor for beauty as for bread, here as elsewhere.

THE GRANDEUR
OF THE YOSEMITE FALL

During the time of the spring floods the best near view of the fall is obtained from Fern Ledge on the east side above the blinding spray at a height of about 400 feet above the base of the fall. A climb of about 1400 feet from the Valley has to be made, and there is no trail, but to any one fond of climbing this will make the ascent all the more delightful. A narrow part of the ledge extends to the side of the fall and back of it, enabling us to approach it as closely as we wish. When the afternoon sunshine is streaming through the throng of comets, ever wasting, ever renewed, the marvelous fineness, firmness and variety of their forms are beautifully revealed. At the top of the fall they seem to burst forth in irregular spurts from some grand, throbbing mountain heart. Now and then one mighty

The Approach to the Valley

throb sends forth a mass of solid water into the free air far beyond the others, which rushes alone to the bottom of the fall with long streaming tail, like combed silk, while the others, descending in clusters, gradually mingle and lose their identity. But they all rush past us with amazing velocity and display of power, though apparently drowsy and deliberate in their movements when observed from a distance of a mile or two. The heads of these comet-like masses are composed of nearly solid water, and are dense white in color like pressed snow, from the friction they suffer in rushing through the air, the portion worn off forming the tail, between the white lustrous threads and films of which faint, grayish pencilings appear, while the outer, finer sprays of water-dust, whirling in sunny eddies, are pearly gray throughout. At the bottom of the fall there is but little distinction of form visible. It is mostly a hissing, clashing, seething, upwhirling mass of scud and spray, through which the light sifts in gray and purple tones, while at times when the sun strikes at the required angle, the whole wild and apparently lawless, stormy, striving mass is changed to brilliant rainbow hues, manifesting finest harmony. The middle portion of the fall is the most openly beautiful; lower, the various forms into which the waters are wrought are more closely and voluminously veiled, while higher, towards the head, the current is comparatively simple and undivided. But even at the bottom, in the boiling clouds of spray, there is no confusion, while the rainbow light makes all divine, adding glorious beauty and peace to glorious power. This noble fall has far the richest, as well as the most powerful, voice of all the falls of the Valley, its tones varying from the sharp hiss and rustle of the wind in the glossy leaves of the live-oaks and the soft, sifting, hushing tones of the pines, to the loudest rush and roar of storm winds and thunder among the crags of the summit peaks. The low bass, booming, reverberating tones, heard under favorable circumstances five or six miles away, are formed by the dashing and exploding of heavy masses mixed with air upon two projecting ledges on the face of the cliff, the one on which we are standing and another about 200 feet above it. The torrent of massive comets is continuous at time of high water, while the explosive, booming notes are wildly intermittent, because, unless influenced by the wind, most of the heavier masses shoot out from the face of the precipice, and pass the ledges upon which at other times they are exploded. Occasionally the whole fall is swayed away from the front of the cliff, then suddenly dashed flat against it, or vibrated from side to side like a pendulum, giving rise to endless variety of forms and sounds.

THE NEVADA FALL

The Nevada Fall is 600 feet high and is usually ranked next to the Yosemite in general interest among the five main falls of the Valley. Coming through the Little Yosemite in tranquil reaches, the river is first broken into rapids on a moraine boulder-bar that crosses the lower end of the Valley. Thence it pursues its way to the head of the fall in a rough, solid rock channel, dashing on side angles, heaving in heavy surging masses against elbow knobs, and swirling and swashing in pot-holes without a moment's rest. Thus, already chafed and dashed to foam, overfolded and twisted, it plunges over the brink of the precipice as if glad to escape into the open air. But before it reaches the bottom it is pulverized yet finer by impinging upon a sloping portion of the cliff about half-way down, thus making it the whitest of all the falls of the Valley, and altogether one of the most wonderful in the world.

On the north side, close to its head, a slab of granite projects over the brink, forming a fine point for a view, over its throng of streamers and wild plunging, into its intensely white bosom, and, through the broad drifts of spray, to the river far below, gathering its spent waters and rushing on again down the cañon in glad exultation into Emerald Pool, where at length it grows calm and gets rest for what still lies before it. All the features of the view correspond with the waters in grandeur and wildness. The glacier-sculptured walls of the cañon on either hand, with the sublime mass of the Glacier Point Ridge in front, form a huge triangular pit-like basin, which, filled with the roaring of the falling river, seems as if it might be the hopper of one of the mills of the gods in which the mountains were being ground.

THE VERNAL FALL

The Vernal, about a mile below the Nevada, is 400 feet high, a staid, orderly, graceful, easy-going fall, proper and exact in every movement and gesture, with scarce a hint of the passionate enthusiasm of the Yosemite or of the impetuous Nevada, whose chafed and twisted waters hurrying over the cliff seem glad to escape into the open air, while its deep, booming, thunder-tones reverberate over the listening landscape. Nevertheless it is a favorite with most visitors, doubtless because it is more accessible than any other, more closely approached and better seen and heard. A good stairway ascends the cliff beside it and the level plateau at the head enables one to saunter safely along the edge of the river as it comes from Emerald Pool and to watch its waters, calmly bending over the brow of the precipice, in a sheet eighty feet wide, changing in color from green to purplish gray and white until dashed on a boulder talus. Thence issuing from beneath its fine broad spray-clouds we see the tremendously adventurous river still unspent, beating its way down the wildest and deepest of all its cañons in gray roaring rapids, dear to the ouzel, and below the confluence of the Illilouette, sweeping around the shoulder of the Half Dome on its approach to the head of the tranquil levels of the Valley.

The Illilouette Fall

The Illilouette in general appearance most resembles the Nevada. The volume of water is less than half as great, but it is about the same height (600 feet) and its waters receive the same kind of preliminary tossing in a rocky, irregular channel. Therefore it is a very white and fine-grained fall. When it is in full springtime bloom it is partly divided by rocks that roughen the lip of the precipice, but this division amounts only to a kind of fluting and grooving of the column, which has a beautiful effect. It is not nearly so grand a fall as the upper Yosemite, or so symmetrical as the Vernal, or so airily graceful and simple as the Bridal Veil, nor does it ever display so tremendous an outgush of snowy magnificence as the Nevada; but in the exquisite fineness and richness of texture of its flowing folds it surpasses them all.

One of the finest effects of sunlight on falling water I ever saw in Yosemite or elsewhere I found on the brow of this beautiful fall. It was in the Indian summer, when the leaf colors were ripe and the great cliffs and domes were transfigured in the hazy golden air. I had scrambled up its rugged talus-dammed cañon, oftentimes stopping to take breath and look back to admire the wonderful views to be had there of the great Half Dome, and to enjoy the extreme purity of the water, which in the motionless pools on this stream is almost perfectly invisible; the colored foliage of the maples, dogwoods, *Rubus* tangles, etc., and the late goldenrods and asters. The voice of the fall was now low, and the grand spring and summer floods had waned to sifting, drifting gauze and thin-broidered folds of linked and arrowy lace-work. When I reached the foot of the fall sunbeams were glinting across its head, leaving all the rest of it in shadow; and on its illumined brow a group of yellow spangles of singular form and beauty were playing, flashing up and dancing in large flame-shaped masses, wavering at times, then steadying, rising and falling in accord with the shifting forms of the water. But the color of the dancing spangles changed not at all. Nothing in clouds or flowers, on bird-wings or the lips of shells, could rival it in fineness. It was the most divinely beautiful mass of rejoicing yellow light I ever beheld—one of Nature's precious gifts that perchance may come to us but once in a lifetime.

THE MINOR FALLS

There are many other comparatively small falls and cascades in the Valley. The most notable are the Yosemite Gorge Fall and Cascades, Tenaya Fall and Cascades, Royal Arch Falls, the two Sentinel Cascades and the falls of Cascade and Tamarack Creeks, a mile or two below the lower end of the Valley. These last are often visited. The others are seldom noticed or mentioned; although in almost any other country they would be visited and described as wonders.

The six intermediate falls in the gorge between the head of the Lower and the base of the Upper Yosemite Falls, separated by a few deep pools and strips of rapids, and three slender, tributary cascades on the west side form a series more strikingly varied and combined than any other in the Valley, yet very few of all the Valley visitors ever see them or hear of them. No available standpoint commands a view of them all. The best general view is obtained from the mouth of the gorge near the head of the Lower Fall. The two lowest of the series, together with one of the three tributary cascades, are visible from this standpoint, but in reaching it the last twenty or thirty feet of the descent is rather dangerous in time of high water, the shelving rocks being then slippery on account of spray, but if one should chance to slip when the water is low, only a bump or two and a harmless plash would be the penalty. No part of the gorge, however, is safe to any but cautious climbers.

Though the dark gorge hall of these rejoicing waters is never flushed by the purple light of morning or evening, it is warmed and cheered by the white light of noonday, which, falling into so much foam and spray of varying degrees of fineness, makes marvelous displays of rainbow colors. So filled, indeed, is it with this precious light, at favorable times it seems to take the place of common air. Laurel bushes shed fragrance into it from above and live-oaks, those fearless mountaineers, hold fast to angular seams and lean out over it with their fringing sprays and bright mirror leaves.

One bird, the ouzel, loves this gorge and flies through it merrily, or cheerily, rather, stopping to sing on foam-washed bosses where other birds could find no rest for their feet. I have even seen a gray squirrel down in the heart of it beside the wild rejoicing water.

One of my favorite night walks was along the rim of this wild gorge in times of high water when the moon was full, to see the lunar bows in the spray.

For about a mile above Mirror Lake the Tenaya Cañon is level, and richly planted with fir, Douglas spruce and libocedrus, forming a remarkably fine grove, at the head of which is the Tenaya Fall. Though seldom seen or described, this is, I think, the most pictur-esque of all the small falls. A considerable distance above it, Tenaya Creek comes hurrying down, white and foamy, over a flat pavement inclined at an angle of about eighteen degrees. In time of high water this sheet of rapids is nearly seventy feet wide, and is varied in a very striking way by three parallel furrows that extend in the direction of its flow. These furrows, worn by the action of the stream upon

116

cleavage joints, vary in width, are slightly sinuous, and have large boulders firmly wedged in them here and there in narrow places, giving rise, of course, to a complicated series of wild dashes, doublings, and upleaping arches in the swift torrent. Just before it reaches the head of the fall the current is divided, the left division making a vertical drop of about eighty feet in a romantic, leafy, flowery, mossy nook, while the other forms a rugged cascade.

The Royal Arch Fall in time of high water is a magnificent object, forming a broad ornamental sheet in front of the arches. The two Sentinel Cascades, 3000 feet high, are also grand spectacles when the snow is melting fast in the spring, but by the middle of summer they have diminished to mere streaks scarce noticeable amid their sublime surroundings.

THE BEAUTY OF THE RAINBOWS

The Bridal Veil and Vernal Falls are famous for their rainbows; and special visits to them are often made when the sun shines into the spray at the most favorable angle. But amid the spray and foam and fine-ground mist ever rising from the various falls and cataracts there is an affluence and variety of iris bows scarcely known to visitors who stay only a day or two. Both day and night, winter and summer, this divine light may be seen wherever water is falling, dancing, singing; telling the heart-peace of Nature amid the wildest displays of her power. In the bright spring mornings the black-walled recess at the foot of the Lower Yosemite Fall is lavishly filled with irised spray; and not simply does this span the dashing foam, but the foam itself, the whole mass of it, beheld at a certain distance, seems to be colored, and drifts and wavers from color to color, mingling with the foliage of the adjacent trees, without sug-

117

gesting any relationship to the ordinary rainbow. This is perhaps the largest and most reservoir-like fountain of iris colors to be found in the Valley.

Lunar rainbows or spray-bows also abound in the glorious affluence of dashing, rejoicing, hurrahing, enthusiastic spring floods, their colors as distinct as those of the sun and regularly and obviously banded, though less vivid. Fine specimens may be found any night at the foot of the Upper Yosemite Fall, glowing gloriously amid the gloomy shadows and thundering waters, whenever there is plenty of moonlight and spray. Even the secondary bow is at times distinctly visible.

The best point from which to observe them is on Fern Ledge. For some time after moonrise, at time of high water, the arc has a span of about five hundred feet, and is set upright; one end planted in the boiling spray at the bottom, the other in the edge of the fall, creeping lower, of course, and becoming less upright as the moon rises higher. This grand arc of color, glowing in mild, shapely beauty in so weird and huge a chamber of night shadows, and amid the rush and roar and tumultuous dashing of this thunder-voiced fall, is one of the most impressive and most cheering of all the blessed mountain evangels.

Smaller bows may be seen in the gorge on the plateau between the Upper and Lower Falls. Once toward midnight, after spending a few hours with the wild beauty of the Upper Fall, I sauntered along the edge of the gorge, looking in here and there, wherever the footing felt safe, to see what I could learn of the night aspects of the smaller falls that dwell there. And down in an exceedingly black, pit-like portion of the gorge, at the foot of the highest of the intermediate falls, into which the moonbeams were pouring through a narrow opening, I saw a well-defined spray-bow, beautifully distinct in colors, spanning the pit from side to side, while pure white foam-waves beneath the beautiful bow were constantly springing up out of the dark into the moonlight like dancing ghosts.

An Unexpected Adventure

A wild scene, but not a safe one, is made by the moon as it appears through the edge of the Yosemite Fall when one is behind it. Once, after enjoying the night-song of the waters and watching the formation of the colored bow as the moon came round the domes and sent her beams into the wild uproar, I ventured out on the narrow bench that extends back of the fall from Fern Ledge and began to admire the dim-veiled grandeur of the view. I could see the fine gauzy threads of the fall's filmy border by having the light in front; and wishing to look at the moon through the meshes of some of the denser portions of the fall, I ventured to creep farther behind it while it was gently wind-swayed, without taking sufficient thought about the consequences of its swaying back to its natural position after the wind-pressure should be removed. The effect was enchanting: fine, savage music sounding above, beneath, around me; while the moon, apparently in the very midst of the rushing waters, seemed to be struggling to keep her place, on account of the ever-varying form and density of the water masses through which she was seen, now darkly veiled or eclipsed by a rush of thick-headed comets, now flashing out through openings between their tails. I was in fairyland between the dark wall and the wild throng of illumined waters, but suffered sudden disenchantment; for, like the witch-scene in Alloway Kirk, "in an instant all was dark." Down came a dash of spent comets, thin and harmless-looking in the distance, but they felt desperately solid and stony when they struck my shoulders, like a mixture of choking spray and gravel and big hailstones. Instinctively dropping on my knees, I gripped an angle of the rock, curled up like a young fern frond with my face pressed against my breast, and in this attitude submitted as best I could to my thundering bath. The heavier masses seemed to strike like cobblestones, and there was a confused noise of many waters about my ears—hissing, gurgling, clashing sounds that were not heard as music. The situation was quickly realized. How fast one's thoughts burn in such times of stress! I was weighing chances of escape. Would the column be swayed a few inches away from the wall, or would it come yet closer? The fall was in flood and not so lightly would its ponderous mass be swayed. My fate seemed to depend on a breath of the "idle wind." It was moved gently forward, the pounding ceased, and I was once more visited by glimpses of the moon. But fearing I might be caught at a disadvantage in making too hasty a retreat, I moved only a few feet along the bench to where a block of ice lay. I wedged myself between the ice and the wall, and lay face downwards, until the steadiness of the light gave encouragement to rise and get away. Somewhat nerve-shaken, drenched, and benumbed, I made out to build a fire, warmed myself, ran home, reached my cabin before daylight, got an hour or two of sleep, and awoke sound and comfortable, better, not worse, for my hard midnight bath.

CLIMATE AND WEATHER

Owing to the westerly trend of the Valley and its vast depth there is a great difference between the climates of the north and south sides—greater than between many countries far apart; for the south wall is in shadow during the winter months, while the north is bathed in sunshine every clear day. Thus there is mild spring weather on one side of the Valley while winter rules the other. Far up the north-side cliffs many a nook may be found closely embraced by sun-beaten rock-bosses in which flowers bloom every month of the year. Even butterflies may be seen in these high winter gardens except when snow-storms are falling

The Approach to the Valley

and a few days after they have ceased. Near the head of the lower Yosemite Fall in January I found the ant lions lying in wait in their warm sand-cups, rock ferns being unrolled, club mosses covered with fresh-growing points, the flowers of the laurel nearly open, and the honeysuckle rosetted with bright young leaves; every plant seemed to be thinking about summer. Even on the shadow-side of the Valley the frost is never very sharp. The lowest temperature I ever observed during four winters was 7° Fahrenheit. The first twenty-four days of January had an average temperature at 9 A.M. of 32°, minimum 22°; at 3 P.M. the average was 40° 30′, the minimum 32°. Along the top of the walls, 7000 and 8000 feet high, the temperature was, of course, much lower. But the difference in temperature between the north and south sides is due not so much to the winter sunshine as to the heat of the preceding summer, stored up in the rocks, which rapidly melts the snow in contact with them. For though summer sun-heat is stored in the rocks of the south side also, the amount is much less because the rays fall obliquely on the south wall even in summer and almost vertically on the north.

The upper branches of the Yosemite streams are buried every winter beneath a heavy mantle of snow, and set free in the spring in magnificent floods. Then, all the fountains, full and overflowing, every living thing breaks forth into singing, and the glad exulting streams, shining and falling in the warm sunny weather, shake everything into music, making all the mountain-world a song.

The great annual spring thaw usually begins in May in the forest region, and in June and July on the high Sierra, varying somewhat both in time and fullness with the weather and the depth of the snow. Toward the end of summer the streams are at their lowest ebb, few even of the strongest singing much above a whisper as they slip and ripple through gravel and boulder-beds from pool to pool in the hollows of their channels, and drop in pattering showers like rain, and slip down precipices and fall in sheets of embroidery, fold over fold. But, however low their singing, it is always ineffably fine in tone, in harmony with the restful time of the year.

The first snow of the season that comes to the help of the streams usually falls in September or October, sometimes even in the latter part of August, in the midst of yellow Indian summer, when the goldenrods and gentians of the glacier meadows are in their prime. This Indian-summer snow, however, soon melts, the chilled flowers spread their petals to the sun, and the gardens as well as the streams are refreshed as if only a warm shower had fallen. The snow-storms that load the mountains to form the main fountain supply for the year seldom set in before the middle or end of November.

WINTER BEAUTY OF THE VALLEY

When the first heavy storms stopped work on the high mountains, I made haste down to my Yosemite den, not to "hole up" and sleep the white months away; I was out every day, and often all night, sleeping but little, studying the so-called wonders and common things ever on show, wading, climbing, sauntering among the blessed storms and calms, rejoicing in almost everything alike that I could see or hear: the glorious brightness of frosty mornings; the sunbeams pouring over the white domes and crags into the groves and waterfalls, kindling marvelous iris fires in the hoarfrost and spray; the great forests and mountains in their deep noon sleep; the good-night alpenglow; the stars; the solemn gazing moon, drawing the huge domes and headlands one by one glowing white out of the shadows hushed and breathless like an audience in awful enthusiasm, while the meadows at their feet sparkle with frost-stars like the sky; the sublime darkness of storm-nights, when all the lights are out; the clouds in whose depths the frail snow-flowers grow; the behavior and many voices of the different kinds of storms, trees, birds, waterfalls, and snow-avalanches in the ever-changing weather.

Every clear, frosty morning loud sounds are heard booming and reverberating from side to side of the Valley at intervals of a few minutes, beginning soon after sunrise and continuing an hour or two like a thunder-storm. In my first winter in the Valley I could not make out the source of this noise. I thought of falling boulders, rock-blasting, etc. Not till I saw what looked like hoarfrost dropping from the side of the Fall was the problem explained. The strange thunder is made by the fall of sections of ice formed of spray that is frozen on the face of the cliff along the sides of the Upper Yosemite Fall—a sort of crystal plaster, a foot or two thick, cracked off by the sunbeams, awakening all the Valley like cock-crowing, announcing the finest weather, shouting aloud Nature's infinite industry and love of hard work in creating beauty.

EXPLORING AN ICE CONE

This frozen spray gives rise to one of the most interesting winter features of the Valley—a cone of ice at the foot of the fall, four or five hundred feet high. From the Fern Ledge standpoint its crater-like throat is seen, down which the fall plunges with deep, gasping explosions of compressed air, and, after being well churned in the stormy interior, the water bursts forth through arched openings at its base, apparently scourged and weary and glad to escape, while belching spray, spouted up out of the throat past the descending current, is wafted away in irised drifts to the adjacent rocks and groves. It is built during the night and early hours of the morning; only in spells of exceptionally cold and cloudy weather is the work

123

continued through the day. The greater part of the spray material falls in crystalline showers direct to its place, something like a small local snow-storm; but a considerable portion is first frozen on the face of the cliff along the sides of the fall and stays there until expanded and cracked off in irregular masses, some of them tons in weight, to be built into the walls of the cone; while in windy, frosty weather, when the fall is swayed from side to side, the cone is well drenched and the loose ice masses and spray-dust are all firmly welded and frozen together. Thus the finest of the downy wafts and curls of spray-dust, which in mild nights fall about as silently as dew, are held back until sunrise to make a store of heavy ice to reinforce the waterfall's thunder-tones.

While the cones is in process of formation, growing higher and wider in the frosty weather, it looks like a beautiful smooth, pure-white hill; but when it is wasting and breaking up in the spring its surface is strewn with leaves, pine branches, stones, sand, etc., that have been brought over the fall, making it look like a heap of avalanche detritus.

Anxious to learn what I could about the structure of this curious hill I often approached it in calm weather and tried to climb it, carrying an ax to cut steps. Once I nearly succeeded in gaining the summit. At the base I was met by a current of spray and wind that made seeing and breathing difficult. I pushed on backward, however, and soon gained the slope of the hill, where by creeping close to the surface most of the choking blast passed over me and I managed to crawl up with but little difficulty. Thus I made my way nearly to the summit, halting at times to peer up through the wild whirls of spray at the veiled grandeur of the fall, or to listen to the thunder beneath me; the whole hill was sounding as if it were a huge, bellowing drum. I hoped that by waiting until the fall was blown aslant I should be able to climb to the lip of the crater and get a view of the interior; but a suffocating blast, half air, half water, followed by the fall of an enormous mass of frozen spray from a spot high up on

The Approach to the Valley

the wall, quickly discouraged me. The whole cone was jarred by the blow and some fragments of the mass sped past me dangerously near; so I beat a hasty retreat, chilled and drenched, and lay down on a sunny rock to dry.

Once during a wind-storm when I saw that the fall was frequently blown westward, leaving the cone dry, I ran up to Fern Ledge hoping to gain a clear view of the interior. I set out at noon. All the way up the storm notes were so loud about me that the voice of the fall was almost drowned by them. Notwithstanding the rocks and bushes everywhere were drenched by the wind-driven spray, I approached the brink of the precipice overlooking the mouth of the ice cone, but I was almost suffocated by the drenching, gusty spray, and was compelled to seek shelter. I searched for some hiding-place in the wall from whence I might run out at some opportune moment when the fall with its whirling spray and torn shreds of comet tails and trailing, tattered skirts was borne westward, as I had seen it carried several times before, leaving the cliffs on the east side and the ice hill bare in the sunlight. I had not long to wait, for, as if ordered so for my special accommodation, the mighty downrush of comets with their whirling drapery swung westward and remained aslant for nearly half an hour. The cone was admirably lighted and deserted by the water, which fell most of the time on the rocky western slopes mostly outside of the cone. The mouth into which the fall pours was, as near as I could guess, about one hundred feet in diameter north and south and about two hundred feet east and west, which is about the shape and size of the fall at its best in its normal condition at this season.

The crater-like opening was not a true oval, but more like a huge coarse mouth. I could see down the throat about one hundred feet or perhaps farther.

The fall precipice overhangs from a height of 400 feet above the base; therefore the water strikes some distance from the base of the cliff, allowing space for the accumulation of a considerable mass of ice between the fall and the wall.

The Water-Ouzel

The waterfalls of the Sierra are frequented by only one bird,—the Ouzel or Water Thrush (*Cinclus Mexicanus,* Sw.). He is a singularly joyous and lovable little fellow, about the size of a robin, clad in a plain waterproof suit of bluish gray, with a tinge of chocolate on the head and shoulders. In form he is about as smoothly plump and compact as a pebble that has been whirled in a pot-hole, the flowing contour of his body being interrupted only by his strong feet and bill, the crisp wing-tips, and the up-slanted wren-like tail.

Among all the countless waterfalls I have met in the course of ten years' exploration in the Sierra, whether among the icy peaks, or warm foot-hills, or in the profound yosemitic cañons of the middle region, not one was found without its Ouzel. No cañon is too cold for this little bird, none too lonely, provided it be rich in falling water. Find a fall, or cascade, or rushing rapid, anywhere upon a clear stream, and there you will surely find its complementary Ouzel, flitting about in the spray, diving in foaming eddies, whirling like a leaf among beaten foam-bells; ever vigorous and enthusiastic, yet self-contained, and neither seeking nor shunning your company.

If disturbed while dipping about in the margin shallows, he either sets off with a rapid whir to some other feeding-ground up or down the stream, or alights on some half-submerged rock or snag out in the current, and immediately begins to nod and courtesy like a wren, turning his head from side to side with many other odd dainty movements that never fail to fix the attention of the observer.

He is the mountain streams' own darling, the humming-bird of blooming waters, loving rocky ripple-slopes and sheets of foam as a bee loves flowers, as a lark loves sunshine and meadows. Among all the mountain birds, none has cheered me so much in my lonely wanderings,—none so unfailingly. For both in winter and summer he sings, sweetly, cheerily, independent alike of sunshine and of love, requiring no other inspiration than the stream on which he dwells. While water sings, so must he, in heat or cold, calm or storm, ever attuning his voice in sure accord; low in the drought of summer and the drought of winter, but never silent.

During the golden days of Indian summer, after most of the snow has been melted, and the mountain streams have become feeble,—a succession of silent pools, linked together by shallow, transparent currents and strips of silvery lacework,—then the song of the Ouzel is at its lowest ebb. But as soon as the winter clouds have bloomed, and the mountain treasuries are once more replenished with snow, the voices of the streams and ouzels increase in strength and richness until the flood season of early summer. Then the torrents chant their noblest anthems, and then is the flood-time of our songster's melody. As for weather, dark days and sun days are the same to him. The voices of most song-birds, however joyous, suffer a long winter eclipse; but the Ouzel sings on through all the seasons and every kind of storm. Indeed no storm can be more violent than those of the waterfalls in the midst of which he delights to dwell. However dark and boisterous the weather, snowing, blowing, or cloudy, all the same he sings, and with never a note of sadness. No need of spring sunshine to thaw *his* song, for it never freezes. Never shall you hear anything wintry from *his* warm breast; no pinched cheeping, no wavering notes between sorrow and joy; his mellow, fluty voice is ever tuned to downright gladness, as free from dejection as cock-crowing.

The Water-Ouzel

It is pitiful to see wee frost-pinched sparrows on cold mornings in the mountain groves shaking the snow from their feathers, and hopping about as if anxious to be cheery, then hastening back to their hidings out of the wind, puffing out their breast-feathers over their toes, and subsiding among the leaves, cold and breakfastless, while the snow continues to fall, and there is no sign of clearing. But the Ouzel never calls forth a single touch of pity; not because he is strong to endure, but rather because he seems to live a charmed life beyond the reach of every influence that makes endurance necessary.

One wild winter morning, when Yosemite Valley was swept its length from west to east by a cordial snow-storm, I sallied forth to see what I might learn and enjoy. A sort of gray, gloaming-like darkness filled the valley, the huge walls were out of sight, all ordinary sounds were smothered, and even the loudest booming of the falls was at times buried beneath the roar of the heavy-laden blast. The loose snow was already over five feet deep on the meadows, making extended walks impossible without the aid of snow-shoes. I found no great difficulty, however, in making my way to a certain ripple on the river where one of my ouzels lived. He was at home, busily gleaning his breakfast among the pebbles of a shallow portion of the margin, apparently unaware of anything extraordinary in the weather. Presently he flew out to a stone against which the icy current was beating, and turning his back to the wind, sang as delightfully as a lark in springtime.

After spending an hour or two with my favorite, I made my way across the valley, boring and wallowing through the drifts, to learn as definitely as possible how the other birds were spending their time. The Yosemite birds are easily found during the winter because all of them excepting the Ouzel are restricted to the sunny north side of the valley, the south side being constantly eclipsed by the great frosty shadow of the wall. And because the Indian Cañon groves, from their peculiar exposure, are the warmest, the birds congregate there, more especially in severe weather.

THE AMERICAN WILDERNESS

I found most of the robins cowering on the lee side of the larger branches where the snow could not fall upon them, while two or three of the more enterprising were making desperate efforts to reach the mistletoe berries by clinging nervously to the under side of the snow-crowned masses, back downward, like woodpeckers. Every now and then they would dislodge some of the loose fringes of the snow-crown, which would come sifting down on them and send them screaming back to camp, where they would subside among their companions with a shiver, muttering in low, querulous chatter like hungry children.

Some of the sparrows were busy at the feet of the larger trees gleaning seeds and benumbed insects, joined now and then by a robin weary of his unsuccessful attempts upon the snow-covered berries. The brave woodpeckers were clinging to the snowless sides of the larger boles and overarching branches of the camp trees, making short flights from side to side of the grove, pecking now and then at the acorns they had stored in the bark, and chattering aimlessly as if unable to keep still, yet evidently putting in the time in a very dull way, like storm-bound travelers at a country tavern. The hardy nut-hatches were threading the open furrows of the trunks in their usual industrious manner, and uttering their quaint notes, evidently less distressed than their neighbors. The Steller jays were of course making more noisy stir than all the other birds combined; ever coming and going with loud bluster, screaming as if each had a lump of melting sludge in his throat, and taking good care to improve the favorable opportunity afforded by the storm to steal from the acorn stores of the woodpeckers. I also noticed one solitary gray eagle braving the storm on the top of a tall pine-stump just outside the main grove. He was standing bolt upright with his back to the wind, a tuft of snow piled on his square shoulders, a monument of passive endurance. Thus every snow-bound bird seemed more or less uncomfortable if not in positive distress. The storm was reflected in every gesture, and not one cheerful note, not to say song, came

The Water-Ouzel

from a single bill; their cowering, joyless endurance offering a striking contrast to the spontaneous, irrepressible gladness of the Ouzel, who could no more help exhaling sweet song than a rose sweet fragrance. He *must* sing though the heavens fall. I remember noticing the distress of a pair of robins during the violent earthquake of the year 1872, when the pines of the Valley, with strange movements, flapped and waved their branches, and beetling rock-brows came thundering down to the meadows in tremendous avalanches. It did not occur to me in the midst of the excitement of other observations to look for the ouzels, but I doubt not they were singing straight on through it all, regarding the terrible rock-thunder as fearlessly as they do the booming of the waterfalls.

What may be regarded as the separate songs of the Ouzel are exceedingly difficult of description, because they are so variable and at the same time so confluent. Though I have been acquainted with my favorite ten years, and during most of this time have heard him sing nearly every day, I still detect notes and strains that seem new to me. Nearly all of his music is sweet and tender, lapsing from his round breast like water over the smooth lip of a pool, then breaking farther on into a sparkling foam of melodious notes, which glow with subdued enthusiasm, yet without expressing much of the strong, gushing ecstasy of the bobolink or skylark.

The more striking strains are perfect arabesques of melody, composed of a few full, round, mellow notes, embroidered with delicate trills which fade and melt in long slender cadences. In a general way his music is that of the streams refined and spiritualized. The deep booming notes of the falls are in it, the trills of rapids, the gurgling of margin eddies, the low whispering of level reaches, and the sweet tinkle of separate drops oozing from the ends of mosses and falling into tranquil pools.

The Ouzel never sings in chorus with other birds, nor with his kind, but only with the streams. And like flowers that bloom beneath the surface of the ground, some of our favorite's best song-blossoms never rise above the surface of the heavier music of the water. I have often observed him singing in the midst of beaten spray, his music completely buried beneath the water's roar; yet I knew he was surely singing by his gestures and the movements of his bill.

His food, as far as I have noticed, consists of all kinds of water insects, which in summer are chiefly procured along shallow margins. Here he wades about ducking his head under water and deftly turning over pebbles and fallen leaves with his bill, seldom choosing to go into deep water where he has to use his wings in diving.

He seems to be especially fond of the larvae of mosquitos, found in abundance attached to the bottom of smooth rock channels where the current is shallow. When feeding in such places he wades upstream, and often while his head is under water the swift current is deflected upward along the glossy curves of his neck and shoulders, in the form of a clear, crystalline shell, which fairly incloses him like a bell-glass, the shell being broken and re-formed as he lifts and dips his head; while ever and anon he sidles out to where the too powerful current carries him off his feet; then he dexterously rises on the wing and goes gleaning again in shallower places.

But during the winter, when the stream-banks are embossed in snow, and the streams themselves are chilled nearly to the freezing-point, so that the snow falling into them in stormy weather is not wholly dissolved, but forms a thin, blue sludge, thus rendering the current opaque—then he seeks the deeper portions of the main rivers, where he may dive to clear water beneath the sludge. Or he repairs to some open lake or millpond, at the bottom of which he feeds in safety.

When thus compelled to betake himself to a lake, he does not plunge into it at once like a duck, but always alights in the first place upon some rock or fallen pine along the shore. Then flying out thirty or forty yards, more or less, according to the character of the bottom, he alights with a dainty glint on the surface, swims about, looks down, finally makes up his mind, and disappears with a sharp stroke of his wings. After feeding for two or three minutes he suddenly reappears, showers the water from his wings with one vigorous shake, and rises abruptly into the air as if pushed up from beneath, comes back to his perch, sings a few minutes, and goes out to dive again; thus coming and going, singing and diving at the same place for hours.

The Ouzel is usually found singly; rarely in pairs, excepting during the breeding season, and *very* rarely in threes or fours. I once observed three thus spending a winter morning in company, upon a small glacier lake, on the Upper Merced, about 7500 feet above the level of the sea. A storm had occurred during the night, but the morning sun shone unclouded, and the shadowy lake, gleaming darkly in its setting of fresh snow, lay smooth and motionless as a mirror. My camp chanced to be within a few feet of the water's edge, opposite a fallen pine, some of the branches of which leaned out over the lake. Here my three dearly welcome visitors took up their station, and at once began to embroider the frosty air with their delicious melody, doubly delightful to me that particular morning, as I had been somewhat apprehensive of danger in breaking my way down through the snow-choked cañons to the lowlands.

The portion of the lake bottom selected for a feeding-ground lies at a depth of fifteen or twenty feet below the surface, and is covered with a short growth of algae and other aquatic plants,—facts I had previously determined while sailing over it on a raft. After alighting on the glassy surface, they occasionally indulged in a little play, chasing one another round about in small circles; then all three would suddenly dive together, and then come ashore and sing.

The Ouzel seldom swims more than a few yards on the surface, for, not being web-footed, he makes rather slow progress, but by means of his strong, crisp wings he swims, or rather flies, with celerity under the surface, often to considerable distances. But it is in withstanding the force of heavy rapids that his strength of wing in this respect is most strikingly manifested. The following may be

133

regarded as a fair illustration of his power of sub-aquatic flight. One stormy morning in winter when the Merced River was blue and green with unmelted snow, I observed one of my ouzels perched on a snag out in the midst of a swift-rushing rapid, singing cheerily, as if everything was just to his mind; and while I stood on the bank admiring him, he suddenly plunged into the sludgy current, leaving his song abruptly broken off. After feeding a minute or two at the bottom, and when one would suppose that he must inevitably be swept far down-stream, he emerged just where he went down, alighted on the same snag, showered the water-beads from his feathers, and continued his unfinished song, seemingly in tranquil ease as if it had suffered no interruption.

The Ouzel alone of all birds dares to enter a white torrent. And though strictly terrestrial in structure, no other is so inseparably related to water, not even the duck, or the bold ocean albatross, or the stormy-petrel. For ducks go ashore as soon as they finish feeding in undisturbed places, and very often make long flights overland from lake to lake or field to field. The same is true of most other aquatic birds. But the Ouzel, born on the brink of a stream, or on a snag or boulder in the midst of it, seldom leaves it for a single moment. For, notwithstanding he is often on the wing, he never flies overland, but whirs with rapid, quail-like beat above the stream, tracing all its windings. Even when the stream is quite small, say from five to ten feet wide, he seldom shortens his flight by crossing a bend, however abrupt it may be; and even when disturbed by meeting some one on the bank, he prefers to fly over one's head, to dodging out over the ground. When, therefore, his flight along a crooked stream is viewed endwise, it appears most strikingly wavered—a description on the air of every curve with lightning-like rapidity.

The vertical curves and angles of the most precipitous torrents he traces with the same rigid fidelity, swooping down the inclines of cascades, dropping sheer over dizzy falls amid the spray, and ascending with the same fearlessness and ease, seldom seeking to lessen the steepness of the acclivity by beginning to ascend before reaching the base of the fall. No matter though it may be several hundred feet in height he holds straight on, as if about to dash headlong into the throng of booming rockets, then darts abruptly upward, and, after alighting at the top of the precipice to rest a moment, proceeds to feed and sing. His flight is solid and impetuous, without any intermission of wing-beats,—one homogeneous buzz like that of a laden bee on its way home. And while thus buzzing freely from fall to fall, he is frequently heard giving utterance to a long outdrawn train of unmodulated notes, in no way connected with his song, but corresponding closely with his flight in sustained vigor.

Were the flights of all the ouzels in the Sierra traced on a chart, they would indicate the direction of the flow of the entire system of ancient glaciers, from about the period of the breaking up of the ice-sheet until near the close of the glacial winter; because the streams which the ouzels so rigidly follow are, with the unimportant exceptions of a few side tributaries, all flowing in channels eroded for them out of the solid flank of the range by the vanished glaciers,—the streams tracing the ancient glaciers, the ouzels tracing the streams. Nor do we find so complete compliance to glacial conditions in the life of any other mountain bird, or animal of any kind. Bears frequently accept the pathways laid down by glaciers as the easiest to travel; but they often leave them and cross over from cañon to cañon. So also, most of the birds trace the moraines to some extent, because the forests are growing on them. But they wander far, crossing the cañons from grove to grove, and draw exceedingly angular and complicated courses.

The Ouzel's nest is one of the most extraordinary pieces of bird architecture I ever saw, odd and novel in design, perfectly fresh and beautiful, and in every way worthy of the genius of the little builder. It is about a foot in diameter, round and bossy in outline, with a neatly arched opening near the bottom, somewhat like an old-fash-

135

ioned brick oven, or Hottentot's hut. It is built almost exclusively of green and yellow mosses, chiefly the beautiful fronded hypnum that covers the rocks and old drift-logs in the vicinity of waterfalls. These are deftly interwoven, and felted together into a charming little hut; and so situated that many of the outer mosses continue to flourish as if they had not been plucked. A few fine, silky-stemmed grasses are occasionally found interwoven with the mosses, but, with the exception of a thin layer lining the floor, their presence seems accidental, as they are of a species found growing with the mosses and are probably plucked with them. The site chosen for this curious mansion is usually some little rock-shelf within reach of the lighter particles of the spray of a waterfall, so that its walls are kept green and growing, at least during the time of high water.

No harsh lines are presented by any portion of the nest as seen in place, but when removed from its shelf, the back and bottom, and sometimes a portion of the top, is found quite sharply angular, because it is made to conform to the surface of the rock upon which and against which it is built, the little architect always taking advantage of slight crevices and protuberances that may chance to offer, to render his structure stable by means of a kind of gripping and dovetailing.

In choosing a building-spot, concealment does not seem to be taken into consideration; yet notwithstanding the nest is large and guilelessly exposed to view, it is far from being easily detected, chiefly because it swells forward like any other bulging moss-cushion growing naturally in such situations. This is more especially the case where the nest is kept fresh by being well sprinkled. Sometimes these romantic little huts have their beauty enhanced by rock-ferns and grasses that spring up around the mossy walls, or in front of the door-sill, dripping with crystal beads.

Furthermore, at certain hours of the day, when the sunshine is poured down at the required angle, the whole mass of the spray enveloping the fairy establishment is brilliantly irised; and it is

The Water-Ouzel

through so glorious a rainbow atmosphere as this that some of our blessed ouzels obtain their first peep at the world.

Ouzels seem so completely part and parcel of the streams they inhabit, they scarce suggest any other origin than the streams themselves; and one might almost be pardoned in fancying they come direct from the living waters, like flowers from the ground. At least, from whatever cause, it never occurred to me to look for their nests until more than a year after I had made the acquaintance of the birds themselves, although I found one the very day on which I began the search. In making my way from Yosemite to the glaciers at the heads of the Merced and Tuolumne rivers, I camped in a particularly wild and romantic portion of the Nevada cañon where in previous excursions I had never failed to enjoy the company of my favorites, who were attracted here, no doubt, by the safe nesting-places in the shelving rocks, and by the abundance of food and falling water. The river, for miles above and below, consists of a succession of small falls from ten to sixty feet in height, connected by flat, plume-like cascades that go flashing from fall to fall, free and almost channelless, over waving folds of glacier-polished granite.

On the south side of one of the falls, that portion of the precipice which is bathed by the spray presents a series of little shelves and tablets caused by the development of planes of cleavage in the granite, and by the consequent fall of masses through the action of the water. "Now here," said I, "of all places, is the most charming spot for an Ouzel's nest." Then carefully scanning the fretted face of the precipice through the spray, I at length noticed a yellowish moss-cushion, growing on the edge of a level tablet within five or six feet of the outer folds of the fall. But apart from the fact of its being situated where one acquainted with the lives of ouzels would fancy an Ouzel's nest ought to be, there was nothing in its appearance visible at first sight, to distinguish it from other bosses of rock-moss similarly situated with reference to perennial spray; and it was not until I had scrutinized it again and again, and had removed my shoes and stockings and crept along the face of the rock within eight or ten feet of it, that I could decide certainly whether it was a nest or a natural growth.

In these moss huts three or four eggs are laid, white like foam-bubbles; and well may the little birds hatched from them sing water songs, for they hear them all their lives, and even before they are born.

I have often observed the young just out of the nest making their odd gestures, and seeming in every way as much at home as their experienced parents, like young bees on their first excursions to the flower fields. No amount of familiarity with people and their ways seems to change them in the least. To all appearance their behavior is just the same on seeing a man for the first time, as when they have seen him frequently.

On the lower reaches of the rivers where mills are built, they sing on through the din of the machinery, and all the noisy confusion of dogs, cattle, and workmen. On one occasion, while a wood-chopper was at work on the river-bank, I observed one cheerily singing within reach of the flying chips. Nor does any kind of unwonted disturbance put him in bad humor, or frighten him out of calm self-possession. In passing through a narrow gorge, I once drove one ahead of me from rapid to rapid, disturbing him four times in quick succession where he could not very well fly past me on account of the narrowness of the channel. Most birds under similar circumstances fancy themselves pursued, and become suspiciously uneasy; but, instead of growing nervous about it, he made his usual dippings, and sang one of his most tranquil strains. When observed within a few yards their eyes are seen to express remarkable gentleness and intelligence; but they seldom allow so near a view unless one wears clothing of about the same color as the rocks and trees, and knows how to sit still. On one occasion, while rambling along the shore of a mountain lake, where the birds, at least those born that season, had never seen a man, I sat down to rest on a large stone

The Water-Ouzel

close to the water's edge, upon which it seemed the ouzels and sandpipers were in the habit of alighting when they came to feed on that part of the shore, and some of the other birds also, when they came down to wash or drink. In a few minutes, along came a whirring ouzel and alighted on the stone beside me, within reach of my hand. Then suddenly observing me, he stooped nervously as if about to fly on the instant, but as I remained as motionless as the stone, he gained confidence, and looked me steadily in the face for about a minute, then flew quietly to the outlet and began to sing. Next came a sandpiper and gazed at me with much the same guileless expression of eye as the Ouzel. Lastly, down with a swoop came a Steller's jay out of a fir-tree, probably with the intention of moistening his noisy throat. But instead of sitting confidingly as my other visitors had done, he rushed off at once, nearly tumbling heels over head into the lake in his suspicious confusion, and with loud screams roused the neighborhood.

Love for song-birds, with their sweet human voices, appears to be more common and unfailing than love for flowers. Every one loves flowers to some extent, at least in life's fresh morning, attracted by them as instinctively as humming-birds and bees. Even the young Digger Indians have sufficient love for the brightest of those found growing on the mountains to gather them and braid them as decorations for the hair. And I was glad to discover, through the few Indians that could be induced to talk on the subject, that they have names for the wild rose and the lily, and other conspicuous flowers, whether available as food or otherwise. Most men, however, whether savage or civilized, become apathetic toward all plants that have no other apparent use than the use of beauty. But fortunately one's first instinctive love of songbirds is never wholly obliterated, no matter what the influences upon our lives may be. I have often been delighted to see a pure, spiritual glow come into the countenances of hard business-men and old miners, when a song-bird chanced to alight near them. Nevertheless, the little mouthful of meat that swells out the breasts of some song-birds is too often the cause of their death. Larks and robins in particular are brought to market in hundreds. But fortunately the Ouzel has no enemy so eager to eat his little body as to follow him into the mountain solitudes. I never knew him to be chased even by hawks.

An acquaintance of mine, a sort of foot-hill mountaineer, had a pet cat, a great, dozy, overgrown creature, about as broad-shouldered as a lynx. During the winter, while the snow lay deep, the mountaineer sat in his lonely cabin among the pines smoking his pipe and wearing the dull time away. Tom was his sole companion, sharing his bed, and sitting beside him on a stool with much the same drowsy expression of eye as his master. The good-natured bachelor was content with his hard fare of soda-bread and bacon, but Tom, the only creature in the world acknowledging dependence on him, must needs be provided with fresh meat. Accordingly he bestirred himself to contrive squirrel-traps, and waded the snowy woods with his gun, making sad havoc among the few winter birds, sparing neither robin, sparrow, nor tiny nuthatch, and the pleasure of seeing Tom eat and grow fat was his great reward.

One cold afternoon, while hunting along the river-bank, he noticed a plain-feathered little bird skipping about in the shallows, and immediately raised his gun. But just then the confiding songster began to sing, and after listening to his summery melody the charmed hunter turned away, saying, "Bless your little heart, I can't shoot you, not even for Tom."

Even so far north as icy Alaska, I have found my glad singer. When I was exploring the glaciers between Mount Fairweather and the Stikeen River, one cold day in November, after trying in vain to force a way through the innumerable icebergs of Sum Dum Bay to the great glaciers at the head of it, I was weary and baffled and sat resting in my canoe convinced at last that I would have to leave this part of my work for another year. Then I began to plan my escape to open water before the young ice which was beginning to form

The Water-Ouzel

should shut me in. While I thus lingered drifting with the bergs, in the midst of these gloomy forebodings and all the terrible glacial desolation and grandeur, I suddenly heard the well-known whir of an ouzel's wings, and, looking up, saw my little comforter coming straight across the ice from the shore. In a second or two he was with me, flying three times round my head with a happy salute, as if saying, "Cheer up, old friend; you see I'm here, and all's well." Then he flew back to the shore, alighted on the topmost jag of a stranded iceberg, and began to nod and bow as though he were on one of his favorite boulders in the midst of a sunny Sierra cascade.

The species is distributed all along the mountain-ranges of the Pacific Coast from Alaska to Mexico, and east to the Rocky Mountains. Nevertheless, it is as yet comparatively little known. Audubon and Wilson did not meet it. Swainson was, I believe, the first naturalist to describe a specimen from Mexico. Specimens were shortly afterward procured by Drummond near the sources of the Athabasca River, between the fifty-fourth and fifty-sixth parallels; and it has been collected by nearly all of the numerous exploring expeditions undertaken of late through our Western States and Territories; for it never fails to engage the attention of naturalists in a very particular manner.

Such, then, is our little cinclus, beloved of every one who is so fortunate as to know him. Tracing on strong wing every curve of the most precipitous torrents from one extremity of the Sierra to the other; not fearing to follow them through their darkest gorges and coldest snow-tunnels; acquainted with every waterfall, echoing their divine music; and throughout the whole of their beautiful lives interpreting all that we in our unbelief call terrible in the utterances of torrents and storms, as only varied expressions of God's eternal love.

141

Winter Storms
and Spring Floods

The Bridal Veil and the Upper Yosemite Falls, on account of their height and exposure, are greatly influenced by winds. The common summer winds that come up the river cañon from the plains are seldom very strong; but the north winds do some very wild work, worrying the falls and the forests, and hanging snow-banners on the comet-peaks. One wild winter morning I was awakened by a storm-wind that was playing with the falls as if they were mere wisps of mist and making the great pines bow and sing with glorious enthusiasm. The Valley had been visited a short time before by a series of fine snow-storms, and the floor and the cliffs and all the region round about were lavishly adorned with its best winter jewelry, the air was full of fine snow-dust, and pine branches, tassels and empty cones were flying in an almost continuous flock.

Soon after sunrise, when I was seeking a place safe from flying branches, I saw the Lower Yosemite Fall thrashed and pulverized from top to bottom into one glorious mass of rainbow dust; while a thousand feet above it the main Upper Fall was suspended on the face of the cliff in the form of an inverted bow, all silvery white and fringed with short wavering strips. Then, suddenly assailed by a tremendous blast, the whole mass of the fall was blown into threads and ribbons, and driven back over the brow of the cliff whence it came, as if denied admission to the Valley. This kind of stormwork was continued about ten or fifteen minutes; then another change in the play of the huge exulting swirls and billows and upheaving domes of the gale allowed the baffled fall to gather and arrange its tattered waters, and sink down again in its place. As the day advanced, the gale gave no sign of dying, excepting brief lulls, the Valley was filled with its weariless roar, and the cloudless sky grew garish-white from myriads of minute, sparkling snow-spicules. In the afternoon, while I watched the Upper Fall from the shelter of a big pine tree, it was suddenly arrested in its descent at a point about half-way down, and was neither blown upward nor driven aside, but simply held stationary in mid-air, as if gravitation below that point in the path of its descent had ceased to act. The ponderous flood, weighing hundreds of tons, was sustained, hovering, hesitating, like a bunch of thistledown, while I counted one hundred and ninety. All this time the ordinary amount of water was coming over the cliff and accumulating in the air, swedging and widening and forming an irregular cone about seven hundred feet high, tapering to the top of the wall, the whole standing still, resting on the invisible arm of the North Wind. At length, as if commanded to go on again, scores of arrowy comets shot forth from the bottom of the suspended mass as if escaping from separate outlets.

The brow of El Capitan was decked with long snow-streamers like hair, Clouds' Rest was fairly enveloped in drifting gossamer films, and the Half Dome loomed up in the garish light like a majestic, living creature clad in the same gauzy, wind-woven drapery, while upward currents meeting at times overhead made it smoke like a volcano.

An Extraordinary Storm and Flood

Glorious as are these rocks and waters arrayed in storm robes, or chanting rejoicing in every-day dress, they are still more glorious when rare weather conditions meet to make them sing with floods. Only once during all the years I have lived in the Valley have I seen it in full flood bloom. In 1871 the early winter weather was delightful; the days all sunshine, the nights all starry and calm, calling forth fine crops of frost-crystals on the pines and withered ferns and grasses for the morning sunbeams to sift through. In the afternoon of December 16, when I was sauntering on the meadows, I noticed a massive crimson cloud growing in solitary grandeur above the Cathedral Rocks, its form scarcely less striking than its color. It had a picturesque, bulging base like an old sequoia, a smooth, tapering stem, and a bossy, down-curling crown like a mushroom; all its parts were colored alike, making one mass of translucent crimson. Wondering what the meaning of that strange, lonely red cloud might be, I was up betimes next morning looking at the weather, but all seemed tranquil as yet. Towards noon gray clouds with a close, curly grain like bird's-eye maple began to grow, and late at night rain fell, which soon changed to snow. Next morning the snow on the meadows was about ten inches deep, and it was still falling in a fine, cordial storm. During the night of the 18th heavy rain fell on the snow, but as the temperature was 34°, the snow-line was only a few hundred feet above the bottom of the Valley, and one had only to climb a little higher than the tops of the pines to get out of the rainstorm into the snow-storm. The streams, instead of being increased in volume by the storm, were diminished, because the snow sponged up part of their waters and choked the smaller tributaries. But about midnight the temperature suddenly rose to 42°, carrying the snow-line far beyond the Valley walls, and next morning Yosemite was rejoicing in a glorious flood. The comparatively warm rain falling on the snow was at first absorbed and held back, and so also was that portion of the snow that the rain melted, and all that was melted by the warm wind, until the whole mass of snow was saturated and became sludgy, and at length slipped and rushed simultaneously from a thousand slopes in wildest extravagance, heaping and swelling flood over flood, and plunging into the Valley in stupendous avalanches.

Awakened by the roar, I looked out and at once recognized the extraordinary character of the storm. The rain was still pouring in torrent abundance and the wind at gale speed was doing all it could with the flood-making rain.

The section of the north wall visible from my cabin was fairly streaked with new falls—wild roaring singers that seemed strangely out of place. Eager to get into the midst of the show, I snatched a piece of bread for breakfast and ran out. The mountain waters, suddenly liberated, seemed to be holding a grand jubilee. The two Sentinel Cascades rivaled the great falls at ordinary stages, and across the Valley by the Three Brothers I caught glimpses of more falls than I could readily count; while the whole Valley throbbed and trembled, and was filled with an awful, massive, solemn, sea-like roar. After gazing a while enchanted with the network of new falls that were adorning and transfiguring every rock in sight, I tried to reach the upper meadows, where the Valley is widest, that I might be able to see the walls on both sides, and thus gain general views. But the river was over its banks and the meadows were flooded, forming an almost continuous lake dotted with blue sludgy islands, while innumerable streams roared like lions across my path and were sweeping forward rocks and logs with tremendous energy over ground where tiny gilias had been growing but a short time before. Climbing into the talus slopes, where these savage torrents were broken among earthquake boulders, I managed to cross them, and force my way up

Winter Storms and Spring Floods

the Valley to Hutchings' Bridge, where I crossed the river and waded to the middle of the upper meadow. Here most of the new falls were in sight, probably the most glorious assemblage of waterfalls ever displayed from any one standpoint. On that portion of the south wall between Hutchings' and the Sentinel there were ten falls plunging and booming from a height of nearly three thousand feet, the smallest of which might have been heard miles away. In the neighborhood of Glacier Point there were six; between the Three Brothers and Yosemite Fall, nine; between Yosemite and Royal Arch Falls, ten; from Washington Column to Mount Watkins, ten; on the slopes of Half Dome and Clouds' Rest, facing Mirror Lake and Tenaya Cañon, eight; on the shoulder of Half Dome, facing the Valley, three: fifty-six new falls occupying the upper end of the Valley, besides a countless host of silvery threads gleaming everywhere. In all the Valley there must have been upwards of a hundred. As if celebrating some great event, falls and cascades in Yosemite costume were coming down everywhere from fountain basins, far and near; and, though newcomers, they behaved and sang as if they had lived here always.

All summer-visitors will remember the comet forms of the Yosemite Fall and the laces of the Bridal Veil and Nevada. In the falls of this winter jubilee the lace forms predominated, but there was no lack of thunder-toned comets. The lower portion of one of the Sentinel Cascades was composed of two main white torrents with the space between them filled in with chained and beaded gauze of intricate pattern, through the singing threads of which the purplish-gray rock could be dimly seen. The series above Glacier Point was still more complicated in structure, displaying every form that one could imagine water might be dashed and combed and woven into. Those on the north wall between Washington Column and the Royal Arch Fall were so nearly related they formed an almost continuous sheet, and these again were but slightly separated from those about Indian Cañon. The group about the Three Brothers and El Capitan, owing to the topography and cleavage of the cliffs back of them, was more broken and irregular. The Tissiack Cascades were comparatively small, yet sufficient to give that noblest of mountain rocks a glorious voice. In the midst of all this extravagant rejoicing the great Yosemite Fall was scarce heard until about three o'clock in the afternoon. Then I was startled by a sudden thundering crash as if a rock avalanche had come to the help of the roaring waters. This was the flood-wave of Yosemite Creek, which had just arrived, delayed by the distance it had to travel, and by the choking snows of its widespread fountains. Now, with volume tenfold increased beyond its spring-time fullness, it took its place as leader of the glorious choir.

And the winds, too, were singing in wild accord, playing on every tree and rock, surging against the huge brows and domes and outstanding battlements, deflected hither and thither and broken into a thousand cascading, roaring currents in the cañons, and low bass, drumming swirls in the hollows. And these again, reacting on the clouds, eroded immense cavernous spaces in their gray depths and swept forward the resulting detritus in ragged trains like the moraines of glaciers. These cloud movements in turn published the work of the winds, giving them a visible body, and enabling us to trace them. As if endowed with independent motion, a detached cloud would rise hastily to the very top of the wall as if on some important errand, examining the faces of the cliffs, and then perhaps as suddenly descend to sweep imposingly along the meadows, trailing its draggled fringes through the pines, fondling the waving spires with infinite gentleness, or, gliding behind a grove or a single tree, bringing it into striking relief, as it bowed and waved in solemn rhythm. Sometimes, as the busy clouds drooped and condensed or dissolved to misty gauze, half of the Valley would be suddenly veiled, leaving here and there some lofty headland cut off from all visible connection with the walls, looming alone, dim, spectral, as if belonging to the sky—visitors, like the new falls, come to take part in the glorious festival. Thus for two days and nights in measureless extravagance the storm went on, and mostly without spectators, at

Winter Storms and Spring Floods

least of a terrestrial kind. I saw nobody out—bird, bear, squirrel, or man. Tourists had vanished months before, and the hotel people and laborers were out of sight, careful about getting cold, and satisfied with views from windows. The bears, I suppose, were in their cañon-boulder dens, the squirrels in their knot-hole nests, the grouse in close fir groves, and the small singers in the Indian Cañon chaparral, trying to keep warm and dry. Strange to say, I did not see even the water-ouzels, though they must have greatly enjoyed the storm.

This was the most sublime waterfall flood I ever saw—clouds, winds, rocks, waters, throbbing together as one. And then to contemplate what was going on simultaneously with all this in other mountain temples; the Big Tuolumne Cañon—how the white waters and the winds were singing there! And in Hetch Hetchy Valley and the great King's River yosemite, and in all the other Sierra cañons and valleys from Shasta to the southernmost fountains of the Kern, thousands of rejoicing flood waterfalls chanting together in jubilee dress.

A Wind-Storm in the Forests

The mountain winds, like the dew and rain, sunshine and snow, are measured and bestowed with love on the forests to develop their strength and beauty. However restricted the scope of other forest influences, that of the winds is universal. The snow bends and trims the upper forests every winter, the lightning strikes a single tree here and there, while avalanches mow down thousands at a swoop as a gardener trims out a bed of flowers. But the winds go to every tree, fingering every leaf and branch and furrowed bole; not one is forgotten; the Mountain Pine towering with outstretched arms on the rugged buttresses of the icy peaks, the lowliest and most retiring tenant of the dells; they seek and find them all, caressing them tenderly, bending them in lusty exercise, stimulating their growth, plucking off a leaf or limb as required, or removing an entire tree or grove, now whispering and cooing through the branches like a sleepy child, now roaring like the ocean; the winds blessing the forests, the forests the winds, with ineffable beauty and harmony as the sure result.

After one has seen pines six feet in diameter bending like grasses before a mountain gale, and ever and anon some giant falling with a crash that shakes the hills, it seems astonishing that any, save the lowest thickset trees, could ever have found a period sufficiently stormless to establish themselves; or, once established, that they should not, sooner or later, have been blown down. But when the storm is over, and we behold the same forests tranquil again, towering fresh and unscathed in erect majesty, and consider what centuries of storms have fallen upon them since they were first planted,—hail, to break the tender seedlings; lightning, to scorch and shatter; snow, winds, and avalanches, to crush and overwhelm,—while the manifest result of all this wild storm-culture is the glorious perfection we behold; then faith in Nature's forestry is established, and we cease to deplore the violence of her most destructive gales, or of any other storm-implement whatsoever.

There are two trees in the Sierra forests that are never blown down, so long as they continue in sound health. These are the Juniper and the Dwarf Pine of the summit peaks. Their stiff, crooked roots grip the storm-beaten ledges like eagles' claws, while their lithe, cord-like branches bend round compliantly, offering but slight holds for winds, however violent. The other alpine conifers—the Needle Pine, Mountain Pine, Two-leaved Pine, and Hemlock Spruce—are never thinned out by this agent to any destructive extent, on account of their admirable toughness and the closeness of their growth. In general the same is true of the giants of the lower zones. The kingly Sugar Pine, towering aloft to a height of more than 200 feet, offers a fine mark to storm-winds; but it is not densely foliaged, and its long, horizontal arms swing round compliantly in the blast, like tresses of green, fluent algae in a brook; while the Silver Firs in most places keep their ranks well together in united strength. The Yellow or Silver Pine is more frequently overturned than any other tree on the Sierra, because its leaves and branches form a larger mass in proportion to its height, while in many places it is planted sparsely, leaving open lanes through which storms may enter with full force. Furthermore, because it is distributed along the lower portion of the range, which was the first to be left bare on the breaking up of the ice-sheet at the close of the glacial winter, the soil it is growing upon has been longer exposed to post-glacial weathering, and consequently is in a

A Wind-Storm in the Forests

more crumbling, decayed condition than the fresher soils farther up the range, and therefore offers a less secure anchorage for the roots.

While exploring the forest zones of Mount Shasta, I discovered the path of a hurricane strewn with thousands of pines of this species. Great and small had been uprooted or wrenched off by sheer force, making a clean gap, like that made by a snow avalanche. But hurricanes capable of doing this class of work are rare in the Sierra, and when we have explored the forests from one extremity of the range to the other, we are compelled to believe that they are the most beautiful on the face of the earth, however we may regard the agents that have made them so.

There is always something deeply exciting, not only in the sounds of winds in the woods, which exert more or less influence over every mind, but in their varied waterlike flow as manifested by the movements of the trees, especially those of the conifers. By no other trees are they rendered so extensively and impressively visible, not even by the lordly tropic palms or tree-ferns responsive to the gentlest breeze. The waving of a forest of the giant Sequoias is indescribably impressive and sublime, but the pines seem to me the best interpreters of winds. They are mighty waving goldenrods, ever in tune, singing and writing wind-music all their long century lives. Little, however, of this noble tree-waving and tree-music will you see or hear in the strictly alpine portion of the forests. The burly Juniper, whose girth sometimes more than equals its height, is about as rigid as the rocks on which it grows. The slender lash-like sprays of the Dwarf Pine stream out in wavering ripples, but the tallest and slenderest are far too unyielding to wave even in the heaviest gales. They only shake in quick, short vibrations. The Hemlock Spruce, however, and the Mountain Pine, and some of the tallest thickets of the Two-leaved species bow in storms with considerable scope and gracefulness. But it is only in the lower and middle zones that the meeting of winds and woods is to be seen in all its grandeur.

One of the most beautiful and exhilarating storms I ever enjoyed in the Sierra occurred in December, 1874, when I happened to be exploring one of the tributary valleys of the Yuba River. The sky and the ground and the trees had been thoroughly rain-washed and were dry again. The day was intensely pure, one of those incomparable bits of California winter, warm and balmy and full of white sparkling sunshine, redolent of all the purest influences of the spring, and at the same time enlivened with one of the most bracing windstorms conceivable. Instead of camping out, as I usually do, I then chanced to be stopping at the house of a friend. But when the storm began to sound, I lost no time in pushing out into the woods to enjoy it. For on such occasions Nature has always something rare to show us, and the danger to life and limb is hardly greater than one would experience crouching deprecatingly beneath a roof.

It was still early morning when I found myself fairly adrift. Delicious sunshine came pouring over the hills, lighting the tops of the pines, and setting free a steam of summery fragrance that contrasted strangely with the wild tones of the storm. The air was mottled with pine-tassels and bright green plumes, that went flashing past in the sunlight like birds pursued. But there was not the slightest dustiness, nothing less pure than leaves, and ripe pollen, and flecks of withered bracken and moss. I heard trees falling for hours at the rate of one every two or three minutes; some uprooted, partly on account of the loose, water-soaked condition of the ground; others broken straight across, where some weakness caused by fire had determined the spot. The gestures of the various trees made a delightful study. Young Sugar Pines, light and feathery as squirrel-tails, were bowing almost to the ground; while the grand old patriarchs, whose massive boles had been tried in a hundred storms, waved solemnly above them, their long, arching branches streaming fluently on the gale, and every needle thrilling and ringing and shedding off keen lances of light like a diamond. The Douglas Spruces, with long sprays drawn out in level tresses, and needles massed in a gray, shimmering glow, presented a most striking appearance as they stood in bold

A Wind-Storm in the Forests

relief along the hilltops. The madroños in the dells, with their red bark and large glossy leaves tilted every way, reflected the sunshine in throbbing spangles like those one so often sees on the rippled surface of a glacier lake. But the Silver Pines were now the most impressively beautiful of all. Colossal spires 200 feet in height waved like supple goldenrods chanting and bowing low as if in worship, while the whole mass of their long, tremulous foliage was kindled into one continuous blaze of white sun-fire. The force of the gale was such that the most steadfast monarch of them all rocked down to its roots with a motion plainly perceptible when one leaned against it. Nature was holding high festival, and every fiber of the most rigid giants thrilled with glad excitement.

I drifted on through the midst of this passionate music and motion, across many a glen, from ridge to ridge; often halting in the lee of a rock for shelter, or to gaze and listen. Even when the grand anthem had swelled to its highest pitch, I could distinctly hear the varying tones of individual trees,—Spruce, and Fir, and Pine, and leafless Oak,—and even the infinitely gentle rustle of the withered grasses at my feet. Each was expressing itself in its own way,—singing its own song, and making its own peculiar gestures,—manifesting a richness of variety to be found in no other forest I have yet seen. The coniferous woods of Canada, and the Carolinas, and Florida, are made up of trees that resemble one another about as nearly as blades of grass, and grow close together in much the same way. Coniferous trees, in general, seldom possess individual character, such as is manifest among Oaks and Elms. But the California forests are made up of a greater number of distinct species than any other in the world. And in them we find, not only a marked differentiation into special groups, but also a marked individuality in almost every tree, giving rise to storm effects indescribably glorious.

Toward midday, after a long, tingling scramble through copses of hazel and ceanothus, I gained the summit of the highest ridge in the neighborhood; and then it occurred to me that it would be a fine thing to climb one of the trees to obtain a wider outlook and get my ear close to the Æolian music of its topmost needles. But under the circumstances the choice of a tree was a serious matter. One whose instep was not very strong seemed in danger of being blown down, or of being struck by others in case they should fall; another was branchless to a considerable height above the ground, and at the same time too large to be grasped with arms and legs in climbing; while others were not favorably situated for clear views. After cautiously casting about, I made choice of the tallest of a group of Douglas Spruces that were growing close together like a tuft of grass, no one of which seemed likely to fall unless all the rest fell with it. Though comparatively young, they were about 100 feet high, and their lithe, brushy tops were rocking and swirling in wild ecstasy. Being accustomed to climb trees in making botanical studies, I experienced no difficulty in reaching the top of this one, and never before did I enjoy so noble an exhilaration of motion. The slender tops fairly flapped and swished in the passionate torrent, bending and swirling backward and forward, round and round, tracing indescribable combinations of vertical and horizontal curves, while I clung with muscles firm braced, like a bobolink on a reed.

In its widest sweeps my tree-top described an arc of from twenty to thirty degrees, but I felt sure of its elastic temper, having seen others of the same species still more severely tried—bent almost to the ground indeed, in heavy snows—without breaking a fiber. I was therefore safe, and free to take the wind into my pulses and enjoy the excited forest from my superb outlook. The view from here must be extremely beautiful in any weather. Now my eye roved over the piny hills and dales as over fields of waving grain, and felt the light running in ripples and broad swelling undulations across the valleys from ridge to ridge, as the shining foliage was stirred by corresponding waves of air. Oftentimes these waves of reflected light would break up suddenly into a kind of beaten foam, and again, after chasing one another in regular order, they would seem to bend

A Wind-Storm in the Forests

forward in concentric curves, and disappear on some hillside, like sea-waves on a shelving shore. The quantity of light reflected from the bent needles was so great as to make whole groves appear as if covered with snow, while the black shadows beneath the trees greatly enhanced the effect of the silvery splendor.

Excepting only the shadows there was nothing somber in all this wild sea of pines. On the contrary, notwithstanding this was the winter season, the colors were remarkably beautiful. The shafts of the pine and libocedrus were brown and purple, and most of the foliage was well tinged with yellow; the laurel groves, with the pale undersides of their leaves turned upward, made masses of gray; and then there was many a dash of chocolate color from clumps of manzanita, and jet of vivid crimson from the bark of the madroños, while the ground on the hillsides, appearing here and there through openings between the groves, displayed masses of pale purple and brown.

The sounds of the storm corresponded gloriously with this wild exuberance of light and motion. The profound bass of the naked branches and boles booming like waterfalls; the quick, tense vibrations of the pine-needles, now rising to a shrill, whistling hiss, now falling to a silky murmur; the rustling of laurel groves in the dells, and the keen metallic click of leaf on leaf—all this was heard in easy analysis when the attention was calmly bent.

The varied gestures of the multitude were seen to fine advantage, so that one could recognize the different species at a distance of several miles by this means alone, as well as by their forms and colors, and the way they reflected the light. All seemed strong and comfortable, as if really enjoying the storm, while responding to its most enthusiastic greetings. We hear much nowadays concerning the universal struggle for existence, but no struggle in the common meaning of the word was manifest here; no recognition of danger by any tree; no deprecation; but rather an invincible gladness as remote from exultation as from fear.

The American Wilderness

I kept my lofty perch for hours, frequently closing my eyes to enjoy the music by itself, or to feast quietly on the delicious fragrance that was streaming past. The fragrance of the woods was less marked than that produced during warm rain, when so many balsamic buds and leaves are steeped like tea; but, from the chafing of resiny branches against each other, and the incessant attrition of myriads of needles, the gale was spiced to a very tonic degree. And besides the fragrance from these local sources there were traces of scents brought from afar. For this wind came first from the sea, rubbing against its fresh, briny waves, then distilled through the redwoods, threading rich ferny gulches, and spreading itself in broad undulating currents over many a flower-enameled ridge of the coast mountains, then across the golden plains, up the purple foot-hills, and into these piny woods with the varied incense gathered by the way.

Winds are advertisements of all they touch, however much or little we may be able to read them; telling their wanderings even by their scents alone. Mariners detect the flowery perfume of land-winds far at sea, and sea-winds carry the fragrance of dulse and tangle far inland, where it is quickly recognized, though mingled with the scents of a thousand land-flowers. As an illustration of this, I may tell here that I breathed sea-air on the Firth of Forth, in Scotland, while a boy; then was taken to Wisconsin, where I remained nineteen years; then, without in all this time having breathed one breath of the sea, I walked quietly, alone, from the middle of the Mississippi Valley to the Gulf of Mexico, on a botanical excursion, and while in Florida, far from the coast, my attention wholly bent on the splendid tropical vegetation about me, I suddenly recognized a sea-breeze, as it came sifting through the palmettos and blooming vine-tangles, which at once awakened and set free a thousand dormant associations, and made me a boy again in Scotland, as if all the intervening years had been annihilated.

Most people like to look at mountain rivers, and bear them in

A Wind-Storm in the Forests

mind; but few care to look at the winds, though far more beautiful and sublime, and though they become at times about as visible as flowing water. When the north winds in winter are making upward sweeps over the curving summits of the High Sierra, the fact is sometimes published with flying snow-banners a mile long. Those portions of the winds thus embodied can scarce be wholly invisible, even to the darkest imagination. And when we look around over an agitated forest, we may see something of the wind that stirs it, by its effects upon the trees. Yonder it descends in a rush of water-like ripples, and sweeps over the bending pines from hill to hill. Nearer, we see detached plumes and leaves, now speeding by on level currents, now whirling in eddies, or, escaping over the edges of the whirls, soaring aloft on grand, upswelling domes of air, or tossing on flame-like crests. Smooth, deep currents, cascades, falls, and swirling eddies, sing around every tree and leaf, and over all the varied topography of the region with telling changes of form, like mountain rivers conforming to the features of their channels.

After tracing the Sierra streams from their fountains to the plains, marking where they bloom white in falls, glide in crystal plumes, surge gray and foam-filled in boulder-choked gorges, and slip through the woods in long, tranquil reaches—after thus learning their language and forms in detail, we may at length hear them chanting all together in one grand anthem, and comprehend them all in clear inner vision, covering the range like lace. But even this spectacle is far less sublime and not a whit more substantial than what we may behold of these storm-streams of air in the mountain woods.

We all travel the milky way together, trees and men; but it never occurred to me until this storm-day, while swinging in the wind, that trees are travelers, in the ordinary sense. They make many journeys, not extensive ones, it is true; but our own little journeys, away and back again, are only little more than tree-wavings—many of them not so much.

When the storm began to abate, I dismounted and sauntered down through the calming woods. The storm-tones died away, and, turning toward the east, I beheld the countless hosts of the forests hushed and tranquil, towering above one another on the slopes of the hills like a devout audience. The setting sun filled them with amber light, and seemed to say, while they listened, "My peace I give unto you."

As I gazed on the impressive scene, all the so-called ruin of the storm was forgotten, and never before did these noble woods appear so fresh, so joyous, so immortal.

Snow-Storms

As has been already stated, the first of the great snow-storms that replenish the Yosemite fountains seldom sets in before the end of November. Then, warned by the sky, wide-awake mountaineers, together with the deer and most of the birds, make haste to the lowlands or foothills; and burrowing marmots, mountain beavers, wood-rats, and other small mountain people, go into winter quarters, some of them not again to see the light of day until the general awakening and resurrection of the spring in June or July. The fertile clouds, drooping and condensing in brooding silence, seem to be thoughtfully examining the forests and streams with reference to the work that lies before them. At length, all their plans perfected, tufted flakes and single starry crystals come in sight, solemnly swirling and glinting to their blessed appointed places; and soon the busy throng fills the sky and makes darkness like night. The first heavy fall is usually from about two to four feet in depth; then with intervals of days or weeks of bright weather storm succeeds storm, heaping snow on snow, until thirty to fifty feet has fallen. But on account of its settling and compacting, and waste from melting and evaporation, the average depth actually found at any time seldom exceeds ten feet in the forest regions, or fifteen feet along the slopes of the summit peaks. After snow-storms come avalanches, varying greatly in form, size, behavior and in the songs they sing;

some on the smooth slopes of the mountains are short and broad; others long and river-like in the side cañons of yosemites and in the main cañons, flowing in regular channels and booming like water-falls, while countless smaller ones fall everywhere from laden trees and rocks and lofty cañon walls. Most delightful it is to stand in the middle of Yosemite on still clear mornings after snow-storms and watch the throng of avalanches as they come down, rejoicing, to their places, whispering, thrilling like birds, or booming and roaring like thunder. The noble yellow pines stand hushed and motionless as if under a spell until the morning sunshine begins to sift through their laden spires; then the dense masses on the ends of the leafy branches begin to shift and fall, those from the upper branches striking the lower ones in succession, enveloping each tree in a hollow conical avalanche of fairy fineness; while the relieved branches spring up and wave with startling effect in the general stillness, as if each tree was moving of its own volition. Hundreds of broad cloud-shaped masses may also be seen, leaping over the brows of the cliffs from great heights, descending at first with regular avalanche speed until, worn into dust by friction, they float in front of the precipices like irised clouds. Those which descend from the brow of El Capitan are particularly fine; but most of the great Yosemite avalanches flow in regular channels like cascades and waterfalls. When the snow first gives way on the upper slopes of their basins, a dull rushing, rumbling sound is heard which rapidly increases and seems to draw nearer with appalling intensity of tone. Presently the white flood comes bounding into sight over bosses and sheer places, leaping from bench to bench, spreading and narrowing and throwing off clouds of whirling dust like the spray of foaming cataracts. Compared with waterfalls and cascades, avalanches are short-lived, few of them lasting more than a minute or two, and the sharp, clashing sounds so common in falling water are mostly wanting; but in their low massy thundertones and purple-tinged whiteness, and in their dress, gait, gestures and general behavior, they are much alike.

AVALANCHES

Besides these common after-storm avalanches that are to be found not only in the Yosemite but in all the deep, sheer-walled cañons of the Range there are two other important kinds, which may be called annual and century avalanches, which still further enrich the scenery. The only place about the Valley where one may be sure to see the annual kind is on the north slope of Clouds' Rest. They are composed of heavy, compacted snow, which has been subjected to frequent alternations of freezing and thawing. They are developed on cañon and mountain-sides at an elevation of from nine to ten thousand feet, where the slopes are inclined at an angle too low to shed off the dry winter snow, and which accumulates until the spring thaws sap their foundations and make them slippery; then away in grand style go the ponderous icy masses without any fine snow-dust. Those of Clouds' Rest descend like thunderbolts for more than a mile.

The great century avalanches and the kind that mow wide swaths through the upper forests occur on mountain-sides about ten or twelve thousand feet high, where under ordinary weather conditions the snow accumulated from winter to winter lies at rest for many years, allowing trees, fifty to a hundred feet high, to grow undisturbed on the slopes beneath them. On their way down through the woods they seldom fail to make a perfectly clean sweep, stripping off the soil as well as the trees, clearing paths two or three hundred yards wide from the timber line to the glacier meadows or lakes, and piling their uprooted trees, head downward, in rows along the sides of the gaps like lateral moraines. Scars and broken branches of the trees standing on the sides of the gaps record the depth of the overwhelming flood; and when we come to count the annual wood-rings on the uprooted trees we learn that some of these immense avalanches occur only once in a century or even at still wider intervals.

A   R I D E   O N   A N   A V A L A N C H E

Few Yosemite visitors ever see snow avalanches and fewer still know the exhilaration of riding on them. In all my mountaineering I have enjoyed only one avalanche ride, and the start was so sudden and the end came so soon I had but little time to think of the danger that attends this sort of travel, though at such times one thinks fast. One fine Yosemite morning after a heavy snowfall, being eager to see as many avalanches as possible and wide views of the forest and summit peaks in their new white robes before the sunshine had time to change them, I set out early to climb by a side cañon to the top of a commanding ridge a little over three thousand feet above the Valley. On account of the looseness of the snow that blocked the cañon I knew the climb would require a long time, some three or four hours as I estimated; but it proved far more difficult than I had anticipated. Most of the way I sank waist deep, almost out of sight in some places. After spending the whole day to within half an hour or so of sundown, I was still several hundred feet below the summit. Then my hopes were reduced to getting up in time to see the sunset. But I was not to get summit views of any sort that day, for deep trampling near the cañon head, where the snow was strained, started an avalanche, and I was swished down to the foot of the cañon as if by enchantment. The wallowing ascent had taken nearly all day, the descent only about a minute. When the avalanche started I threw myself on my back and spread my arms to try to keep from sinking. Fortunately, though the grade of the cañon is very steep, it is not interrupted by precipices large enough to cause out-bounding or free plunging. On no part of the rush was I buried. I was only moderately imbedded on the surface or at times a little below it, and covered with a veil of back-streaming dust particles; and as the whole mass beneath and about me joined in the flight there was no friction, though I was tossed here and there and lurched from side to side. When the avalanche swedged and came to rest I found myself on top of the crumpled pile without a bruise or scar. This was a fine experience. Hawthorne says somewhere that steam has spiritualized travel; though unspiritual smells, smoke, etc., still attend steam travel. This flight in what might be called a milky way of snow-stars was the most spiritual and exhilarating of all the modes of motion I have ever experienced. Elijah's flight in a chariot of fire could hardly have been more gloriously exciting.

THE STREAMS
IN OTHER SEASONS

In the spring, after all the avalanches are down and the snow is melting fast, then all the Yosemite streams, from their fountains to their falls, sing their grandest songs. Countless rills make haste to the rivers, running and singing soon after sunrise, louder and louder with increasing volume until sundown; then they gradually fail through the frosty hours of the night. In this way the volume of the upper branches of the river is nearly doubled during the day, rising and falling as regularly as the tides of the sea. Then the Merced overflows its banks, flooding the meadows, sometimes almost from wall to wall in some places, beginning to rise towards sundown just when the streams on the fountains are beginning to diminish, the difference in time of the daily rise and fall being caused by the distance the upper flood streams have to travel before reaching the Valley. In the warmest weather they seem fairly to shout for joy and clash their upleaping waters together like clapping of hands; racing down the cañons with white manes flying in glorious exuberance of strength, compelling huge, sleeping boulders to wake up and join in their dance and song, to swell their exulting chorus.

In early summer, after the flood season, the Yosemite streams are in their prime, running crystal clear, deep and full but not overflowing their banks—about as deep through the night as the day, the difference in volume so marked in spring being now too slight to be noticed. Nearly all the weather is cloudless and everything is at its brightest—lake, river, garden and forest with all their life. Most of the plants are in full flower. The blessed ouzels have built their mossy huts and are now singing their best songs with the streams.

In tranquil, mellow autumn, when the year's work is about done and the fruits are ripe, birds and seeds out of their nests, and all the landscape is glowing like a benevolent countenance, then the streams are at their lowest ebb, with scarce a memory left of their wild spring floods. The small tributaries that do not reach back to the lasting snow fountains of the summit peaks shrink to whispering, tinkling currents. After the snow is gone from the basins, excepting occasional thunder-showers, they are now fed only by small springs whose waters are mostly evaporated in passing over miles of warm pavements, and in feeling their way slowly from pool to pool through the midst of boulders and sand. Even the main rivers are so low they may easily be forded, and their grand falls and cascades, now gentle and approachable, have waned to sheets of embroidery.

Snow Banners

But it is on the mountain tops, when they are laden with loose, dry snow and swept by a gale from the north, that the most magnificent storm scenery is displayed. The peaks along the axis of the Range are then decorated with resplendent banners, some of them more than a mile long, shining, streaming, waving with solemn exuberant enthusiasm as if celebrating some surpassingly glorious event.

The snow of which these banners are made falls on the high Sierra in most extravagant abundance, sometimes to a depth of fifteen or twenty feet, coming from the fertile clouds not in large tangled flakes such as one oftentimes sees in Yosemite, seldom even in complete crystals, for many of the starry blossoms fall before they are ripe, while most of those that attain perfect development as six-petaled flowers are more or less broken by glinting and chafing against one another on the way down to their work. This dry frosty snow is prepared for the grand banner-waving celebrations by the action of the wind. Instead of at once finding rest like that which falls into the tranquil depths of the forest, it is shoved and rolled and beaten against boulders and out-jutting rocks, swirled in pits and hollows like sand in river pot-holes, and ground into sparkling dust. And when storm winds find this snow-dust in a loose condition on the slopes above the timber-line they toss it back into the sky and sweep

167

it onward from peak to peak in the form of smooth regular banners, or in cloudy drifts, according to the velocity and direction of the wind, and the conformation of the slopes over which it is driven. While thus flying through the air a small portion escapes from the mountains to the sky as vapor; but far the greater part is at length locked fast in bossy overcurling cornices along the ridges, or in stratified sheets in the glacier cirques, some of it to replenish the small residual glaciers and remain silent and rigid for centuries before it is finally melted and sent singing down home to the sea.

But, though snow-dust and storm-winds abound on the mountains, regular shapely banners are, for causes we shall presently see, seldom produced. During the five winters that I spent in Yosemite I made many excursions to high points above the walls in all kinds of weather to see what was going on outside; from all my lofty outlooks I saw only one banner-storm that seemed in every way perfect. This was in the winter of 1873, when the snow-laden peaks were swept by a powerful norther. I was awakened early in the morning by a wild storm-wind and of course I had to make haste to the middle of the Valley to enjoy it. Rugged torrents and avalanches from the main wind-flood overhead were roaring down the side cañons and over the cliffs, arousing the rocks and the trees and the streams alike into glorious hurrahing enthusiasm, shaking the whole Valley into one huge song. Yet inconceivable as it must seem even to those who love all Nature's wildness, the storm was telling its story on the mountains in still grander characters.

A Wonderful Winter Scene

I had long been anxious to study some points in the structure of the ice-hill at the foot of the Upper Yosemite Fall, but, as I have already explained, blinding spray had hitherto prevented me from getting sufficiently near it. This morning the entire body of the Fall was oftentimes torn into gauzy strips and blown horizontally along the face of the cliff, leaving the ice-hill dry; and while making my way to the top of Fern Ledge to seize so favorable an opportunity to look down its throat, the peaks of the Merced group came in sight over the shoulder of the South Dome, each waving a white glowing banner against the dark blue sky, as regular in form and firm and fine in texture as if it were made of silk. So rare and splendid a picture, of course, smothered everything else and I at once began to scramble and wallow up the snow-choked Indian Cañon to a ridge about 8000 feet high, commanding a general view of the main summits along the axis of the Range, feeling assured I should find them bannered still more gloriously; nor was I in the least disappointed. I reached the top of the ridge in four or five hours, and through an opening in the woods the most imposing windstorm effect I ever beheld came full in sight; unnumbered mountains rising sharply into the cloudless sky, their bases solid white, their sides plashed with snow, like ocean rocks with foam, and on every summit a magnificent silvery banner, from two thousand to six thousand feet in length, slender at the point of attachment, and widening gradually until about a thousand or fifteen hundred feet in breadth, and as shapely and as substantial looking in texture as the banners of the finest silk, all streaming and waving free and clear in the sun-glow with nothing to blur the sublime picture they made.

Fancy yourself standing beside me on this Yosemite Ridge. There is a strange garish glitter in the air and the gale drives wildly overhead, but you feel nothing of its violence, for you are looking out through a sheltered opening in the woods, as through a window. In the immediate foreground there is a forest of silver firs, their foliage warm yellow-green, and the snow beneath them is strewn with their plumes, plucked off by the storm; and beyond a broad, ridgy, cañon-furrowed, dome-dotted middle ground, darkened here and there with belts of pines, you behold the lofty snow-laden mountains in glorious array, waving their banners with jubilant enthusiasm as if shouting aloud for joy. They are twenty miles away, but you would not wish them nearer, for every feature is distinct, and the whole wonderful show is seen in its right proportions, like a painting on the sky.

And now after this general view, mark how sharply the ribs and buttresses and summits of the mountains are defined, excepting the portions veiled by the banners; how gracefully and nobly the banners are waving in accord with the throbbing of the wind-flood; how trimly each is attached to the very summit of its peak like a streamer at a mast-head; how bright and glowing white they are, and how finely their fading fringes are penciled on the sky! See how solid white and opaque they are at the point of attachment and how filmy and translucent toward the end, so that the parts of the peaks past which they are streaming look dim as if seen through a veil of ground glass. And see how some of the longest of the banners on the highest peaks are streaming perfectly free from peak to peak across intervening notches or passes, while others overlap and partly hide one another.

As to their formation, we find that the main causes of the wondrous beauty and perfection of those we are looking at are the favorable direction and force of the wind, the abundance of snow-dust, and the form of the north sides of the peaks. In general, the north sides are concave in both their horizontal and vertical sections, having been sculptured into this shape by the residual glaciers that lingered in the protecting northern shadows, while the sun-beaten south sides, having never been subjected to this kind of glaciation, are convex or irregular. It is essential, therefore, not only that the wind should move with great velocity and steadiness to supply a sufficiently copious and continuous stream of snow-dust, but that it should come from the north. No perfect banner is ever hung on the Sierra peaks by the south wind. Had the gale today blown from the south, leaving the other conditions unchanged, only swirling, interfering, cloudy drifts would have been produced; for the snow, instead of being spouted straight up and over the tops of the peaks in condensed currents to be drawn out as streamers, would have been driven over the convex southern slopes from peak to peak like white pearly fog.

It appears, therefore, that shadows in great part determine not only the forms of lofty ice mountains, but also those of the snow banners that the wild winds hang upon them.

EARTHQUAKE STORMS

The avalanche taluses, leaning against the walls at intervals of a mile or two, are among the most striking and interesting of the secondary features of the Valley. They are from about three to five hundred feet high, made up of huge, angular, well-preserved, unshifting boulders, and instead of being slowly weathered from the cliffs like ordinary taluses, they were all formed suddenly and simultaneously by a great earthquake that occurred at least three centuries ago. And though thus hurled into existence in a few seconds or minutes, they are the least changeable of all the Sierra soil-beds. Excepting those which were launched directly into the channels of swift rivers, scarcely one of their wedged and interlacing boulders has moved since the day of their creation; and though mostly made up of huge blocks of granite, many of them from ten to fifty feet cube, weighing thousands of tons with only a few small chips, trees and shrubs make out to live and thrive on them and even delicate herbaceous plants—draperia, collomia, zauschneria, etc., soothing and coloring their wild rugged slopes with gardens and groves.

I was long in doubt on some points concerning the origin of these taluses. Plainly enough they were derived from the cliffs above them, because they are of the size of scars on the wall, the rough angular surface of which contrasts with the rounded, glaciated, unfractured parts. It was plain, too, that instead of being made up of material slowly and gradually weathered from the cliffs like ordinary taluses, almost every one of them had been formed suddenly in a single avalanche, and had not been increased in size during the last three or four centuries, for trees three or four hundred years old are growing on them, some standing at the top close to the wall without a bruise or broken branch, showing that scarcely a single boulder had ever fallen among them. Furthermore, all these taluses throughout the Range seemed by the trees and lichens growing on them to be of the same age. All the phenomena thus pointed straight to a grand ancient earthquake. But for years I left the question open, and went on from cañon to cañon, observing again and again; measuring the heights of taluses throughout the Range on both flanks, and the variations in the angles of their surface slopes; studying the way their boulders had been assorted and related and brought to rest, and their correspondence in size with the cleavage joints of the cliffs from whence they were derived, cautious about making up my mind. But at last all doubt as to their formation vanished.

At half-past two o'clock of a moonlit morning in March, I was awakened by a tremendous earthquake, and though I had never before enjoyed a storm of this sort, the strange thrilling motion could not be mistaken, and I ran out of my cabin, both glad and frightened, shouting, "A noble earthquake! A noble earthquake!" feeling sure I was going to learn something. The shocks were so violent and varied, and succeeded one another so closely, that I had to balance myself carefully in walking as if on the deck of a ship among waves, and it seemed impossible that the high cliffs of the Valley could escape being shattered. In particular, I feared that the sheer-fronted Sentinel Rock, towering above my cabin, would be shaken down, and I took shelter back of a large yellow pine, hoping that it might protect me from at least the smaller outbounding boulders. For a minute or two the shocks became more and more violent—flashing horizontal thrusts mixed with a few twists and battering, explosive, upheaving jolts,—as if Nature were wrecking her Yosemite temple, and getting ready to build a still better one.

I was now convinced before a single boulder had fallen that earthquakes were the talus-makers and positive proof soon came. It was a calm moonlight night, and no sound was heard for the first minute or so, save low, muffled, underground, bubbling rumblings, and the whispering and rustling of the agitated trees, as if Nature were holding her breath. Then, suddenly, out of the strange silence and strange motion there came a tremendous roar. The Eagle Rock on the south wall, about a half mile up the Valley, gave way and I saw it falling in thousands of the great boulders I had so long been studying, pouring to the Valley floor in a free curve luminous from friction, making a terribly sublime spectacle—an arc of glowing, passionate fire, fifteen hundred feet span, as true in form and as serene in beauty as a rainbow in the midst of the stupendous, roaring rock-storm. The sound was so tremendously deep and broad and earnest, the whole earth like a living creature seemed to have at last found a voice and to be calling to her sister planets. In trying to tell something of the size of this awful sound it seems to me that if all the thunder of all the storms I had ever heard were condensed into one roar it would not equal this rock-roar at the birth of a mountain talus. Think, then, of the roar that arose to heaven at the simultaneous birth of all the thousands of ancient cañon-taluses throughout the length and breadth of the Range!

The first severe shocks were soon over, and eager to examine the new-born talus I ran up the Valley in the moonlight and climbed upon it before the huge blocks, after their fiery flight, had come to complete rest. They were slowly settling into their places, chafing, grating against one another, groaning, and whispering; but no motion was visible except in a stream of small fragments pattering down the face of the cliff. A cloud of dust particles, lighted by the moon, floated out across the whole breadth of the Valley, forming a ceiling that lasted until after sunrise, and the air was filled with the odor of crushed Douglas spruces from a grove that had been mowed down and mashed like weeds.

After the ground began to calm I ran across the meadow to the river to see in what direction it was flowing and was glad to find that *down* the Valley was still down. Its waters were muddy from portions of its banks having given way, but it was flowing around its curves and over its ripples and shallows with ordinary tones and gestures. The mud would soon be cleared away and the raw slips on the banks would be the only visible record of the shaking it suffered.

The Upper Yosemite Fall, glowing white in the moonlight, seemed to know nothing of the earthquake, manifesting no change in form or voice, as far as I could see or hear.

After a second startling shock, about half-past three o'clock, the ground continued to tremble gently, and smooth, hollow rumbling sounds, not always distinguishable from the rounded, bumping, explosive tones of the falls, came from deep in the mountains in a northern direction.

The few Indians fled from their huts to the middle of the Valley, fearing that angry spirits were trying to kill them; and, as I afterward learned, most of the Yosemite tribe, who were spending the winter at their village on Bull Creek forty miles away, were so terrified that they ran into the river and washed themselves,—getting themselves clean enough to say their prayers, I suppose, or to die. I asked Dick, one of the Indians with whom I was acquainted, "What made the ground shake and jump so much?" He only shook his head and said, "No good. No good," and looked appealingly to me to give him hope that his life was to be spared.

In the morning I found the few white settlers assembled in front of the old Hutchings Hotel comparing notes and meditating flight to the lowlands, seemingly as sorely frightened as the Indians. Shortly after sunrise a low, blunt, muffled rumbling, like distant thunder, was followed by another series of shocks, which, though not nearly so severe as the first, made the cliffs and domes tremble like jelly, and the big pines and oaks thrill and swish and wave their branches with startling effect. Then the talkers were suddenly hushed, and the solemnity on their faces was sublime. One in particular of these winter neighbors, a somewhat speculative thinker with whom I had often conversed, was a firm believer in the cataclysmic origin of the Valley; and I now jokingly remarked that his wild tumble-down-and-engulfment hypothesis might soon be proved, since these underground rumblings and shakings might be the forerunners of another Yosemite-making cataclysm, which would perhaps double the depth of the Valley by swallowing the floor, leaving the ends of the roads and trails dangling three or four thousand feet in the air. Just then came the third series of shocks, and it was fine to see how awfully silent and solemn he became. His belief in the existence of a mysterious abyss, into which the suspended floor of the Valley and all the domes and battlements of the walls might at any moment go roaring down, mightily troubled him. To diminish his fears and laugh him into something like reasonable faith, I said, "Come, cheer up; smile a little and clap your hands, now that kind Mother Earth is trotting us on her knee to amuse us and make us good." But the well-meant joke seemed irreverent and utterly failed, as if only prayerful terror could rightly belong to the wild beauty-making business. Even after all the heavier shocks were over I could do nothing to reassure him. On the contrary, he handed me the keys of his little store to keep, saying that with a companion of like mind he was going to the lowlands to stay until the fate of poor, trembling Yosemite was settled. In vain I rallied them on their fears, calling attention to the strength of the granite walls of our Valley home, the very best and solidest masonry in the world, and less likely to collapse and sink than the sedimentary lowlands to which they were looking for safety; and saying that in any case they sometime would have to die, and so grand a burial was not to be slighted. But they were too seriously panic-stricken to get comfort from anything I could say.

During the third severe shock the trees were so violently shaken that the birds flew out with frightened cries. In particular, I noticed two robins flying in terror from a leafless oak, the branches of which swished and quivered as if struck by a heavy battering-ram. Exceedingly interesting were the flashing and quivering of the elastic needles of the pines in the sunlight and the waving up and down of the branches while the trunks stood rigid. There was no swaying, waving or swirling as in wind-storms, but quick, quivering jerks, and at times the heavy tasseled branches moved as if they had all been pressed down against the trunk and suddenly let go, to spring up and vibrate until they came to rest again. Only the owls seemed to be undisturbed. Before the rumbling echoes had died away a hollow-voiced owl began to hoot in philosophical tranquillity from near the edge of the new talus as if nothing extraordinary had occurred, although, perhaps, he was curious to know what all the noise was about. His "hoot-too-hoot-too-whoo" might have meant, "what's a' the steer, kimmer?"

It was long before the Valley found perfect rest. The rocks trembled more or less every day for over two months, and I kept a bucket of water on my table to learn what I could of the movements. The blunt thunder in the depths of the mountains was usually followed by sudden jarring, horizontal thrusts from the northward, often succeeded by twisting, upjolting movements. More than a month after the first great shock, when I was standing on a fallen tree up the

Snow Banners

Valley near Lamon's winter cabin, I heard a distinct bubbling thunder from the direction of Tenaya Cañon. Carlo, a large intelligent St. Bernard dog standing beside me seemed greatly astonished, and looked intently in that direction with mouth open and uttered a low *Wouf!* as if saying, "What's that?" He must have known that it was not thunder, though like it. The air was perfectly still, not the faintest breath of wind perceptible, and a fine, mellow, sunny hush pervaded everything, in the midst of which came that subterranean thunder. Then, while we gazed and listened, came the corresponding shocks, distinct as if some mighty hand had shaken the ground. After the sharp horizontal jars died away, they were followed by a gentle rocking and undulating of the ground so distinct that Carlo looked at the log on which he was standing to see who was shaking it. It was the season of flooded meadows and the pools about me, calm as sheets of glass, were suddenly thrown into low ruffling waves.

Judging by its effects, this Yosemite, or Inyo earthquake, as it is sometimes called, was gentle as compared with the one that gave rise to the grand talus system of the Range and did so much for the cañon scenery. Nature, usually so deliberate in her operations, then created, as we have seen, a new set of features, simply by giving the mountains a shake—changing not only the high peaks and cliffs, but the streams. As soon as these rock avalanches fell, the streams began to sing new songs; for in many places thousands of boulders were hurled into their channels, roughening and half-damming them, compelling the waters to surge and roar in rapids where before they glided smoothly. Some of the streams were completely dammed; driftwood, leaves, etc., gradually filling the interstices between the boulders, thus giving rise to lakes and level reaches; and these again, after being gradually filled in, were changed to meadows, through which the streams are now silently meandering; while at the same time some of the taluses took the places of old meadows and groves. Thus rough places were made smooth, and smooth places rough.

But, on the whole, by what at first sight seemed pure confounded confusion and ruin, the landscapes were enriched; for gradually every talus was covered with groves and gardens, and made a finely proportioned and ornamental base for the cliffs. In this work of beauty, every boulder is prepared and measured and put in its place more thoughtfully than are the stones of temples. If for a moment you are inclined to regard these taluses as mere draggled, chaotic dumps, climb to the top of one of them, and run down without any haggling, puttering hesitation, boldly jumping from boulder to boulder with even speed. You will then find your feet playing a tune, and quickly discover the music and poetry of these magnificent rock piles—a fine lesson; and all Nature's wildness tells the same story— the shocks and outbursts of earthquakes, volcanoes, geysers, roaring, thundering waves and floods, the silent uprush of sap in plants, storms of every sort—each and all are the orderly beauty-making love-beats of Nature's heart.

Burned Area, Glacier National Park, Montana

Glacier National Park, Montana

Glacier National Park, Montana

Mount Moran and Mount Jackson,
Lake from Signal Hill,
Grand Teton National Park, Wyoming

Grand Teton National Park, Wyoming

Glacier National Park, Montana

Snake River, Grand Teton National Park

Unnamed Peak, Kings Canyon National Park, California

Paradise Valley, Kings Canyon National Park, California

Rocky Mountain National Park, Colorado

Long's Peak, Rocky Mountain National Park, Colorado

Long's Peak, Rocky Mountain National Park, Colorado

Long's Peak, Rocky Mountain National Park, Colorado

Ferns, Glacier National Park, Montana

Leaves, Glacier National Park, Montana

The Douglas Squirrel

(Sciurus Douglasii)

The Douglas Squirrel is by far the most interesting and influential of the California sciuridae, surpassing every other species in force of character, numbers, and extent of range, and in the amount of influence he brings to bear upon the health and distribution of the vast forests he inhabits.

Go where you will throughout the noble woods of the Sierra Nevada, among the giant pines and spruces of the lower zones, up through the towering Silver Firs to the storm-bent thickets of the summit peaks, you everywhere find this little squirrel the master-existence. Though only a few inches long, so intense is his fiery vigor and restlessness, he stirs every grove with wild life, and makes himself more important than even the huge bears that shuffle through the tangled underbrush beneath him. Every wind is fretted by his voice, almost every bole and branch feels the sting of his sharp feet. How much the growth of the trees is stimulated by this means it is not easy to learn, but his action in manipulating their seeds is more appreciable. Nature has made him master forester and committed most of her coniferous crops to his paws. Probably over fifty per cent of all the cones ripened on the Sierra are cut off and handled by the Douglas alone, and of those of the Big Trees perhaps ninety per cent pass through his hands: the greater portion is of course stored away for food to last during the winter and spring, but some of them are

179

tucked separately into loosely covered holes, where some of the seeds germinate and become trees. But the Sierra is only one of the many provinces over which he holds sway, for his dominion extends over all the Redwood Belt of the Coast Mountains, and far northward throughout the majestic forests of Oregon, Washington, and British Columbia. I make haste to mention these facts, to show upon how substantial a foundation the importance I ascribe to him rests.

The Douglas is closely allied to the Red Squirrel or Chickaree of the eastern woods. Ours may be a lineal descendant of this species, distributed westward to the Pacific by way of the Great Lakes and the Rocky Mountains, and thence southward along our forested ranges. This view is suggested by the fact that our species becomes redder and more Chickaree-like in general, the farther it is traced back along the course indicated above. But whatever their relationship, and the evolutionary forces that have acted upon them, the Douglas is now the larger and more beautiful animal.

From the nose to the root of the tail he measures about eight inches; and his tail, which he so effectively uses in interpreting his feelings, is about six inches in length. He wears dark bluish-gray over the back and half-way down the sides, bright buff on the belly, with a stripe of dark gray, nearly black, separating the upper and under colors; this dividing stripe, however, is not very sharply defined. He has long black whiskers, which gives him a rather fierce look when observed closely, strong claws, sharp as fish-hooks, and the brightest of bright eyes, full of telling speculation.

A King's River Indian told me that they call him "Pillillooeet," which, rapidly pronounced with the first syllable heavily accented, is not unlike the lusty exclamation he utters on his way up a tree when excited. Most mountaineers in California call him the Pine Squirrel; and when I asked an old trapper whether he knew our little forester, he replied with brightening countenance: "Oh, yes, of course I know him; everybody knows him. When I'm huntin' in the woods, I often

The Douglas Squirrel

find out where the deer are by his barkin' at 'em. I call 'em Lightnin' Squirrels, because they're so mighty quick and peert."

All the true squirrels are more or less birdlike in speech and movements; but the Douglas is preëminently so, possessing, as he does, every attribute peculiarly squirrelish enthusiastically concentrated. He is the squirrel of squirrels, flashing from branch to branch of his favorite evergreens crisp and glossy and undiseased as a sunbeam. Give him wings and he would outfly any bird in the woods. His big gray cousin is a looser animal, seemingly light enough to float on the wind; yet when leaping from limb to limb, or out of one treetop to another, he sometimes halts to gather strength, as if making efforts concerning the upshot of which he does not always feel exactly confident. But the Douglas, with his denser body, leaps and glides in hidden strength, seemingly as independent of common muscles as a mountain stream. He threads the tasseled branches of the pines, stirring their needles like a rustling breeze; now shooting across openings in arrowy lines; now launching in curves, glinting deftly from side to side in sudden zigzags, and swirling in giddy loops and spirals around the knotty trunks; getting into what seem to be the most impossible situations without sense of danger; now on his haunches, now on his head; yet ever graceful, and punctuating his most irrepressible outbursts of energy with little dots and dashes of perfect repose. He is, without exception, the wildest animal I ever saw,—a fiery, sputtering little bolt of life, luxuriating in quick oxygen and the woods' best juices. One can hardly think of such a creature being dependent, like the rest of us, on climate and food. But, after all, it requires no long acquaintance to learn he is human, for he works for a living. His busiest time is in the Indian summer. Then he gathers burs and hazelnuts like a plodding farmer, working continuously every day for hours; saying not a word; cutting off the ripe cones at the top of his speed, as if employed by the job, and examining every branch in regular order, as if careful that not one should escape him; then, descending, he stores them away beneath logs and stumps, in anticipation of the pinching hunger days of winter. He seems himself a kind of coniferous fruit,—both fruit and flower. The resiny essences of the pines pervade every pore of his body, and eating his flesh is like chewing gum.

One never tires of this bright chip of nature,—this brave little voice crying in the wilderness,—of observing his many works and ways, and listening to his curious language. His musical, piny gossip is as savory to the ear as balsam to the palate; and, though he has not exactly the gift of song, some of his notes are as sweet as those of a linnet—almost flute-like in softness, while others prick and tingle like thistles. He is the mocking-bird of squirrels, pouring forth mixed chatter and song like a perennial fountain; barking like a dog, screaming like a hawk, chirping like a blackbird or a sparrow; while in bluff, audacious noisiness he is a very jay.

In descending the trunk of a tree with the intention of alighting on the ground, he preserves a cautious silence, mindful, perhaps, of foxes and wildcats; but while rocking safely at home in the pine-tops there is no end to his capers and noise; and woe to the gray squirrel or chipmunk that ventures to set foot on his favorite tree! No matter how slyly they trace the furrows of the bark, they are speedily discovered, and kicked down-stairs with comic vehemence, while a torrent of angry notes comes rushing from his whiskered lips that sounds remarkably like swearing. He will even attempt at times to drive away dogs and men, especially if he has had no previous knowledge of them. Seeing a man for the first time, he approaches nearer and nearer, until within a few feet; then, with an angry outburst, he makes a sudden rush, all teeth and eyes, as if about to eat you up. But, finding that the big, forked animal doesn't scare, he prudently beats a retreat, and sets himself up to reconnoiter on some over-hanging branch, scrutinizing every movement you make with ludi-crous solemnity. Gathering courage, he ventures down the trunk again, churring and chirping, and jerking nervously up and down in curious loops, eyeing you all the time, as if showing off and demand-

The Douglas Squirrel

ing your admiration. Finally, growing calmer, he settles down in a comfortable posture on some horizontal branch commanding a good view, and beats time with his tail to a steady "Chee-up! chee-up!" or, when somewhat less excited, "Pee-ah!" with the first syllable keenly accented, and the second drawn out like the scream of a hawk,—repeating this slowly and more emphatically at first, then gradually faster, until a rate of about 150 words a minute is reached; usually sitting all the time on his haunches, with paws resting on his breast, which pulses visibly with each word. It is remarkable, too, that, though articulating distinctly, he keeps his mouth shut most of the time, and speaks through his nose. I have occasionally observed him even eating Sequoia seeds and nibbling a troublesome flea, without ceasing or in any way confusing his "Pee-ah! pee-ah!" for a single moment.

While ascending trees all his claws come into play, but in descending the weight of his body is sustained chiefly by those of the hind feet; still in neither case do his movements suggest effort, though if you are near enough you may see the bulging strength of his short, bear-like arms, and note his sinewy fists clinched in the bark.

Whether going up or down, he carries his tail extended at full length in line with his body, unless it be required for gestures. But while running along horizontal limbs or fallen trunks, it is frequently folded forward over the back, with the airy tip daintily upcurled. In cool weather it keeps him warm. Then, after he has finished his meal, you may see him crouched close on some level limb with his tail-robe neatly spread and reaching forward to his ears, the electric, outstanding hairs quivering in the breeze like pine-needles. But in wet or very cold weather he stays in his nest, and while curled up there his comforter is long enough to come forward around his nose. It is seldom so cold, however, as to prevent his going out to his stores when hungry.

Once as I lay storm-bound on the upper edge of the timber line on Mount Shasta, the thermometer nearly at zero and the sky thick with driving snow, a Douglas came bravely out several times from one of the lower hollows of a Dwarf Pine near my camp, faced the wind without seeming to feel it much, frisked lightly about over the mealy snow, and dug his way down to some hidden seeds with wonderful precision, as if to his eyes the thick snow-covering were glass.

No other of the Sierra animals of my acquaintance is better fed, not even the deer, amid abundance of sweet herbs and shrubs, or the mountain sheep, or omnivorous bears. His food consists of grass-seeds, berries, hazel-nuts, chinquapins, and the nuts and seeds of all the coniferous trees without exception,—Pine, Fir, Spruce, Libocedrus, Juniper, and Sequoia,—he is fond of them all, and they all agree with him, green or ripe. No cone is too large for him to manage, none so small as to be beneath his notice. The smaller ones, such as those of the Hemlock, and the Douglas Spruce, and the Two-leaved Pine, he cuts off and eats on a branch of the tree, without allowing them to fall; beginning at the bottom of the cone and cutting away the scales to expose the seeds; not gnawing by guess, like a bear, but turning them round and round in regular order, in compliance with their spiral arrangement.

When thus employed, his location in the tree is betrayed by a dribble of scales, shells, and seed-wings, and, every few minutes, by the fall of the stripped axis of the cone. Then of course he is ready for another, and if you are watching you may catch a glimpse of him as he glides silently out to the end of a branch and see him examining the cone-clusters until he finds one to his mind; then, leaning over, pull back the springy needles out of his way, grasp the cone with his paws to prevent its falling, snip it off in an incredibly short time, seize it with jaws grotesquely stretched, and return to his chosen seat near the trunk. But the immense size of the cones of the Sugar Pine—from fifteen to twenty inches in length—and those of the Jeffrey variety of the Yellow Pine compel him to adopt a quite different method. He cuts them off without attempting to hold

The Douglas Squirrel

them, then goes down and drags them from where they have chanced to fall up to the bare, swelling ground around the instep of the tree, where he demolishes them in the same methodical way, beginning at the bottom and following the scale-spirals to the top.

From a single Sugar Pine cone he gets from two to four hundred seeds about half the size of a hazelnut, so that in a few minutes he can procure enough to last a week. He seems, however, to prefer those of the two Silver Firs above all others; perhaps because they are most easily obtained, as the scales drop off when ripe without needing to be cut. Both species are filled with an exceedingly pungent, aromatic oil, which spices all his flesh, and is of itself sufficient to account for his lightning energy.

You may easily know this little workman by his chips. On sunny hillsides around the principal trees they lie in big piles,—bushels and basketfuls of them, all fresh and clean, making the most beautiful kitchen-middens imaginable. The brown and yellow scales and nut-shells are as abundant and as delicately penciled and tinted as the shells along the sea-shore; while the beautiful red and purple seed-wings mingled with them would lead one to fancy that innumerable butterflies had there met their fate.

He feasts on all the species long before they are ripe, but is wise enough to wait until they are matured before he gathers them into his barns. This is in October and November, which with him are the two busiest months of the year. All kinds of burs, big and little, are now cut off and showered down alike, and the ground is speedily covered with them. A constant thudding and bumping is kept up; some of the larger cones chancing to fall on old logs make the forest reëcho with the sound. Other nut-eaters less industrious know well what is going on, and hasten to carry away the cones as they fall. But however busy the harvester may be, he is not slow to descry the pilferers below, and instantly leaves his work to drive them away. The little striped tamias is a thorn in his flesh, stealing persistently, punish him as he may. The large Gray Squirrel gives trouble also, although the Douglas has been accused of stealing from him. Generally, however, just the opposite is the case.

The excellence of the Sierra evergreens is well known to nurserymen throughout the world, consequently there is considerable demand for the seeds. The greater portion of the supply has hitherto been procured by chopping down the trees in the more accessible sections of the forest alongside of bridle-paths that cross the range. Sequoia seeds at first brought from twenty to thirty dollars per pound, and therefore were eagerly sought after. Some of the smaller fruitful trees were cut down in the groves not protected by government, especially those of Fresno and King's River. Most of the Sequoias, however, are of so gigantic a size that the seedsmen have to look for the greater portion of their supplies to the Douglas, who soon learns he is no match for these freebooters. He is wise enough, however, to cease working the instant he perceives them, and never fails to embrace every opportunity to recover his burs whenever they happen to be stored in any place accessible to him, and the busy seedsman often finds on returning to camp that the little Douglas has exhaustively spoiled the spoiler. I know one seed-gatherer who, whenever he robs the squirrels, scatters wheat or barley beneath the trees as conscience-money.

The want of appreciable life remarked by so many travelers in the Sierra forests is never felt at this time of year. Banish all the humming insects and the birds and quadrupeds, leaving only Sir Douglas, and the most solitary of our so-called solitudes would still throb with ardent life. But if you should go impatiently even into the most populous of the groves on purpose to meet him, and walk about looking up among the branches, you would see very little of him. But lie down at the foot of one of the trees and straightway he will come. For, in the midst of the ordinary forest sounds, the falling of burs, piping of quails, the screaming of the Clark Crow, and the rustling of deer and bears among the chaparral, he is quick to detect your strange footsteps, and will hasten to make a good, close inspec-

The Douglas Squirrel

tion of you as soon as you are still. First, you may hear him sounding a few notes of curious inquiry, but more likely the first intimation of his approach will be the prickly sounds of his feet as he descends the tree overhead, just before he makes his savage onrush to frighten you and proclaim your presence to every squirrel and bird in the neighborhood. If you remain perfectly motionless, he will come nearer and nearer, and probably set your flesh a-tingle by frisking across your body. Once, while I was seated at the foot of a Hemlock Spruce in one of the most inaccessible of the San Joaquin yosemites engaged in sketching, a reckless fellow came up behind me, passed under my bended arm, and jumped on my paper. And one warm afternoon, while an old friend of mine was reading out in the shade of his cabin, one of his Douglas neighbors jumped from the gable upon his head, and then with admirable assurance ran down over his shoulder and on to the book he held in his hand.

Our Douglas enjoys a large social circle; for, besides his numerous relatives, *Sciurus fossor, Tamias quadrivitatus, T. Townsendii, Spermophilus Beecheyi, S. Douglasii,* he maintains intimate relations with the nut-eating birds, particularly the Clark Crow (*Picicorvus columbianus*) and the numerous woodpeckers and jays. The two spermophiles are astonishingly abundant in the lowlands and lower foot-hills, but more and more sparingly distributed up through the Douglas domains,—seldom venturing higher than six or seven thousand feet above the level of the sea. The gray sciurus ranges but little higher than this. The little striped tamias alone is associated with him everywhere. In the lower and middle zones, where they all meet, they are tolerably harmonious—a happy family, though very amusing skirmishes may occasionally be witnessed. Wherever the ancient glaciers have spread forest soil there you find our wee hero, most abundant where depth of soil and genial climate have given rise to a corresponding luxuriance in the trees, but following every kind of growth up the curving moraines to the highest glacial fountains.

Though I cannot of course expect all my readers to sympathize

187

fully in my admiration of this little animal, few, I hope, will think this sketch of his life too long. I cannot begin to tell here how much he has cheered my lonely wanderings during all the years I have been pursuing my studies in these glorious wilds; or how much unmistakable humanity I have found in him. Take this for example: One calm, creamy Indian summer morning, when the nuts were ripe, I was camped in the upper pinewoods of the south fork of the San Joaquin, where the squirrels seemed to be about as plentiful as the ripe burs. They were taking an early breakfast before going to their regular harvest-work. While I was busy with my own breakfast I heard the thudding fall of two or three heavy cones from a Yellow Pine near me. I stole noiselessly forward within about twenty feet of the base of it to observe. In a few moments down came the Douglas. The breakfast-burs he had cut off had rolled on the gently sloping ground into a clump of ceanothus bushes, but he seemed to know exactly where they were, for he found them at once, apparently without searching for them. They were more than twice as heavy as himself, but after turning them into the right position for getting a good hold with his long sickle-teeth he managed to drag them up to the foot of the tree from which he had cut them, moving backward. Then seating himself comfortably, he held them on end, bottom up, and demolished them at his ease. A good deal of nibbling had to be done before he got anything to eat, because the lower scales are barren, but when he had patiently worked his way up to the fertile ones he found two sweet nuts at the base of each, shaped like trimmed hams, and spotted purple like birds' eggs. And notwithstanding these cones were dripping with soft balsam, and covered with prickles, and so strongly put together that a boy would be puzzled to cut them open with a jack-knife, he accomplished his meal with easy dignity and cleanliness, making less effort apparently than a man would in eating soft cookery from a plate.

188

Breakfast done, I whistled a tune for him before he went to work, curious to see how he would be affected by it. He had not seen me

The Douglas Squirrel

all this while; but the instant I began to whistle he darted up the tree nearest to him, and came out on a small dead limb opposite me, and composed himself to listen. I sang and whistled more than a dozen airs, and as the music changed his eyes sparkled, and he turned his head quickly from side to side, but made no other response. Other squirrels, hearing the strange sounds, came around on all sides, also chipmunks and birds. One of the birds, a handsome, speckle-breasted thrush, seemed even more interested than the squirrels. After listening for awhile on one of the lower dead sprays of a pine, he came swooping forward within a few feet of my face, and re-mained fluttering in the air for half a minute or so, sustaining him-self with whirring wing-beats, like a humming-bird in front of a flower, while I could look into his eyes and see his innocent wonder.

By this time my performance must have lasted nearly half an hour. I sang or whistled "Bonnie Doon," "Lass o' Gowrie," "O'er the Water to Charlie," "Bonnie Woods o' Cragie Lee," etc., all of which seemed to be listened to with bright interest, my first Douglas sitting patiently through it all, with his telling eyes fixed upon me until I ventured to give the "Old Hundredth," when he screamed his Indian name, Pillillooeet, turned tail, and darted with ludicrous haste up the tree out of sight, his voice and actions in the case leaving a somewhat profane impression, as if he had said, "I'll be hanged if you get me to hear anything so solemn and unpiny." This acted as a signal for the general dispersal of the whole hairy tribe, though the birds seemed willing to wait further developments, music being nat-urally more in their line.

What there can be in that grand old church-tune that is so offen-sive to birds and squirrels I can't imagine. A year or two after this High Sierra concert, I was sitting one fine day on a hill in the Coast Range where the common Ground Squirrels were abundant. They were very shy on account of being hunted so much; but after I had been silent and motionless for half an hour or so they began to venture out of their holes and to feed on the seeds of the grasses and thistles around me as if I were no more to be feared than a tree-stump. Then it occurred to me that this was a good opportunity to find out whether they also disliked "Old Hundredth." Therefore I began to whistle as nearly as I could remember the same familiar airs that had pleased the mountaineers of the Sierra. They at once stopped eating, stood erect, and listened patiently until I came to "Old Hundredth," when with ludicrous haste every one of them rushed to their holes and bolted in, their feet twinkling in the air for a moment as they vanished.

No one who makes the acquaintance of our forester will fail to admire him; but he is far too self-reliant and warlike ever to be taken for a darling.

How long the life of a Douglas Squirrel may be, I don't know. The young seem to sprout from knot-holes, perfect from the first, and as enduring as their own trees. It is difficult, indeed, to realize that so condensed a piece of sun-fire should ever become dim or die at all. He is seldom killed by hunters, for he is too small to encourage much of their attention, and when pursued in settled regions becomes excessively shy, and keeps close in the furrows of the highest trunks, many of which are of the same color as himself. Indian boys, however, lie in wait with unbounded patience to shoot them with arrows. In the lower and middle zones a few fall a prey to rattle-snakes. Occasionally he is pursued by hawks and wildcats, etc. But, upon the whole, he dwells safely in the deep bosom of the woods, the most highly favored of all his happy tribe. May his tribe increase!

Hetch Hetchy Valley

Yosemite is so wonderful that we are apt to regard it as an exceptional creation, the only valley of its kind in the world; but Nature is not so poor as to have only one of anything. Several other yosemites have been discovered in the Sierra that occupy the same relative positions on the Range and were formed by the same forces in the same kind of granite. One of these, the Hetch Hetchy Valley, is in the Yosemite National Park about twenty miles from Yosemite and is easily accessible to all sorts of travelers by a road and trail that leaves the Big Oak Flat road at Bronson Meadows a few miles below Crane Flat, and to mountaineers by way of Yosemite Creek basin and the head of the middle fork of the Tuolumne.

It is said to have been discovered by Joseph Screech, a hunter, in 1850, a year before the discovery of the great Yosemite. After my first visit to it in the autumn of 1871, I have always called it the "Tuolumne Yosemite," for it is a wonderfully exact counterpart of the Merced Yosemite, not only in its sublime rocks and waterfalls but in the gardens, groves and meadows of its flowery park-like floor. The floor of Yosemite is about 4000 feet above the sea; the Hetch Hetchy floor about 3700 feet. And as the Merced River flows through Yosemite, so does the Tuolumne through Hetch Hetchy. The walls of both are of gray granite, rise abruptly from the floor, are sculptured in the same style and in both every rock is a glacier monument.

Standing boldly out from the south wall is a strikingly picturesque rock called by the Indians, Kolana, the outermost of a group 2300 feet high, corresponding with the Cathedral Rocks of Yosemite both in relative position and form. On the opposite side of the Valley, facing Kolana, there is a counterpart of the El Capitan that rises sheer and plain to a height of 1800 feet, and over its massive brow flows a stream which makes the most graceful fall I have ever seen. From the edge of the cliff to the top of an earthquake talus it is perfectly free in the air for a thousand feet before it is broken into cascades among talus boulders. It is in all its glory in June, when the snow is melting fast, but fades and vanishes toward the end of summer. The only fall I know with which it may fairly be compared is the Yosemite Bridal Veil; but it excels even that favorite fall both in height and airy-fairy beauty and behavior. Lowlanders are apt to suppose that mountain streams in their wild career over cliffs lose control of themselves and tumble in a noisy chaos of mist and spray. On the contrary, on no part of their travels are they more harmonious and self-controlled. Imagine yourself in Hetch Hetchy on a sunny day in June, standing waist-deep in grass and flowers (as I have often stood), while the great pines sway dreamily with scarcely perceptible motion. Looking northward across the Valley you see a plain, gray granite cliff rising abruptly out of the gardens and groves to a height of 1800 feet, and in front of it Tueeulala's silvery scarf burning with irised sun-fire. In the first white outburst at the head there is abundance of visible energy, but it is speedily hushed and concealed in divine repose, and its tranquil progress to the base of the cliff is like that of a downy feather in a still room. Now observe the fineness and marvelous distinctness of the various sun-illumined fabrics into which the water is woven; they sift and float from form to form down the face of that grand gray rock in so leisurely and unconfused a manner that you can examine their texture, and patterns and tones of color as you would a piece of embroidery held in the hand. Toward the top of the fall you see groups of booming, comet-like masses, their solid, white heads separate, their tails like combed silk interlacing among delicate gray and purple shadows, ever forming and dissolving, worn out by friction in their rush through the air. Most of these vanish a few hundred feet below the summit, changing to varied forms of cloud-like drapery. Near the bottom the width of the fall has increased from about twenty-five feet to a hundred feet. Here it is composed of yet finer tissues, and is still without a trace of disorder—air, water and sunlight woven into stuff that spirits might wear.

So fine a fall might well seem sufficient to glorify any valley; but here, as in Yosemite, Nature seems in nowise moderate, for a short distance to the eastward of Tueeulala booms and thunders the great Hetch Hetchy Fall, Wapama, so near that you have both of them in full view from the same standpoint. It is the counterpart of the Yosemite Fall, but has a much greater volume of water, is about 1700 feet in height, and appears to be nearly vertical, though considerably inclined, and is dashed into huge outbounding bosses of foam on projecting shelves and knobs. No two falls could be more unlike—Tueeulala out in the open sunshine descending like thistledown; Wapama in a jagged, shadowy gorge roaring and thundering, pounding its way like an earthquake avalanche.

Besides this glorious pair there is a broad, massive fall on the main river a short distance above the head of the Valley. Its position is something like that of the Vernal in Yosemite, and its roar as it plunges into a surging trout-pool may be heard a long way, though it is only about twenty feet high. On Rancheria Creek, a large stream, corresponding in position with the Yosemite Tenaya Creek, there is a chain of cascades joined here and there with swift flashing plumes like the one between the Vernal and Nevada Falls, making magnificent shows as they go their glacier-sculptured way, sliding, leaping, hurrahing, covered with crisp clashing spray made glorious with sifting sunshine. And besides all these a few small streams come over the walls at wide intervals, leaping from ledge to ledge with birdlike song and watering many a hidden cliff-garden and fernery, but they are too unshowy to be noticed in so grand a place.

The correspondence between the Hetch Hetchy walls in their trends, sculpture, physical structure, and general arrangement of the main rock-masses and those of the Yosemite Valley has excited the wondering admiration of every observer. We have seen that the El Capitan and Cathedral rocks occupy the same relative positions in both valleys; so also do their Yosemite points and North Domes. Again, that part of the Yosemite north wall immediately to the east of the Yosemite Fall has two horizontal benches, about 500 and 1500 feet above the floor, timbered with golden-cup oak. Two benches similarly situated and timbered occur on the same relative portion of the Hetch Hetchy north wall, to the east of Wapama Fall, and on no other. The Yosemite is bounded at the head by the great Half Dome. Hetch Hetchy is bounded in the same way, though its head rock is incomparably less wonderful and sublime in form.

The floor of the Valley is about three and a half miles long, and from a fourth to half a mile wide. The lower portion is mostly a level meadow about a mile long, with the trees restricted to the sides and the river banks, and partially separated from the main, upper, forested portion by a low bar of glacier-polished granite across which the river breaks in rapids.

The principal trees are the yellow and sugar pines, digger pine, incense cedar, Douglas spruce, silver fir, the California and golden-cup oaks, balsam cottonwood, Nuttall's flowering dogwood, alder, maple, laurel, tumion, etc. The most abundant and influential are the great yellow or silver pines like those of Yosemite, the tallest over two hundred feet in height, and the oaks assembled in magnificent groves with massive rugged trunks four to six feet in diameter, and broad, shady, wide-spreading heads. The shrubs forming conspicuous flowery clumps and tangles are manzanita, azalea, spiraea, brier-rose, several species of ceanothus, calycanthus, philadelphus, wild cherry, etc.; with abundance of showy and fragrant herbaceous

Hetch Hetchy Valley

plants growing about them or out in the open in beds by themselves —lilies, Mariposa tulips, brodiaeas, orchids, iris, spraguea, draperia, collomia, collinsia, castilleja, nemophila, larkspur, columbine, goldenrods, sunflowers, mints of many species, honeysuckle, etc. Many fine ferns dwell here also, especially the beautiful and interesting rock-ferns—pellaea, and cheilanthes of several species—fringing and rosetting dry rock-piles and ledges; woodwardia and asplenium on damp spots with fronds six or seven feet high; the delicate maidenhair in mossy nooks by the falls, and the sturdy, broad-shouldered pteris covering nearly all the dry ground beneath the oaks and pines.

It appears, therefore, that Hetch Hetchy Valley, far from being a plain, common, rock-bound meadow, as many who have not seen it seem to suppose, is a grand landscape garden, one of Nature's rarest and most precious mountain temples. As in Yosemite, the sublime rocks of its walls seem to glow with life, whether leaning back in repose or standing erect in thoughtful attitudes, giving welcome to storms and calms alike, their brows in the sky, their feet set in the groves and gay flowery meadows, while birds, bees, and butterflies help the river and waterfalls to stir all the air into music—things frail and fleeting and types of permanence meeting here and blending, just as they do in Yosemite, to draw her lovers into close and confiding communion with her.

Sad to say, this most precious and sublime feature of the Yosemite National Park, one of the greatest of all our natural resources for the uplifting joy and peace and health of the people, is in danger of being dammed and made into a reservoir to help supply San Francisco with water and light, thus flooding it from wall to wall and burying its gardens and groves one or two hundred feet deep. This grossly destructive commercial scheme has long been planned and urged (though water as pure and abundant can be got from outside of the people's park, in a dozen different places), because of the comparative cheapness of the dam and of the territory which it is sought to divert from the great uses to which it was dedicated in the Act of 1890 establishing the Yosemite National Park.

The making of gardens and parks goes on with civilization all over the world, and they increase both in size and number as their value is recognized. Everybody needs beauty as well as bread, places to play in and pray in, where Nature may heal and cheer and give strength to body and soul alike. This natural beauty-hunger is made manifest in the little window-sill gardens of the poor, though perhaps only a geranium slip in a broken cup, as well as in the carefully tended rose and lily gardens of the rich, the thousands of spacious city parks and botanical gardens, and in our magnificent National parks—the Yellowstone, Yosemite, Sequoia, etc.—Nature's sublime wonderlands, the admiration and joy of the world. Nevertheless, like anything else worth while, from the very beginning, however well guarded, they have always been subject to attack by despoiling gainseekers and mischiefmakers of every degree from Satan to Senators, eagerly trying to make everything immediately and selfishly commercial, with schemes disguised in smug-smiling philanthropy, industriously, shampiously crying, "Conservation, conservation, panutilization," that man and beast may be fed and the dear Nation made great. Thus long ago a few enterprising merchants utilized the Jerusalem temple as a place of business instead of a place of prayer, changing money, buying and selling cattle and sheep and doves; and earlier still, the first forest reservation, including only one tree, was likewise despoiled. Ever since the establishment of the Yosemite National Park, strife has been going on around its borders and I suppose this will go on as part of the universal battle between right and wrong, however much its boundaries may be shorn, or its wild beauty destroyed.

The first application to the Government by the San Francisco Supervisors for the commercial use of Lake Eleanor and the Hetch Hetchy Valley was made in 1903, and on December 22nd of that year

Hetch Hetchy Valley

it was denied by the Secretary of the Interior, Mr. Hitchcock, who truthfully said:

> Presumably the Yosemite National Park was created such by law because of the natural objects of varying degrees of scenic importance located within its boundaries, inclusive alike of its beautiful small lakes, like Eleanor, and its majestic wonders, like Hetch Hetchy and Yosemite Valley. It is the aggregation of such natural scenic features that makes the Yosemite Park a wonderland which the Congress of the United States sought by law to reserve for all coming time as nearly as practicable in the condition fashioned by the hand of the Creator—a worthy object of national pride and a source of healthful pleasure and rest for the thousands of people who may annually sojourn there during the heated months.

In 1907 when Mr. Garfield became Secretary of the Interior the application was renewed and granted; but under his successor, Mr. Fisher, the matter has been referred to a Commission, which as this volume goes to press still has it under consideration.

The most delightful and wonderful camp grounds in the Park are its three great valleys—Yosemite, Hetch Hetchy, and Upper Tuolumne; and they are also the most important places with reference to their positions relative to the other great features—the Merced and Tuolumne Cañons, and the High Sierra peaks and glaciers, etc., at the head of the rivers. The main part of the Tuolumne Valley is a spacious flowery lawn four or five miles long, surrounded by magnificent snowy mountains, slightly separated from other beautiful meadows, which together make a series about twelve miles in length, the highest reaching to the feet of Mount Dana, Mount Gibbs, Mount Lyell and Mount McClure. It is about 8500 feet above the sea, and forms the grand central High Sierra camp ground from which excursions are made to the noble mountains, domes, glaciers, etc.; across the Range to the Mono Lake and volcanoes and down the Tuolumne Cañon to Hetch Hetchy. Should Hetch Hetchy be submerged for a reservoir, as proposed, not only would it be utterly destroyed, but the sublime cañon way to the heart of the High Sierra would be hopelessly blocked and the great camping ground, as the watershed of a city drinking system, virtually would be closed to the public. So far as I have learned, few of all the thousands who have seen the park and seek rest and peace in it are in favor of this outrageous scheme.

One of my later visits to the Valley was made in the autumn of 1907 with the late William Keith, the artist. The leaf-colors were then ripe, and the great godlike rocks in repose seemed to glow with life. The artist, under their spell, wandered day after day along the river and through the groves and gardens, studying the wonderful scenery; and, after making about forty sketches, declared with enthusiasm that although its walls were less sublime in height, in picturesque beauty and charm Hetch Hetchy surpassed even Yosemite.

That any one would try to destroy such a place seems incredible; but sad experience shows that there are people good enough and bad enough for anything. The proponents of the dam scheme bring forward a lot of bad arguments to prove that the only righteous thing to do with the people's parks is to destroy them bit by bit as they are able. Their arguments are curiously like those of the devil, devised for the destruction of the first garden—so much of the very best Eden fruit going to waste; so much of the best Tuolumne water and Tuolumne scenery going to waste. Few of their statements are even partly true, and all are misleading.

Thus, Hetch Hetchy, they say, is a "low-lying meadow." On the contrary, it is a high-lying natural landscape garden, as the photographic illustrations show.

"It is a common minor feature, like thousands of others." On the contrary it is a very uncommon feature; after Yosemite, the rarest and in many ways the most important in the National Park.

"Damming and submerging it 175 feet deep would enhance its beauty by forming a crystal-clear lake." Landscape gardens, places of recreation and worship, are never made beautiful by destroying and burying them. The beautiful sham lake, forsooth, would be only an eyesore, a dismal blot on the landscape, like many others to be seen in the Sierra. For, instead of keeping it at the same level all the year, allowing Nature centuries of time to make new shores, it would, of course, be full only a month or two in the spring, when the snow is melting fast; then it would be gradually drained, exposing the slimy sides of the basin and shallower parts of the bottom, with the gathered drift and waste, death and decay of the upper basins, caught here instead of being swept on to decent natural burial along the banks of the river or in the sea. Thus the Hetch Hetchy dam-lake would be only a rough imitation of a natural lake for a few of the spring months, an open sepulcher for the others.

"Hetch Hetchy water is the purest of all to be found in the Sierra, unpolluted, and forever unpollutable." On the contrary, excepting that of the Merced below Yosemite, it is less pure than that of most of the other Sierra streams, because of the sewerage of camp grounds draining into it, especially of the Big Tuolumne Meadows camp ground, occupied by hundreds of tourists and mountaineers, with their animals, for months every summer, soon to be followed by thousands from all the world.

These temple destroyers, devotees of ravaging commercialism, seem to have a perfect contempt for Nature, and, instead of lifting their eyes to the God of the mountains, lift them to the Almighty Dollar.

Dam Hetch Hetchy! As well dam for water-tanks the people's cathedrals and churches, for no holier temple has ever been consecrated by the heart of man.

The American Forests

The forests of America, however slighted by man, must have been a great delight to God; for they were the best he ever planted. The whole continent was a garden, and from the beginning it seemed to be favored above all the other wild parks and gardens of the globe. To prepare the ground, it was rolled and sifted in seas with infinite loving deliberation and forethought, lifted into the light, submerged and warmed over and over again, pressed and crumpled into folds and ridges, mountains, and hills, subsoiled with heaving volcanic fires, ploughed and ground and sculptured into scenery and soil with glaciers and rivers—every feature growing and changing from beauty to beauty, higher and higher. And in the fullness of time it was planted in groves, and belts, and broad, exuberant, mantling forests, with the largest, most varied, most fruitful, and most beautiful trees in the world. Bright seas made its border, with wave embroidery and icebergs; gray deserts were outspread in the middle of it, mossy tundras on the north, savannas on the south, and blooming prairies and plains; while lakes and rivers shone through all the vast forests and openings, and happy birds and beasts gave delightful animation. Everywhere, everywhere over all the blessed continent, there were beauty and melody and kindly, wholesome, foodful abundance.

These forests were composed of about five hundred species of trees, all of them in some way useful to man, ranging in size from twenty-five feet in height and less than one foot in diameter at the ground to four hundred feet in height and more than twenty feet in diameter—lordly monarchs proclaiming the gospel of beauty like apostles. For many a century after the ice-ploughs were melted, Nature fed them and dressed them every day—working like a man, a loving, devoted, painstaking gardener; fingering every leaf and flower and mossy furrowed bole; bending, trimming, modeling, balancing; painting them with the loveliest colors; bringing over them now clouds with cooling shadows and showers, now sunshine; fanning them with gentle winds and rustling their leaves; exercising them in every fibre with storms, and pruning them; loading them with flowers and fruit, loading them with snow, and ever making them more beautiful as the years rolled by. Wide-branching oak and elm in endless variety, walnut and maple, chestnut and beech, ilex and locust, touching limb to limb, spread a leafy translucent canopy along the coast of the Atlantic over the wrinkled folds and ridges of the Alleghenies—a green billowy sea in summer, golden and purple in autumn, pearly gray like a steadfast frozen mist of interlacing branches and sprays in leafless, restful winter.

To the southward stretched dark, level-topped cypresses in knobby, tangled swamps, grassy savannas in the midst of them like lakes of light, groves of gay, sparkling spice-trees, magnolias and palms, glossy-leaved and blooming and shining continually. To the northward, over Maine and Ottawa, rose hosts of spiry, rosiny evergreens—white pine and spruce, hemlock and cedar, shoulder to shoulder, laden with purple cones, their myriad needles sparkling and shimmering, covering hills and swamps, rocky headlands and domes, ever bravely aspiring and seeking the sky; the ground in their shade now snow-clad and frozen, now mossy and flowery; beaver meadows here and there, full of lilies and grass; lakes gleaming like eyes, and a silvery embroidery of rivers and creeks watering and brightening all the vast glad wilderness.

The American Forests

Thence westward were oak and elm, hickory and tupelo, gum and liriodendron, sassafras and ash, linden and laurel, spreading on ever wider in glorious exuberance over the great fertile basin of the Mississippi, over damp level bottoms, low dimpling hollows, and round dotting hills, embosoming sunny prairies and cheery park openings, half sunshine, half shade; while a dark wilderness of pines covered the region around the Great Lakes. Thence still westward swept the forests to right and left around grassy plains and deserts a thousand miles wide: irrepressible hosts of spruce and pine, aspen and willow, nut-pine and juniper, cactus and yucca, caring nothing for drought, extending undaunted from mountain to mountain, over mesa and desert, to join the darkening multitudes of pines that covered the high Rocky ranges and the glorious forests along the coast of the moist and balmy Pacific, where new species of pine, giant cedars and spruces, silver firs and Sequoias, kings of their race, growing close together like grass in a meadow, poised their brave domes and spires in the sky, three hundred feet above the ferns and the lilies that enameled the ground; towering serene through the long centuries, preaching God's forestry fresh from heaven.

Here the forests reached their highest development. Hence they went wavering northward over icy Alaska, brave spruce and fir, poplar and birch, by the coasts and the rivers, to within sight of the Arctic Ocean. American forests! the glory of the world! Surveyed thus from the east to the west, from the north to the south, they are rich beyond thought, immortal, immeasurable, enough and to spare for every feeding, sheltering beast and bird, insect and son of Adam; and nobody need have cared had there been no pines in Norway, no cedars and deodars in Lebanon and the Himalayas, no vine-clad selvas in the basin of the Amazon. With such variety, harmony, and triumphant exuberance, even Nature, it would seem, might have rested content with the forests of North America, and planted no more.

So they appeared a few centuries ago when they were rejoicing in wildness. The Indians with stone axes could do them no more harm than could gnawing beavers and browsing moose. Even the fires of the Indians and the fierce shattering lightning seemed to work together only for good in clearing spots here and there for smooth garden prairies, and openings for sunflowers seeking the light. But when the steel axe of the white man rang out on the startled air their doom was sealed. Every tree heard the bodeful sound, and pillars of smoke gave the sign in the sky.

I suppose we need not go mourning the buffaloes. In the nature of things they had to give place to better cattle, though the change might have been made without barbarous wickedness. Likewise many of Nature's five hundred kinds of wild trees had to make way for orchards and cornfields. In the settlement and civilization of the country, bread more than timber or beauty was wanted; and in the blindness of hunger, the early settlers, claiming Heaven as their guide, regarded God's trees as only a larger kind of pernicious weed, extremely hard to get rid of. Accordingly, with no eye to the future, these pious destroyers waged interminable forest wars; chips flew thick and fast; trees in their beauty fell crashing by millions, smashed to confusion, and the smoke of their burning has been rising to heaven more than two hundred years. After the Atlantic coast from Maine to Georgia had been mostly cleared and scorched into melancholy ruins, the overflowing multitude of bread and money seekers poured over the Alleghenies into the fertile middle West, spreading ruthless devastation ever wider and farther over the rich valley of the Mississippi and the vast shadowy pine region about the Great Lakes. Thence still westward, the invading horde of destroyers called settlers made its fiery way over the broad Rocky Mountains, felling and burning more fiercely than ever, until at last it has reached the wild side of the continent, and entered the last of the great aboriginal forests on the shores of the Pacific.

Surely, then, it should not be wondered at that lovers of their country, bewailing its baldness, are now crying aloud, "Save what is left of the forests!" Clearing has surely now gone far enough; soon timber will be scarce, and not a grove will be left to rest in or pray in. The remnant protected will yield plenty of timber, a perennial harvest for every right use, without further diminution of its area, and will continue to cover the springs of the rivers that rise in the mountains and give irrigating waters to the dry valleys at their feet, prevent wasting floods, and be a blessing to everybody forever.

Every other civilized nation in the world has been compelled to care for its forests, and so must we if waste and destruction are not to go on to the bitter end, leaving America as barren as Palestine or Spain. In its calmer moments, in the midst of bewildering hunger and war and restless over-industry, Prussia has learned that the forest plays an important part in human progress, and that the advance in civilization only makes it more indispensable. It has, therefore, as shown by Mr. Pinchot, refused to deliver its forests to more or less speedy destruction by permitting them to pass into private ownership. But the state woodlands are not allowed to lie idle. On the contrary, they are made to produce as much timber as is possible without spoiling them. In the administration of its forests, the state righteously considers itself bound to treat them as a trust for the nation as a whole, and to keep in view the common good of the people for all time.

In France no government forests have been sold since 1870. On the other hand, about one half of the fifty million francs spent on forestry has been given to engineering works, to make the replanting of denuded areas possible. The disappearance of the forests in the first place, it is claimed, may be traced in most cases directly to mountain pasturage. The provisions of the Code concerning private woodlands are substantially these: no private owner may clear his woodlands without giving notice to the government at least four months in advance, and the forest service may forbid the clearing on the following grounds—to maintain the soil on mountains, to defend the soil against erosion and flooding by rivers or torrents, to insure the existence of springs or watercourses, to protect the dunes and sea-shore, etc. A proprietor who has cleared his forest without permission is subject to heavy fine, and in addition may be made to replant the cleared area.

In Switzerland, after many laws like our own had been found wanting, the Swiss forest school was established in 1865, and soon after the federal forest law was enacted, which is binding over nearly two thirds of the country. Under its provisions, the cantons must appoint and pay the number of suitably educated foresters required for the fulfillment of the forest law; and in the organization of a normally stocked forest, the object of first importance must be the cutting each year of an amount of timber equal to the total annual increase, and no more.

The Russian government passed a law in 1888, declaring that clearing is forbidden in protected forests, and is allowed in others "only when its effects will not be to disturb the suitable relations which should exist between forest and agricultural lands."

Even Japan is ahead of us in the management of her forests. They cover an area of about twenty-nine million acres. The feudal lords valued the woodlands, and enacted vigorous protective laws; and when, in the latest civil war, the Mikado government destroyed the feudal system, it declared the forests that had belonged to the feudal lords to be the property of the state, promulgated a forest law binding on the whole kingdom, and founded a school of forestry in Tokyo. The forest service does not rest satisfied with the present proportion of woodland, but looks to planting the best forest trees it can find in any country, if likely to be useful and to thrive in Japan.

In India systematic forest management was begun about forty years ago, under difficulties—presented by the character of the country, the prevalence of running fires, opposition from lumber-men, settlers, etc.—not unlike those which confront us now. Of the total area of government forests, perhaps seventy million acres, fifty-five million acres have been brought under the control of the forestry department—a larger area than that of all our national parks and reservations. The chief aims of the administration are effective protection of the forests from fire, an efficient system of regeneration, and cheap transportation of the forest products; the results so far have been most beneficial and encouraging.

It seems, therefore, that almost every civilized nation can give us a lesson on the management and care of forests. So far our government has done nothing effective with its forests, though the best in the world, but is like a rich and foolish spendthrift who has inherited a magnificent estate in perfect order, and then has left his fields and meadows, forests and parks, to be sold and plundered and wasted at will, depending on their inexhaustible abundance. Now it is plain that the forests are not inexhaustible, and that quick measures must be taken if ruin is to be avoided. Year by year the remnant is growing smaller before the axe and fire, while the laws in existence provide neither for the protection of the timber from destruction nor for its use where it is most needed.

As is shown by Mr. E. A. Bowers, formerly Inspector of the Public Land Service, the foundation of our protective policy, which has never protected, is an act passed March 1, 1817, which authorized the Secretary of the Navy to reserve lands producing live-oak and cedar, for the sole purpose of supplying timber for the navy of the United States. An extension of this law by the passage of the act of March 2, 1831, provided that if any person should cut live-oak or red cedar trees or *other timber* from the lands of the United States for any other purpose than the construction of the navy, such person should pay a fine not less than triple the value of the timber cut, and be imprisoned for a period not exceeding twelve months. Upon this old law, as Mr. Bowers points out, having the construction of a wooden navy in view, the United States government has to-day chiefly to rely in protecting its timber throughout the arid regions of the West, where none of the naval timber which the law had in mind is to be found.

By the act of June 3, 1878, timber can be taken from public lands not subject to entry under any existing laws except for minerals, by *bona fide* residents of the Rocky Mountain states and territories and the Dakotas. Under the timber and stone act, of the same date, land in the Pacific States and Nevada, valuable mainly for timber, and unfit for cultivation if the timber is removed, can be purchased for two dollars and a half an acre, under certain restrictions. By the act of March 3, 1875, all land-grant and right-of-way railroads are authorized to take timber from the public lands adjacent to their lines for construction purposes; and they have taken it with a vengeance, destroying a hundred times more than they have used, mostly by allowing fires to run in the woods. The settlement laws, under which a settler may enter lands valuable for timber as well as for agriculture, furnish another means of obtaining title to public timber.

With the exception of the timber culture act, under which, in consideration of planting a few acres of seedlings, settlers on the treeless plains got 160 acres each, the above is the only legislation aiming to protect and promote the planting of forests. In no other way than under some one of these laws can a citizen of the United States make any use of the public forests. To show the results of the timber-planting act, it need only be stated that of the thirty-eight million acres entered under it, less than one million acres have been patented. This means that less than fifty thousand acres have been planted with stunted, woebegone, almost hopeless sprouts of trees, while at the same time the government has allowed millions of acres of the grandest forest trees to be stolen or destroyed, or sold for nothing. Under the act of June 3, 1878, settlers in Colorado and the Territories were allowed to cut timber for mining and educational purposes from mineral land, which in the practical West means both cutting and burning anywhere and everywhere, for any purpose, on any sort of public land. Thus, the prospector, the miner, and mining and railroad companies are allowed by law to take all the timber they like for their mines and roads, and the forbidden settler, if there are

208

no mineral lands near his farm or stock-ranch, or none that he knows of, can hardly be expected to forbear taking what he needs wherever he can find it. Timber is as necessary as bread, and no scheme of management failing to recognize and properly provide for this want can possibly be maintained. In any case, it will be hard to teach the pioneers that it is wrong to steal government timber. Taking from the government is with them the same as taking from Nature, and their consciences flinch no more in cutting timber from the wild forests than in drawing water from a lake or river. As for reservation and protection of forests, it seems as silly and needless to them as protection and reservation of the ocean would be, both appearing to be boundless and inexhaustible.

The special land agents employed by the General Land Office to protect the public domain from timber depredations are supposed to collect testimony to sustain prosecution and to superintend such prosecution on behalf of the government, which is represented by the district attorneys. But timber thieves of the Western class are seldom convicted, for the good reason that most of the jurors who try such cases are themselves as guilty as those on trial. The effect of the present confused, discriminating, and unjust system has been to place almost the whole population in opposition to the government; and as conclusive of its futility, as shown by Mr. Bowers, we need only state that during the seven years from 1881 to 1887 inclusive, the value of the timber reported stolen from the government lands was $36,719,935, and the amount recovered was $478,073, while the cost of the services of special agents alone was $455,000, to which must be added the expense of the trials. Thus for nearly thirty-seven million dollars' worth of timber the government got less than nothing; and the value of that consumed by running fires during the same period, without benefit even to thieves, was probably over two hundred millions of dollars. Land commissioners and Secretaries of the Interior have repeatedly called attention to this ruinous state of affairs, and asked Congress to enact the requisite legislation for reasonable reform. But, busied with tariffs, etc., Congress has given no heed to these or other appeals, and our forests, the most valuable and the most destructible of all the natural resources of the country, are being robbed and burned more rapidly than ever. The annual appropriation for so-called "protection service" is hardly sufficient to keep twenty-five timber agents in the field, and as far as any efficient protection of timber is concerned these agents themselves might as well be timber.

That a change from robbery and ruin to a permanent rational policy is urgently needed nobody with the slightest knowledge of American forests will deny. In the East and along the northern Pacific coast, where the rainfall is abundant, comparatively few care keenly what becomes of the trees so long as fuel and lumber are not noticeably dear. But in the Rocky Mountains and California and Arizona, where the forests are inflammable, and where the fertility of the lowlands depends upon irrigation, public opinion is growing stronger every year in favor of permanent protection by the federal government of all the forests that cover the sources of the streams. Even lumbermen in these regions, long accustomed to steal, are now willing and anxious to buy lumber for their mills under cover of law: some possibly from a late second growth of honesty, but most, especially the small mill-owners, simply because it no longer pays to steal where all may not only steal, but also destroy, and in particular because it costs about as much to steal timber for one mill as for ten, and, therefore, the ordinary lumberman can no longer compete with the large corporations. Many of the miners find that timber is already becoming scarce and dear on the denuded hills around their mills, and they, too, are asking for protection of forests, at least against fire. The slow-going, unthrifty farmers, also, are beginning to realize that when the timber is stripped from the mountains the irrigating streams dry up in summer, and are destructive in winter; that soil, scenery, and everything slips off with the trees: so of course they are coming into the ranks of tree-friends.

The American Forests

Of all the magnificent coniferous forests around the Great Lakes, once the property of the United States, scarcely any belong to it now. They have disappeared in lumber and smoke, mostly smoke, and the government got not one cent for them; only the land they were growing on was considered valuable, and two and a half dollars an acre was charged for it. Here and there in the Southern States there are still considerable areas of timbered government land, but these are comparatively unimportant. Only the forests of the West are significant in size and value, and these, although still great, are rapidly vanishing. Last summer, of the unrivaled redwood forests of the Pacific Coast Range, the United States Forestry Commission could not find a single quarter-section that remained in the hands of the government.

Under the timber and stone act of 1878, which might well have been called the "dust and ashes act," any citizen of the United States could take up to one hundred and sixty acres of timber land, and by paying two dollars and a half an acre for it obtain title. There was some virtuous effort made with a view to limit the operations of the act by requiring that the purchaser should make affidavit that he was entering the land exclusively for his own use, and by not allowing any association to enter more than one hundred and sixty acres. Nevertheless, under this act wealthy corporations have fraudulently obtained title to from ten thousand to twenty thousand acres or more. The plan was usually as follows: A mill company, desirous of getting title to a large body of redwood or sugar-pine land, first blurred the eyes and ears of the land agents, and then hired men to enter the land they wanted, and immediately deed it to the company after a nominal compliance with the law; false swearing in the wilderness against the government being held of no account. In one case which came under the observation of Mr. Bowers, it was the practice of a lumber company to hire the entire crew of every vessel which might happen to touch at any port in the redwood belt, to enter one hundred and sixty acres each and immediately deed the land to the company, in consideration of the company's paying all expenses and giving the jolly sailors fifty dollars apiece for their trouble.

By such methods have our magnificent redwoods and much of the sugar-pine forests of the Sierra Nevada been absorbed by foreign and resident capitalists. Uncle Sam is not often called a fool in business matters, yet he has sold millions of acres of timber land at two dollars and a half an acre on which a single tree was worth more than a hundred dollars. But this priceless land has been patented, and nothing can be done now about the crazy bargain. According to the everlasting law of righteousness, even the fraudulent buyers at less than one per cent of its value are making little or nothing, on account of fierce competition. The trees are felled, and about half of each giant is left on the ground to be converted into smoke and ashes; the better half is sawed into choice lumber and sold to citizens of the United States or to foreigners: thus robbing the country of its glory and impoverishing it without right benefit to anybody—a bad, black business from beginning to end.

The redwood is one of the few conifers that sprout from the stump and roots, and it declares itself willing to begin immediately to repair the damage of lumberman and also that of the forest-burner. As soon as a redwood is cut down or burned it sends up a crowd of eager, hopeful shoots, which, if allowed to grow, would in a few decades attain a height of a hundred feet, and the strongest of them would finally become giants as great as the original tree. Gigantic second and third growth trees are found in the redwoods, forming magnificent temple-like circles around charred ruins more than a thousand years old. But not one denuded acre in a hundred is allowed to raise a new forest growth. On the contrary, all the brains, religion, and superstition of the neighborhood are brought into play to prevent a new growth. The sprouts from the roots and stumps are cut off again and again, with zealous concern as to the best time and method of making death sure. In the clearings of one of the largest mills on the coast we found thirty men at work, last summer, cutting off redwood shoots "in the dark of the moon," claiming that all the stumps and roots cleared at this auspicious time would send up no more shoots. Anyhow, these vigorous, almost immortal trees are killed at last, and black stumps are now their only monuments over most of the chopped and burned areas.

The redwood is the glory of the Coast Range. It extends along the western slope, in a nearly continuous belt about ten miles wide, from beyond the Oregon boundary to the south of Santa Cruz, a distance of nearly four hundred miles, and in massive, sustained grandeur and closeness of growth surpasses all the other timber woods of the world. Trees from ten to fifteen feet in diameter and three hundred feet high are not uncommon, and a few attain a height of three hundred and fifty feet or even four hundred, with a diameter at the base of fifteen to twenty feet or more, while the ground beneath them is a garden of fresh, exuberant ferns, lilies, gaultheria, and rhododendron. This grand tree, Sequoia sempervirens, is surpassed in size only by its near relative, Sequoia gigantea, or Big Tree, of the Sierra Nevada, if, indeed, it is surpassed. The sempervirens is certainly the taller of the two. The gigantea attains a greater girth, and is heavier, more noble in port, and more sublimely beautiful. These two Sequoias are all that are known to exist in the world, though in former geological times the genus was common and had many species. The redwood is restricted to the Coast Range, and the Big Tree to the Sierra.

As timber the redwood is too good to live. The largest sawmills ever built are busy along its seaward border, "with all the modern improvements," but so immense is the yield per acre it will be long ere the supply is exhausted. The Big Tree is also, to some extent, being made into lumber. It is far less abundant than the redwood, and is, fortunately, less accessible, extending along the western flank of the Sierra in a partially interrupted belt, about two hundred and fifty miles long, at a height of from four to eight thousand feet above the sea. The enormous logs, too heavy to handle, are blasted into manageable dimensions with gunpowder. A large portion of the best timber is thus shattered and destroyed, and, with the huge, knotty tops, is left in ruins for tremendous fires that kill every tree within their range, great and small. Still, the species is not in danger of extinction. It has been planted and is flourishing over a great part of Europe, and magnificent sections of the aboriginal forests have been reserved as national and State parks—the Mariposa Sequoia Grove, near Yosemite, managed by the State of California, and the General Grant and Sequoia national parks on the Kings, Kaweah, and Tule rivers, efficiently guarded by a small troop of United States cavalry under the direction of the Secretary of the Interior. But there is not a single specimen of the redwood in any national park. Only by gift or purchase, so far as I know, can the government get back into its possession a single acre of this wonderful forest.

The legitimate demands on the forests that have passed into private ownership, as well as those in the hands of the government, are increasing every year with the rapid settlement and upbuilding of the country, but the methods of lumbering are as yet grossly wasteful. In most mills only the best portions of the best trees are used, while the ruins are left on the ground to feed great fires, which kill much of what is left of the less desirable timber, together with the seedlings, on which the permanence of the forest depends. Thus every mill is a centre of destruction far more severe from waste and fire than from use. The same thing is true of the mines, which consume and destroy indirectly immense quantities of timber with their innumerable fires, accidental or set to make open ways, and often without regard to how far they run. The prospector deliberately sets fires to clear off the woods just where they are densest, to lay the rocks bare and make the discovery of mines easier. Sheep-owners and their shepherds also set fires everywhere through the woods in the fall to facilitate the march of their countless flocks the next summer, and perhaps in some places to improve the pasturage.

The American Forests

The axe is not yet at the root of every tree, but the sheep is, or was before the national parks were established and guarded by the military, the only effective and reliable arm of the government free from the blight of politics. Not only do the shepherds, at the driest time of the year, set fire to everything that will burn, but the sheep consume every green leaf, not sparing even the young conifers, when they are in a starving condition from crowding, and they rake and dibble the loose soil of the mountain sides for the spring floods to wash away, and thus at last leave the ground barren.

Of all the destroyers that infest the woods, the shake-maker seems the happiest. Twenty or thirty years ago, shakes, a kind of long, boardlike shingles split with a mallet and a frow, were in great demand for covering barns and sheds, and many are used still in preference to common shingles, especially those made from the sugar-pine, which do not warp or crack in the hottest sunshine. Drifting adventurers in California, after harvest and threshing are over, often-times meet to discuss their plans for the winter, and their talk is interesting. Once, in a company of this kind, I heard a man say, as he peacefully smoked his pipe: "Boys, as soon as this job's done I'm goin' into the duck business. There's big money in it, and your grub costs nothing. Tule Joe made five hundred dollars last winter on mallard and teal. Shot 'em on the Joaquin, tied 'em in dozens by the neck, and shipped 'em to San Francisco. And when he was tired wading in the sloughs and touched with rheumatiz, he just knocked off on ducks, and went to the Contra Costa hills for dove and quail. It's a mighty good business, and you're your own boss, and the whole thing's fun."

Another of the company, a bushy-bearded fellow, with a trace of brag in his voice, drawled out: "Bird business is well enough for some, but bear is my game, with a deer and a California lion thrown in now and then for change. There's always market for bear grease, and sometimes you can sell the hams. They're good as hog hams any day. And you are your own boss in my business, too, if the bears ain't too big and too many for you. Old grizzlies I despise—they want cannon to kill 'em; but the blacks and browns are beauties for grease, and when once I get 'em just right, and draw a bead on 'em, I fetch 'em ever time." Another said he was going to catch up a lot of mustangs as soon as the rains set in, hitch them to a gang-plough, and go to farming on the San Joaquin plans for wheat. But most preferred the shake business, until something more profitable and as sure could be found, with equal comfort and independence.

With a cheap mustang or mule to carry a pair of blankets, a sack of flour, a few pounds of coffee, and an axe, a frow, and a cross-cut saw, the shake-maker ascends the mountains to the pine belt where it is most accessible, usually by some mine or mill road. Then he strikes off into the virgin woods, where the sugar pine, king of all the hundred species of pines in the world in size and beauty, towers on the open sunny slopes of the Sierra in the fullness of its glory. Selecting a favorable spot for a cabin near a meadow with a stream, he unpacks his animal and stakes it out on the meadow. Then he chops into one after another of the pines, until he finds one that he feels sure will split freely, cuts this down, saws off a section four feet long, splits it, and from this first cut, perhaps seven feet in diameter, he gets shakes enough for a cabin and its furniture—walls, roof, door, bedstead, table, and stool. Besides his labor, only a few pounds of nails are required. Sapling poles form the frame of the airy building, usually about six feet by eight in size, on which the shakes are nailed, with the edges overlapping. A few bolts from the same section that the shakes were made from are split into square sticks and built up to form a chimney, the inside and interspaces being plastered and filled in with mud. Thus, with abundance of fuel, shelter and comfort by his own fireside are secured. Then he goes to work sawing and splitting for the market, tying the shakes in bundles of fifty or a hundred. They are four feet long, four inches wide, and about one fourth of an inch thick. The first few thousands he sells or trades at the nearest mill or store, getting provisions in exchange. Then he advertises, in whatever way he can, that he has excellent sugar-pine shakes for sale, easy of access and cheap.

Only the lower, perfectly clear, free-splitting portions of the giant pines are used—perhaps ten to twenty feet from a tree two hundred and fifty in height; all the rest is left a mass of ruins, to rot or to feed the forest fires, while thousands are hacked deeply and rejected in proving the grain. Over nearly all of the more accessible slopes of the Sierra and Cascade mountains in southern Oregon, at a height of from three to six thousand feet above the sea, and for a distance of about six hundred miles, this waste and confusion extends. Happy robbers! dwelling in the most beautiful woods, in the most salubrious climate, breathing delightful odors both day and night, drinking cool living water—roses and lilies at their feet in the spring, shedding fragrance and ringing bells as if cheering them on in their desolating work. There is none to say them nay. They buy no land, pay no taxes, dwell in a paradise with no forbidding angel either from Washington or from heaven. Every one of the frail shake shanties is a centre of destruction, and the extent of the ravages wrought in this quiet way is in the aggregate enormous.

It is not generally known that, notwithstanding the immense quantities of timber cut every year for foreign and home markets and mines, from five to ten times as much is destroyed as is used, chiefly by running forest fires that only the federal government can stop. Travelers through the West in summer are not likely to forget the fire-work displayed along the various railway tracks. Thoreau, when contemplating the destruction of the forests on the east side of the continent, said that soon the country would be so bald that every man would have to grow whiskers to hide its nakedness, but he thanked God that at least the sky was safe. Had he gone West he would have found out that the sky was not safe; for all through the summer months, over most of the mountain regions, the smoke of mill and forest fires is so thick and black that no sunbeam can pierce it. The whole sky, with clouds, sun, moon, and stars, is simply blotted out. There is no real sky and no scenery. Not a mountain is left in the landscape. At least none is in sight from the lowlands, and they all might as well be on the moon, as far as scenery is concerned.

The half-dozen transcontinental railroad companies advertise the beauties of their lines in gorgeous many-colored folders, each claiming its as the "scenic route." "The route of superior desolation"—the smoke, dust, and ashes route—would be a more truthful description. Every train rolls on through dismal smoke and barbarous, melancholy ruins; and the companies might well cry in their advertisements: "Come! travel our way. Ours is the blackest. It is the only genuine Erebus route. The sky is black and the ground is black, and on either side there is a continuous border of black stumps and logs and blasted trees appealing to heaven for help as if still half alive, and their mute eloquence is most interestingly touching. The blackness is perfect. On account of the superior skill of our workmen, advantages of climate, and the kind of trees, the charring is generally deeper along our line, and the ashes are deeper, and the confusion and desolation displayed can never be rivaled. No other route on this continent so fully illustrates the abomination of desolation." Such a claim would be reasonable, as each seems the worst, whatever route you chance to take.

Of course a way had to be cleared through the woods. But the felled timber is not worked up into firewood for the engines and into lumber for the company's use; it is left lying in vulgar confusion, and is fired from time to time by sparks from locomotives or by the workmen camping along the line. The fires, whether accidental or set, are allowed to run into the woods as far as they may, thus assuring comprehensive destruction. The directors of a line that guarded against fires, and cleared a clean gap edged with living trees, and fringed and mantled with the grass and flowers and beautiful seedlings that are ever ready and willing to spring up, might justly boast of the beauty of their road; for nature is always ready to heal every scar. But there is no such road on the western side of the continent. Last summer, in the Rocky Mountains, I saw six fires started by sparks from a locomotive within a distance of three miles, and nobody was in sight to prevent them from spreading. They might run into the adjacent forests and burn the timber from hundreds of square miles; not a man in the State would care to spend an hour in fighting them, as long as his own fences and buildings were not threatened.

Notwithstanding all the waste and use which have been going on unchecked like a storm for more than two centuries, it is not yet too late—though it is high time—for the government to begin a rational administration of its forests. About seventy million acres it still owns —enough for all the country, if wisely used. These residual forests are generally on mountain slopes, just where they are doing the most good, and where their removal would be followed by the greatest number of evils; the lands they cover are too rocky and high for agriculture, and can never be made as valuable for any other crop as for the present crop of trees. It has been shown over and over again that if these mountains were to be stripped of their trees and underbrush, and kept bare and sodless by hordes of sheep and the innumerable fires the shepherds set, besides those of the millmen, prospectors, shake-makers, and all sorts of adventurers, both lowlands and mountains would speedily become little better than deserts, compared with their present beneficent fertility. During heavy rainfalls and while the winter accumulations of snow were melting, the larger streams would swell into destructive torrents, cutting deep, rugged-edged gullies, carrying away the fertile humus and soil as well as sand and rocks, filling up and overflowing their lower channels, and covering the lowland fields with raw detritus. Drought and barrenness would follow.

In their natural condition, or under wise management, keeping out destructive sheep, preventing fires, selecting the trees that should be cut for lumber, and preserving the young ones and the shrubs and sod of herbaceous vegetation, these forests would be a never failing fountain of wealth and beauty. The cool shades of the forest give rise to moist beds and currents of air, and the sod of grasses and the various flowering plants and shrubs thus fostered, together with the network and sponge of tree roots, absorb and hold back the rain and the waters from melting snow, compelling them to ooze and percolate and flow gently through the soil in streams that never dry. All the pine needles and rootlets and blades of grass, and the fallen, decaying trunks of trees, are dams, storing the bounty of the clouds and dispensing it in perennial life-giving streams, instead of allowing it to gather suddenly and rush headlong in short-lived devastating floods. Everybody on the dry side of the continent is beginning to find this out, and, in view of the waste going on, is growing more and more anxious for government protection. The outcries we hear against forest reservations come mostly from thieves who are wealthy and steal timber by wholesale. They have so long been allowed to steal and destroy in peace that any impediment to forest robbery is denounced as a cruel and irreligious interference with "vested rights," likely to endanger the repose of all ungodly welfare.

Gold, gold, gold! How strong a voice that metal has!

'O wae for the siller, it is sae preva'lin'!'

Even in Congress a sizable chunk of gold, carefully concealed, will outtalk and outfight all the nation on a subject like forestry, well smothered in ignorance, and in which the money interests of only a few are conspicuously involved. Under these circumstances, the bawling, blethering oratorical stuff drowns the voice of God himself. Yet the dawn of a new day in forestry is breaking. Honest citizens see that only the rights of the government are being trampled, not those of the settlers. Only what belongs to all alike is reserved, and every acre that is left should be held together under the federal government as a basis for a general policy of administration for the public good. The people will not always be deceived by selfish opposition,

The American Forests

whether from lumber and mining corporations or from sheepmen and prospectors, however cunningly brought forward underneath fables and gold.

Emerson says that things refuse to be mismanaged long. An exception would seem to be found in the case of our forests, which have been mismanaged rather long, and now come desperately near being like smashed eggs and spilt milk. Still, in the long run the world does not move backward. The wonderful advance made in the last few years, in creating four national parks in the West, and thirty forest reservations, embracing nearly forty million acres; and in the planting of the borders of streets and highways and spacious parks in all the great cities, to satisfy the natural taste and hunger for landscape beauty and righteousness that God has put, in some measure, into every human being and animal, shows the trend of awakening public opinion. The making of the far-famed New York Central Park was opposed by even good men, with misguided pluck, perseverance, and ingenuity; but straight right won its way, and now that park is appreciated. So we confidently believe it will be with our great national parks and forest reservations. There will be a period of indifference on the part of the rich, sleepy with wealth, and of the toiling millions, sleepy with poverty, most of whom never saw a forest; a period of screaming protest and objection from the plunderers, who are as unconscionable and enterprising as Satan. But light is surely coming, and the friends of destruction will preach and bewail in vain.

The United States government has always been proud of the welcome it has extended to good men of every nation, seeking freedom and homes and bread. Let them be welcomed still as Nature welcomes them, to the woods as well as to the prairies and plains. No place is too good for good men, and still there is room. They are invited to heaven, and may well be allowed in America. Every place is made better by them. Let them be as free to pick gold and gems from the hills, to cut and hew, dig and plant, for homes and bread, as the birds are to pick berries from the wild bushes, and moss and leaves for nests. The ground will be glad to feed them, and the pines will come down from the mountains for their homes as willingly as the cedars came from Lebanon for Solomon's temple. Nor will the woods be the worse for this use, or their benign influences be diminished any more than the sun is diminished by shining. Mere destroyers, however, tree-killers, wool and mutton men, spreading death and confusion in the fairest groves and gardens ever planted—let the government hasten to cast them out and make an end of them. For it must be told again and again, and be burningly borne in mind, that just now, while protective measures are being deliberated languidly, destruction and use are speeding on faster and farther every day. The axe and saw are insanely busy, chips are flying thick as snowflakes, and every summer thousands of acres of priceless forests, with their underbrush, soil, springs, climate, scenery, and religion, are vanishing away in clouds of smoke, while, except in the national parks, not one forest guard is employed.

All sorts of local laws and regulations have been tried and found wanting, and the costly lessons of our own experience, as well as that of every civilized nation, show conclusively that the fate of the remnant of our forests is in the hands of the federal government, and that if the remnant is to be saved at all, it must be saved quickly.

Any fool can destroy trees. They cannot run away; and if they could, they would still be destroyed—chased and hunted down as long as fun or a dollar could be got out of their bark hides, branching horns, or magnificent bole backbones. Few that fell trees plant them; nor would planting avail much towards getting back anything like the noble primeval forests. During a man's life only saplings can be grown, in the place of the old trees—tens of centuries old—that have been destroyed. It took more than three thousand years to make some of the trees in these Western woods—trees that are still standing in perfect strength and beauty, waving and singing in the mighty forests of the Sierra. Through all the wonderful, eventful centuries since Christ's time—and long before that—God has cared for these trees, saved them from drought, disease, avalanches, and a thousand straining, leveling tempests and floods; but he cannot save them from fools—only Uncle Sam can do that.